¿Que es la vida? Un frenesí.
¿Que es la vida? Una ilusión.
...
Que toda la vida es sueño
Y los sueños, sueños son.

Sofía Casanova (1861-1958):

Spanish Poet, Journalist and Author

Scripta Humanistica ®

Directed by
BRUNO M. DAMIANI
The Catholic University of America

ADVISORY BOARD

Sofía Casanova (1861-1958):

Spanish Poet, Journalist and Author

𝔖cripta 𝔥umanistica
89

Library of Congress Cataloging-in-Publication Data

Alayeto, Ofelia.
    Sofía Casanova (1861-1958) : Spanish woman poet, journalist, and
author / Ofelia Alayeto.
        p.   cm. -- (Scripta Humanistica ; 89)
    Includes bibliographical references and index.
    ISBN 0-916379-95-7 : $54.50
    1. Casanova, Sofía, 1861-1958. 2. Authors, Spanish--20th century-
-Biography. 3. Journalists--Spain--Biography.   I. Title.
II. Series: Scripta Humanistica (Series) ; 89.
PQ6605.A826Z53 1992
861'.62--dc20
[B]   92-22741
                                                              CIP

Publisher and Distributor:
SCRIPTA HUMANISTICA
1383 Kersey Lane
Potomac, Maryland 20854 U. S. A.

Table of Contents

Acknowledgements

As I finish this book, I am reminded that no one does anything alone. What began as an isolated academic exercise became an exhilarating process of discovery shared by many people, most of them unknown to me before I began my research on Sofía Casanova. I'm happy to acknowledge the contributions of the many people and organizations in the United States, Poland and Spain who have helped me research and write this book.

The late Martin Nozick, then Executive Officer of the Spanish Department at the Graduate Center of the City University of New York, sparked my interest in Sofía Casanova. He agreed with the late Don Emilio González López, and with Don Juan Naya (then President of the *Real Academia de la Lengua Gallega*) that Sofía Casanova's life was a topic overdue for study within a comparative context. Prof. Nozick challenged me to "break new ground!" with my dissertation. Now, largely thanks to Janet Pérez's long-distance guidance and encouragement, that dissertation has become a book. Sections on Casanova's poetry appeared initially in "The Poetry of Sofía Casanova" in *Monographic Review/Revista Monográfica*, Vol. VI (1990), edited by Janet and Genaro Pérez. "Sofía Casanova: An Annotated Bibliography," appeared in slightly different form in *Bulletin of Bibliography* 44 (1987). Thanks also to Dan Gerould for his participation on my dissertation committee. My gratitude to Halina Czarnocka for her help with Polish references. My good friend and editor, Sherry Symington, provided essential support. I am indebted to Szilvia Szmuk for countless hours of counseling and advice on the telephone between Manhattan and San Francisco.

Personal interviews, conversations and correspondence with members of Casanova's Polish family comprise a fair part of the new information contained in this book. Krystina Niklewicz (Sofía Casanova's granddaughter) and the late Halita Meissner (Casanova's youngest daughter) gave me invaluable information and direction during my visit to Poland and later on through correspondence. I particularly thank Prof. Niklewicz for reading my dissertation and sending me her useful observations. Peter Niklewicz (Sofía Casanova's great-grandson), now of Washington, D. C., became a friend and adviser, and deserves special mention for his help during my original trip to Warsaw, and afterwards. General Romuald Wolikowski of Alberta, Canada added valuable information about his late wife, Izabela Lutosławska and his mother-in-law Sofía Casanova. Brother Adalbert Meissner, one of Casanova's grandchildren, filled in details about the last years of her life in Communist Poland.

In addition, I have had conversations and correspondence over time with my distinguished friend Alex Jordan of Coral Gables, Florida (only son of Wincenty Lutosławski, Sofia Casanova's husband and a noted Polish-American writer and translator) which rounded out my understanding of his father's life. I am grateful for the use of a copy of Henry James' correspondence with his father (the original letters are held at Yale's Beinecke Library). Dr. Halina Wittlin (widow of Józef Wittlin, the Polish author) revealed details about Casanova's reputation in Poland. The late Clément Jedrzewski (one of Professor Lutosławski's students in turn-of-the century Cracow) enlightened me about Wincenty Lutosławski's activities during that time, and on the role that the Lutosławskis played in Polish intellectual life. I want to thank them and many other Polish friends who have brought Poland close to my life.

Jorge Dezcallar of the Uruguayan Diplomatic Corps helped me contact Casanova's Polish family in Warsaw, and Maria Teresa Zapiain of the Spanish Diplomatic Service made my stay there more productive. The Library of the University of Warsaw opened its doors to me. Head Librarian Maria Bohonos-Zagórska, and Librarians Franciszka Gałczyńska, Mieczysław Kret and Ewa Truskolaska were also of help. Father Bill Faix, O.S.A., of the Akademia Teologii Katolickiej, and Yagoda Niklewicz also made my experiences there more pleasant and understandable.

In Madrid, I was able to draw on the resources of the Biblioteca Nacional, which holds almost every work of Casanova's, and on the archives of the Hemeroteca Nacional. I especially want to thank *ABC* and its Director, Don Rafael de Góngora, for their help.

Back home in New York City, I made use of the Research Libraries of the New York City Public Library, and of the Hispanic Society of America. S. L. Cranston, Murray T. Bloom, S. Jordanowski and Dr. R. Krystina Dietrich responded to my notice in the *New York Times Sunday Book Review* and gave me further leads. I am happy to acknowledge the support of the staff of the City University of New York Graduate School Library (now Mina Rees Library). Carol Fitzgerald in particular was always ready to facilitate anything needed for the completion of this work. For her professional support and editorial encouragement, all my gratitude.

Several colleagues at Herbert H. Lehman College, City University of New York, including Carmen de Zulueta and Nadine Savage, and other New York friends and colleagues including Dave Gearey, Dr. Florian A. Mikulski, Laura Madison and J. P. Leppert gave me leads, advice and technical support towards completing my dissertation.

After I returned to teaching and further research in San Francisco, Deirdre Cornell and Virginie Pelletier became my research assistants, readers, and much more. My writing group in San Francisco has helped me reach these final stages. Hans Hollitscher did some light-handed copyediting. At the University of San Francisco I thank Anne Barrows, Nancy Vogeley, and the Gleeson Library staff for their help. Mónica Contreras de Rioja and Jackie Shapiro have helped me with organization, setting and reaching goals. I must thank my students in New York and California - they have taught me a great deal.

Closer to home I thank my parents, Pedro and Ofelia Alayeto for moral and material support. My sister Elena Alayeto met me during my original research trip to Spain, and later spent many Saturdays in Manhattan libraries as I completed my research. She has developed her own interests in Polish language and culture, and has just returned from a visit to Warsaw as I write these lines. Only recently have I realized that this book reflects our family experiences and values as part of the Cuban diaspora.

To my sons Greg and Seth Solomonow, who have finally become interested in Sofía Casanova: thank you for your high spirits and insouciance, and for all your practical help. You have kept my feet on the ground. Thanks also to my father-in-law and premier proofreader Lt. Col. (Ret.) Joseph Solomonow, and to my dear mother-in-law Fran Solomonow, who tells me that I will survive the moment and will write other books someday. Blessings to Allan Solomonow, guru, editor and sounding board: it wouldn't have happened without you.

This book is dedicated to the late Hannah E. Bergman, who was able to read only the first chapter, but whose spirit is behind every page. I think she would have approved of the rest. Hannah encouraged her students to ignore boundaries between literatures and disciplines, and to explore new authors and genres. I learned a great deal from her exacting scholarly and linguistic standards. My appreciation to John Bergman for his support.

A note on format: In preparing this book, I interviewed many individuals, in various languages, over a period of several years. Certain sections of the book, because of their subject matter, draw heavily on these interviews and conversations, rather than on books, family papers, correspondence or other printed sources. Therefore, statements attributed to an individual, unless otherwise noted, have been extracted from that individual's interviews, and translated into English by the author.

An additional note on references: In parenthetical documentation, short titles have generally been used. I direct readers to the Table of Abbreviations on page iii for a key to abbreviations of frequently cited titles of works by Casanova and others. Textual quotes from Casanova's works are clearly documented as such. To facilitate reference, abbreviated titles of Casanova's works are listed with their date of first appearance, since they are listed chronologically in the *Annotated Bibliography of her works*. For future reference, I have listed alphabetically works on Casanova by other authors in the Selected Bibliography, whether referred to or not in the text. An additional list of specific Works Cited is also listed alphabetically.

Summaries of Casanova's major works are included in the *Annotated Bibliography*. I cite and translate Casanova's Spanish quotations, but due to space limitations, give only the English for most Polish and other foreign language quotes. Any errors of translation, fact or opinion, unless otherwise stated, are my own.

> Esta verdadera historia
> Aquí, amigos, se acaba,
> Recibid nuestros deseos
> Y perdonad nuestras faltas.

San Francisco
Summer 1992

Preface

Sofía Casanova: A Forgotten Legend

Born in 1861 at the beginning of the Civil War in the United States, Sofía Casanova was formed by the nineteenth century ambient of her upbringing and early adulthood, absorbing its outlook and values. Yet she lived well into the second half of the twentieth century, chronicling World War I and the Bolshevik Revolution as a foreign correspondent, surviving World War II in Eastern Europe, and spending her last two decades behind the Iron Curtain in Communist Poland. Her vast historical experience is echoed by equally wide-ranging geographical and cultural settings: from the remote, almost medieval Galician village of her birth and first twelve years, to the provincial, bourgeois atmosphere of Pérez Galdós's Madrid where she resided some fifteen years until her marriage, Casanova moved to become a world citizen, travelling throughout Europe and becoming sufficiently well assimilated into Polish culture to publish in that language and to play a prominent role in Poland's most select literary and political circles.

Casanova's extensive literary and journalistic output is equally wide-ranging, from early post-Romantic poetry and somber, pessimistic Parnassist verse to novels of the frivolous international elite in the years between the wars and narratives of ideological conflict between Bolsheviks and counter-revolutionaries. She enjoyed Royal patronage along with the friendship of Liberal literati, descended from the conservative rural Galician aristocracy, yet lived to become an impartial international observer of social revolution. During her marriage to a Polish political activist and visionary philosopher of eugenics, she lived in places as diverse as an oriental, provincial Russian town in Central Asia, an isolated fishing hamlet on the Galician coast, a rural manor north of Warsaw, and the old Polish university town of Cracow. From her early admiration of Rosalía de Castro to acquaintance with major writers of European and Polish Modernism, from translating Nobel prize-winning Polish novelists to becoming Spain's first female war correspondent, Casanova lived an extraordinary intellectual life of exceptional achievement. As the major conduit whereby the Spanish public learned of Poland, Russian and Eastern Europe, as well as Spain's primary interpreter for peoples of the East, she exercised incalculable political and cultural influence.

In the literary and cultural life of turn-of-the century Spain, Casanova maintained a salon frequented by the likes of Galdós, Pardo Bazán, the

Machado brothers and Benavente; wrote in Madrid dailies on topics ranging from Polish culture, history and politics to art and public hygiene, campaigned against negative stereotypes of Spanish women in European literature and became a social activist on behalf of preventive medicine and public health in Spain. She wrote on the prevention of tuberculosis and joined the Spanish Red Cross while earning her living and caring for her children as a journalist. Her lectures, collections of poetry, and books of short and long fiction were sufficiently well received that she became a member of the Real Academia Gallega (1906) and the Academia de Poesía Española (1910).

Casanova, a convinced pacifist, volunteered as a Red Cross nurse and Sister of Charity in Warsaw during 1914-1915, riding military trains into battle zones to bring back the wounded, and wrote a series of anti-war articles for Madrid's most influential daily, *ABC*. Her eyewitness accounts, widely reprinted throughout Spain and Latin America, were produced in a violently politicized context, yet she maintained her objectivity. Amid rampant anti-Semitism in Poland, mocked by friends and relatives for her views, she defended Jews, and having detailed the horrors of the evacuation of Warsaw, returned to report the city's apocalyptic fall to the Germans. Working for war relief while in exile in Russia, she reported on the 1917 Revolution in Petrograd --the first accounts to reach Spain-- and her columns were headlined on the front pages of *ABC*. She even interviewed Trotsky at Bolshevik headquarters, a journalistic coup, only days before the October takeover. She lived through the German siege of Petrograd, the Red Terror of 1918, managing through diplomatic contacts to escape with her family back to German-held Warsaw, and later portrayed these world-shaking events in her novels.

Casanova's literary and journalistic achievements were remarkable by any yardstick, and notwithstanding her long years of expatriation, it seems incredible that she could have been so completely forgotten by Spain's literary and cultural establishment. She is among the first to be rescued by the joint publishing program initiated by the Instituto de la Mujer and Editorial Castalia, which has recently reprinted one of her novels, and included one of her stories in a collection of short fiction by women. Ofelia Alayeto's sensitive intellectual and literary biography of Casanova, a ground-breaking achievement, represents a major contribution to the understanding of one of this century's truly great women.

Janet Pérez

ii

Table of Abbreviations

Works by Sofía Casanova

Bartek	Bartek el Vencedor, 1902.
Cancionero	El Cancionero de la dicha, 1911.
Catacumbas	Las catacumbas de Rusia roja, 1933.
Corte	En la corte de los zares, 1924.
Lo eterno	Lo eterno, 1908.
Exóticas	Exóticas, 1913.
Fugaces	Fugaces, 1898.
Guerra	De la guerra, 1916.
Idilio	Idilio epistolar, 1931
Impresiones	"Impresiones... en el frente oriental," 1919.
Inéd.	Poesías Inéditas. La Coruña, 1973.
Madeja	"La madeja," 1913.
Martirio	El martirio de Polonia, 1945.
Mujer	"La mujer española en el extranjero," 1910.
Nihilista	Una nihilista, 1909.
Pecado	El Pecado, 1911.
Poesías	Poesías, 1885.
Rev. bol.	La revolución bolchevista, 1920.
Rev. rus.	De la revolución rusa en 1917, 1918.
Rusia	De Rusia: amores y confidencias, 1927.
Wolski	El doctor Wolski, 1894.
Viajes	Viajes y aventuras, 1920.
Vida	Como en la vida, 1931.
Volga	Sobre el Volga helado,1903.

Works by Other Authors

EUIEA	Enciclopedia Universal Ilustrada Europeo Americana.
EG	Enciclopedia Gallega.
PSB	Polski Słownik Biograficzny.
VG	Vida Gallega.

Sofía Casanova - A Chronology

1861   Sofía Casanova born in Almeiras, La Coruña, 30 September.

1875   Casanova family moves to Madrid.

1875   Casanova writes first poem after grandfather's death.

1885   *Poesías*. Death of Rosalía de Castro in Galicia, 15 July.

1887   Marriage to Wincenty Lutosławski. Travel to Lisbon, London, Paris, Poland, Estonia.

1887   Dorpat, Estonia. Birth of daughter Marie ("Mania", "Mañita")

1888   First visit to Moscow. Birth of daughter Izabela ("Bela").

1889   Kazan.

1889   1890 - Casanova and family in London.

1890   Kazan.

1891   Birth of daughter Jadwiga.

1893   Visit to Madrid. London. *El doctor Wolski*.

1894   Madrid.

1895   Drozdowo. Death of Jadwiga, September 17. Mera, Galicia.

1897   Birth of daughter Halina ("Halita").

1898   Spanish-Cuban-American War. Loss of Cuba, Philippines. End of Spanish Empire.

1899   Cracow.

1903	*Sobre el Volga helado. Bartek el vencedor.*
1905	Casanova moves to Madrid for extended stay.
1907	"El pino del Norte" (zarzuela): collaboration with Vicente Casanova.
1908	*Lo eterno. ¿Quo Vadis?* (Translation). *Más que amor* published in Madrid and Warsaw, censored by czarist military authorities.
1909	"Tragic Week" in Barcelona. *Una nihilista.* (Translation).
1910	Conference in the Ateneo de Madrid: "La mujer española en el extranjero."
1911	*El pecado. El cancionero de la dicha.*
1912	*Exóticas.*
1913	"La madeja," Teatro Español.
1914	Beginning of World War I, 1 August. Casanova begins as foreign correspondent for *ABC*, 23 April.
1915	Flight to Minsk and Moscow.
1916	Petrograd. *De la guerra. Crónicas de Polonia y Rusia.*
1917	Russian Revolution.
1918	Moscow: Józef and Marian Lutosławski executed by Bolsheviks. Escape from Russia. Armistice signed. *De la Revolución rusa en 1917.*
1919	Polish independence restored. Triumphal return to Spain. "Impresiones de una mujer en el frente Oriental."
1920	Warsaw. Polish-Soviet War. *La Revolución bolchevista. Lo eterno (re-issue). Viajes y aventuras de una muñeca española. Triunfo de amor.*

1921   *Episodio de guerra*. Death of Emilia Pardo Bazán. Bela marries Colonel Romuald Wolikowski.

1922   *Princesa rusa*. Halita marries Doctor Czesław Meissner.

1923   *Kola el bandido*. Madrid: Primo de Rivera *coup d'état*.

1924   *Obras Completas. En la corte de los Zares* (Vol. I).

1925   Madrid. Galicia. *El dolor de reinar*.

1926   Madrid.

1928   *De Rusia: Amores y confidencias*.

1929   Lecture: "Algo de poesia." *En la corte de los Zares* (2nd Ed.). Death of Queen María Cristina.

1930   Proclamation of Second Spanish Republic.

1931   *Como en la vida*.

1933   *Las catacumbas de Rusia roja*.

1934   Poland: Death of Marshall Piłsudski.

1936   Spanish Civil War, July 19. *ABC* shut down, re-opened as Republican newspaper.

1938   January: Sofía Casanova's last visit to Spain. La Coruña, Bilbao, San Sebastián

1939   Warsaw. *Blitzkrieg*. Nazi occupation of Poland.

1944   Soviet Army invades Poland. Warsaw uprising. German defeat.

1945   Sofía Casanova moves to Posnań.

1946   Madrid: Unauthorized publication of *El martirio de Polonia*.

1947   New Polish constitution proclaims Communist state. "Iron Curtain" falls around Poland. Sofía Casanova cut off from Spain and the rest of the world.

1955   Death of Professor Wincenty Lutosławski, Cracow (29 December).

1958   Death of Sofía Casanova in Posnań (16 January) .

Introduction

Sofía Casanova (1861-1958): Time for a New Approach

Poet, journalist of war and revolution, prolific novelist, translator, playwright, respected society figure: Sofía Casanova intrigued and influenced the Spanish reading public for over fifty years. She was an outspoken political commentator, a conservative feminist, a nexus of Spanish and Polish cultures, and Spain's sole envoy at the heart of Europe. Above all, she was a rarity: a successful professional woman in a patriarchal society. Sofía Casanova's unique achievements should have drawn considerable critical and scholarly notice. Yet today her life and works remain largely unexamined or ignored. It is the purpose of this book to reintroduce Sofía Casanova to the scholarly world and general public.

It would be reasonable to describe Sofía Casanova not only as one of the most remarkable Spanish women who has ever lived, but almost as a force of nature. She married a distinguished Polish philosopher, left Spain and spent most of her life as an expatriate. Yet even as she became conversant with Eastern European politics, she remained active in the world of Spanish letters. She reached fame thanks to her brilliant foreign correspondence during World War I and the Bolshevik Revolution; she did pioneering social work on behalf of Spanish women during the first decade of the century; she succeeded at having both a family and a professional career; she managed a prodigious journalistic and literary output between 1917 and 1945. Finally, she reached the age of ninety-five as an active if suppressed writer. Sofía Casanova has few peers in Spanish history, or indeed in the history of her time.

Why, then, has so little critical notice been taken of this extraordinary woman? Even now, over thirty years after her death, when so many Spanish woman writers of the past have been discovered or reexamined, one of Spain's most accomplished and celebrated women remains virtually unknown in the country that once venerated her.

During most of her long life, thanks to her talent, versatility and sheer persistence, Sofía Casanova's work was appreciated by succeeding generations of Spanish readers. At the height of her poetic career, her fellow poets made her one of the few Spanish women accepted by literary academies (the *Real Academia Gallega* in 1906 and the "alternative" *Academia de Poesía Española* in 1911). In an enthusiastic review of her third book of poetry, *Cancionero de la dicha* (1912), Ramón Pérez de

1

Ayala called her "una poetisa completa" (Pérez de Ayala 1299).

In later years, her journalistic work during World War I and the Russian revolution brought her enormous popularity and one of Spain's most prestigious awards, the country's highest medal for service to humanity, "La Gran Cruz de Beneficencia" 'The Great Cross of Charity'. In 1925, she was nominated by Spain for the 1925 Nobel Prize in Literature by Don Antonio Maura (then President of the Royal Academy of the Spanish Language) and Don Emilio Cotarelo y Mori, the famous scholar. That same year, she was awarded the Alfonso XII medal, Spain's highest recognition of intellectual achievement. Clearly, for several decades Sofía Casanova was one of Spain's best known and most respected women writers.

But today Sofía Casanova's poems, lauded in their time by the *Modernistas*, are not included in anthologies of Spanish poetry. Her long and brilliant career as Spain's first female war correspondent and political polemicist is not mentioned in histories of Spanish journalism. Her vast production of over thirty books (novels, travel narratives, collections of essays and short stories, a play) does not merit even a footnote in Spanish literary histories. And, despite the recurring concern for women's issues that appears in her writing, feminist scholars have just begun to examine her works.[1]

At first, the abrupt decline and disappearance of Casanova's reputation might appear natural. At least in part, it was caused by the usual loss of public recognition an author suffers after death, the changing literary trends after the Spanish Civil War, and the fact that Casanova lived and died in an area of Europe that remains linguistically, culturally and geographically remote from Spain.

To be fair, one must also mention that although most of her books and almost all of her many articles are to be found in Spanish libraries and archives, until fairly recently the political situations of Spain and Poland hindered research and evaluation of her life and works. Spanish secondary sources on her were limited to sketchy encyclopedia entries, newspaper obituaries, and a handful of scholarly articles of limited usefulness. In Poland, outside of her family's archives, there was even less available. Given conditions in both Spanish and Polish society during the 1950s and 1960s, it would have been difficult, if not impossible, to put Casanova's tumultuous life and vast but scattered works into proper historical and literary context.

Another problem in approaching Casanova lies in her diversity of genres. She was both the salon poet who enjoyed *succès d'estime* from a handful of her peers, and a popular journalist whose work found its way

2

into homes all over Spain and Latin America. She wrote Parnassist verse and sentimental romances, ideological novels (such as *El Doctor Wolski* and *Las catacumbas de Rusia roja*) and children's books (*Viajes de una muñeca española*). Some of her works focus on Eastern European politics, others on narrow Galician topics. Another deterrent is her amazing productivity: Casanova wrote over eight hundred and thirty articles for the Spanish newspaper *ABC* alone (See *Sofía Casanova: An Annotated Bibliography*, "Articles by Sofía Casanova in *ABC*).

Anyone familiar with the history of Spanish literature knows that Casanova's obscurity is not unique. With the appearance of Carolyn Galerstein's *Women Writers of Spain* (1986), it became clear that Casanova was part of a larger company of "forgotten" women writers that merited critical attention. And as Janet Pérez observed three years later in *Contemporary Women Writers of Spain* (which placed Casanova in the "Turn of the Century Generation"), some of these women writers suffered not only from obscurity, but also from critical misperception and condescension:

> Spain's conservative, traditionalist society has long held rigid and narrow views concerning women's roles and proper activities. Critical distortion... (has) combined with patriarchal scholarship to bury the works of many women or to devalue their ideas. (6)

Corroborating Pérez's observation, it is easy to detect that after her death, Casanova suffered from two kinds of misperception. On one hand, she was widely misrepresented by the Spanish establishment as the epitome of patriotic Spanish womanhood. On the other hand, Spanish and Polish intellectuals and scholars perceived her as a Franco supporter who had also been a minor penwoman. In the larger analysis, she did not seem to merit serious study.

Madrid, 1958

When Casanova died in Posnań on January 16, 1958, after almost twenty years of expatriation in Communist Poland, Spanish officialdom and Galician cultural organizations acknowledged her passing with anecdotes, sentimentality and nationalist rhetoric that were short on facts and critical evaluation. Newspapers ranging from Madrid's *ABC*, *Pueblo* and *¡Arriba!* to the regional *El Faro de Vigo* and *Voz de Galicia* reported her death with prominent articles and illustrations. She was described in Spanish letters as a "legendary figure" who had remained loyal to Spain and its Catholic values while imprisoned behind the Iron Curtain. These commentators focused on her longevity (she died at age ninety-five), her bygone fame, her aristocratic heritage, and the nationalist and anti-Communist ideas she had proclaimed during her later years. They said nothing about the actual content of her writings.

There were two distinguishable trends in this public recasting of the Sofía Casanova legend. The first tendency was to portray Casanova as a Spanish icon, with the uncomplicated story line and saccharine style often used to portray a saint's life. The second focused on her Galician birth, and identified her as a second Rosalía de Castro (1837-1885), another *gallega* who had lived "tragically".

"...ángel de hospitales, apóstol de humildad"

The Spanish establishment's praise was reverential, but too vague: "poetisa, novelista, conferenciante, cronista de revoluciones y guerras, ángel de hospitales, apóstol de humildad" 'angel of hospitals, poet, novelist, lecturer, chronicler of revolutions and wars, apostle of humility' (*ABC*, 25 January 1958). Their admiration was fulsome, undocumented and unconvincing, and discouraged a more meaningful examination of Casanova's life and writings.

Critics avoided the fact that Sofía Casanova's personal life had been extraordinarily active, diverse, intellectual, and self-reliant. She had married outside of her culture and lived abroad most of her life, far from the strictures of Spanish society. After separating permanently from her husband in 1912, she supported herself and her family as a writer for many years.

Some contemporary critics went to great lengths to make her path-breaking past conform to Francoist Spain's rigid ideas about the role of women. Casanova had enjoyed a varied writing career between 1887 (the year she married and left Spain) and 1919 (the year she returned to Spain in triumph as a national heroine). During that time she had published two books of poetry, several novels, many travel narratives and articles, and had a play produced at the Teatro Español at the request of Benito Pérez Galdós. Any of these achievements, particularly the last, would have been outstanding for a woman of her time.

But after the Spanish Civil War, laws had been passed that forbade Spanish married women from working outside the home. In an article published in the *Boletín de la Biblioteca de Menéndez Pelayo*, noted Hispanist Camille Pitollet made Casanova fit this new paradigm.

4

Pitollet claimed that due to "Polish customs," after her marriage Casanova had found it necessary to "borrar su personalidad y acogerse a la familia de su marido...¿que hacer, pues, sino dedicarse...a la educación de sus hijas?" 'to erase her personality and to take shelter within her husband's family...what else to do, but to dedicate herself to her daughters' education?' He continued:

> todas las glorias que le proporcionara la fama conquistada en España no pesaban, en definitiva, en la balanza de su existencia nueva, lo que significaba el cumplimiento de los deberes del hogar. (135)

> All the glories given by the fame she conquered in Spain did not weigh, in the scales of her new life, as much as the fulfillment of her domestic duties.

According to his account, Casanova had not picked up her pen "sino para escribir cartas" 'except to write letters' between her marriage and the time she became a grandmother in 1918 (135).

In addition, in the politically cautious atmosphere of 1958, Casanova's works were viewed as a Pandora's box of explosive subjects and ideas better left alone. As an avowed pacifist, Casanova had written openly about Spain's "neutrality" during World War I and condemned anti-Semitism in Poland and everywhere. She had advocated better education and equal rights for Spanish women, briefly sympathized with the Russian revolution and criticized Spain for allying itself with Nazi Germany. She had often dwelt on Spain's cultural, social and economic underdevelopment in relation to the rest of Europe, and been a passionate participant in Spain's pre-Civil War polemics. Perhaps worst of all to critics of the fifties, she had been an ardent Catholic who heeded the social call of the Gospels. She had often boldly called herself "socialista, como lo fue Cristo" 'a Socialist, as Christ was' (*ABC*, 20 April 1919; Niklewicz, K. interview).

To resurrect these taboo subjects in the wary atmosphere of 1958 Spanish journalism was impossible. Spanish readers had to wait until 1975 for Professor Alfonso Lazo's scholarly study, *La revolución rusa en el diario ABC de la época*, for an analysis of Casanova's important role in influencing Spanish public opinion during this period.

Contemporary critics basically ignored Sofía Casanova's unique qualities: her bold contributions to Spanish journalism during World War I and the Russian Revolution; her influence on Spanish politics through her columns for *ABC*; her radical Catholicism; her espousal of pacifism; her admirable stands against anti-Semitism; her conservative feminism; her youthful Liberal leanings and even her lapse into Fascism in later life. In effect, a true picture of Casanova's life and works threatened these critics

5

with a woman too active and self-defining to conform to accepted notions of appropriate female behavior and political orthodoxy.

Galicia: "La santa que murió de saudade"

A second, regional tendency linked Casanova to the legends surrounding Rosalía de Castro. According to these critics, like Rosalía, Casanova's psychologically-oriented poetry was not a product of her individual talent, but of a regional and collective form of expression that reflected human suffering in a singularly Galician way.[2] These critics held that Rosalía was the quintessence of *saudade* (a Galician mixture of love and sorrow that can mean general nostalgia for the past, for those who are far away, or for something that one misses from a distance like one's native village.).

This perception of Casanova as a second Rosalía was reflected in José María de Cossío's monumental *Cincuenta años de poesía española* (1962), written while Casanova was still alive. Cossío affiliated her with a school of nineteenth-century Galician *saudade* of which Rosalía was the leading exemplar, and Casanova a disciple. After her death, *ABC* reprinted Cossío's patronizing observations which featured her as "la santa que murió de *saudade*" (*ABC* 2 April 1958). Amid other tributes from the Galician community, *Vida Gallega* followed with "Sofía Casanova, gloria de España en la *saudade*".

This was an unfortunate and limiting approach to Casanova's individual merit as a poet and writer. Rosalía de Castro and Sofía Casanova were both *gallegas*, and their lives had much in common. But Rosalía's poetry centered on Galicia, unlike Casanova's. Her writing, particularly *Cantares gallegos* (1863), culminated a tradition of regional lyric. At the beginning of her career, she emerged as a voice for what was considered a marginal culture: she had no interest in obliging the Castilian literary elite.

Casanova admired and emulated Rosalía de Castro, and some of her early poetry is clearly derivative of the older poet's. On the other hand, she also read and imitated Cuban poet Gertrudis Gómez de Avellaneda and the Spanish Carolina Coronado (Casanova's first book, like theirs, was titled *Poesías*). Several other Spanish and European poets of both genders influenced her poetry.

After all, Sofía Casanova had left Galicia at the age of twelve, lived in Madrid until her marriage in 1887, and after that travelled and lived throughout Europe, spending almost her entire life outside of Galicia and

Spain. Her poetry dealt almost exclusively with Spanish, European and personal subjects and topics. Although she often visited her *patria chica* 'native province' and wrote about it with great feeling in her prose works, she never thought of it as "home" or as the focus of her writing. She wrote in Castilian (with the exception of one single poem in *gallego*), vigorously sought admission into Madrid's literary circles, cultivated Castilian literary lions, and from abroad stayed abreast of mainstream, national literary movements such as *Modernismo*. As is typical with expatriates, a lifetime abroad made her consider herself even more Spanish.

Amid Galician adulation and sentiment, there was one Galician scholar, José Luis Bugallal, an old family friend, who did some pioneering bio-bibliographical research. Immediately after her death, he had written several affectionate articles featuring her as the epitome of *saudade* and as "la última de las excepcionales hembras gallegas que descollaron en España...a lo largo de la segunda mitad del siglo xix y primera del actual." (*VG*) 'The last of the exceptional Galician females that stood out in Spain...during the second half of the nineteenth century and the first half of the twentieth.'

Later on, Bugallal's admiring memoir, "Sofía Casanova: Un siglo de glorias y dolores," was published in 1964 in the *Boletín de la Real Academia Gallega*. It attempted to place her in her literary and historical context, and proved valuable for later research. But, in the political atmosphere of 1958, it was easier for Casanova to be labelled and isolated as a regional poet or as a stereotypical sorrowful *gallega*.

It is unfortunate that Sofía Casanova received such hollow tributes from Spanish sources at the end of her life. Their vacuousness and narrow partisanship created an "ideology gap" between Sofía Casanova and potential readers, and discouraged serious Spanish and Hispanist scholars from exploring her works until very recently.

Polish Secondary Sources

Before World War II, Casanova had been a well-known albeit exotic figure in Poland's highest literary and political circles. During her many decades in Poland, she was frequently mentioned in books, memoirs and the press (for an example, see *Świat* 31 May 1913, a glowing account of the premiere of her play "La Madeja" in Madrid). Nonetheless, after 1945 her anti-Communist and pro-Franco past made her a non-person in the Communist government's judgment. At the same time, her family ties to the Bourbons in Spain and to pre-war nationalist political groups gave her a reputation considered "plutôt antipathique" 'rather unsympathetic' in progressive intellectual circles, where she was also not favored (Wittlin, H. interview).

Reaction to her death was muted by political circumstances. Daily papers noted her death with obituaries and brief articles. Shortly afterwards, *Kierunki*, the Warsaw Catholic literary journal, published a long article about her life, including the text of "Krople Wody," (a brilliant Polish version of her most famous poem, "Gotas de Agua"), written at the turn of the century by Antoni Lange, a distinguished literary figure. In 1961, S. Pieczara, a Polish literary scholar, published a short, two-page bibliography of her works, "Polonica, hiszpańskie". Finally, in 1973 she was the subject of a page-long entry in the *Polski Słownik Biograficzny*, Poland's standard biographical reference work. Written by her granddaughter, Prof. Krystina Niklewicz, a professor and scholar of Spanish language and literature, this entry became, along with Bugallal's memoir, the most complete and accurate bio-bibliographical account of Casanova's work to date.

Sofía Casanova: Time for a New Approach

As we mentioned above, Casanova's unresolved problems of inaccessibility, public image and critical neglect are not hers alone. But now, more than thirty years after her death in 1958, Sofía Casanova's literary corpus demands critical notice and reevaluation, the kind of scrutiny and consideration given to other Spanish women writers. The recent reissue of *La revolución bolchevista* (Castalia, 1989) reflects growing interest in her work.

There is now a wealth of information, contexts, bibliographical resources and approaches available to contemporary scholars. An initial examination of Casanova's far-ranging works has to question earlier critical assumptions based on political alignment, outdated secondary sources, Galician regionalism, or even Casanova's own seductive personality. Her texts must be examined both internally and in the setting of their time. We must develop a more complex and appropriate context, to give their due to Casanova's literary talents, her often contradictory social and political ideas, her path-breaking work as a gender writer, and her sometimes uneven works in different genres. It is time to discover Casanova's unique place within Spanish and European letters.

This is easier said than done. All-too admiring critics ranging from

8

Ramón de Campoamor and Benito Pérez Galdós to the Machado brothers, Eugenio d'Ors (874) and even Francisco Franco himself, who described her as "Spain's intellectual ambassador to Eastern Europe" (Niklewicz, K. interview; Wolikowski, R. interview), have tried to fit Casanova's extraordinary life and talents into their artistic or political schemes. But her personality and achievements were so unique and varied that they are hard to categorize

In conclusion, we know that Casanova's reputation is emerging from the obscurity imposed upon her writings. We hope that new generations of scholars will recognize her uniqueness, and through further analysis, enrich our understanding of her work and ideas.

Chapter 1

Childhood and Early Career

Sofía Guadalupe Pérez Eguía Casanova was born in the village of Almeiras, near La Coruña, in Galicia, on September 30, 1861. Her parents, Don Vicente Pérez Eguía and Doña Rosa Casanova Estomper, descended from the old Galician aristocracy. She was born in the *Pazo del Hombre*, a rambling, ivy-covered old *pazo* ("palace" in Galician). Her mother's father, Don Juan Bautista Casanova de Plá y Cancela, a retired colonel, rented the aristocratic manor house from his friend the Marquis of Almeiras. Casanova was probably baptized in the *pazo*'s private chapel, but her baptismal certificate disappeared early in her life, and she was never sure of the exact place and date (Niklewicz, K. interview).

Both sides of her family had been involved in Galicia's political life, but from opposing points of view. Although Casanova's father was a Liberal, he descended from an ultra-conservative *Carlista* family with two generals in its lineage.

One of them, Don Francisco Ramón de Eguía (1750-1827), was accused of cruelty by his many enemies. He countered that, in serving the king, one had to be "justo e inflexible," 'just and unyielding.' He was rewarded by his ruler with the title of first Count of Real Aprecio (Suárez de Tangil 201).

The other ancestral general, the more famous Nazario Eguía (1777-1865) was an "exaltado absolutista," 'a passionate absolutist', and by all accounts, an authoritarian, fanatical and ruthless individual (Risco 233). Eguía became a field marshal at a relatively early age, then ruled Galicia with an iron fist as its military commander-in-chief, relentlessly persecuting the Liberals. Enemies punished his zeal by sending him the first letter bomb in recorded history. He lost his right hand and three fingers from his left, but remained unrepentant (*EUIEA*).

After the death of Fernando VII, General Eguía became a fervent *Carlista*, and was rewarded by the Pretender Don Carlos with the title of Count of the House of Eguía. After Eguía's death, the title passed to his daughter, Doña Bernarda Eguía. Her son (Sofía Casanova's father), Don Vicente Pérez Eguía, could have claimed the title, but apparently decided it went against his political beliefs (Niklewicz, K. interview).

The maternal side of the family had more progressive political ideas. Sofía Casanova's grandfather, Colonel Juan Bautista Casanova, was related to some of the oldest families in Galicia. Like many *hidalgos* 'members of the landed nobility,' Juan Bautista Casanova was a Liberal, even at one time a Mason. Nevertheless, sometime after the return of Fernando VII in 1823 and the ensuing repression, Colonel Casanova and hundreds of Galician Liberals were forced into exile.Under assumed names, he and his wife Doña Isabel de Estomper fled to America (Niklewicz, K. interview). Their daughter Rosa Casanova, Sofía's mother, was born in New Orleans, Louisiana, and learned English at an early age (Casanova Marriage Certificate).

Sofía Casanova's grandparents probably did not return to La Coruña until the death of Fernando VII in 1833, when the political situation eased. Almost a century later, Sofía Casanova drew a loving portrait of Don Juan Bautista in one of her novels, *Como en la vida* (1931). According to her testimony and to family recollections, her grandfather was an old *hidalgo* of refined and skeptical mind. His support of education for women, equality between the sexes, and other "progressive" ideas were startling notions in provincial La Coruña. Don Juan Bautista played a role in Casanova's life similar to that of another progressive Galician, the father of novelist Emilia Pardo Bazán, who encouraged his daughter to pursue an education far beyond what was considered adequate for a woman.

Thus, Sofía Casanova's family heritage included the extreme Right and the Liberal Left, aristocratic ancestry but little money, tension between sternly traditional ideas and progressive beliefs. In her writings and political thinking, she would always be torn between extremes, self-contradicting and ambivalent about her final allegiances. But Juan Bautista Casanova's Liberal influence was strong, and his granddaughter inherited his keen interest in politics. Sofía and her brother Vicente adopted his last name as their own.

Sofía Casanova vaguely remembered her father, Don Vicente Pérez Eguía, as an affectionate parent, albeit impractical. Gentle and absent-minded, he was a contrast to his energetic and more worldly wife, Doña Rosa. The couple lived in her parents' rented *pazo*, where Sofía was born on September 30, 1861, Vicente on April 14, 1864, and Juan sometime in 1865 (*Enciclopedia Gallega*).

Don Vicente was passionate about politics and poetry. He had befriended Prime Minister Cánovas del Castillo and other well-known Galician politicians. Don Vicente did not go into politics himself (Bugallal, *Siglo* 6) but tried his hand at poetry, and submitted a poem in one of the literary "tournaments" popular at the time. In 1862, the poem was included in an acclaimed anthology of Galician poetry, next to poems by Rosalía de Castro, Concepción Arenal and other famous Galician authors (*Álbum de la Caridad* 231).

Despite his many talents, like other *gallegos* Don Vicente could not make a living in Galicia. After several years of struggle, he decided to try his luck in America, perhaps Cuba. In 1865, when Sofía Casanova was four years old, he set out alone, with plans for the rest of the family to follow. Shortly afterward his family received news that his ship had foundered, and that only a few passengers had survived. After anxious days, a list of survivors and victims reached La Coruña. To the Casanovas' despair, Don Vicente was not listed in either category. This raised troubling questions that added to their grief. Perhaps he had taken an alias to protect his family's aristocratic name from the approaching dishonor of work, and was listed under a different name among the dead. Of course, under this different name he could have survived, and gone on to America. Or perhaps going to America had been a subterfuge. Could he have planned to desert his family, and never boarded the ship, but simply left Galicia? The Casanovas agonized over this mystery for years, but it was never solved, and had a profound effect on their lives (Lutosławski, Żywot 134; Niklewicz, K. interview; Meissner, H. interview).

Casanova's grandfather had a military pension, but it was not enough to support the entire family. Money had to be found to educate the three children. The family was forced to sell possessions and heirlooms. A treasured necklace was sold, pearl by pearl. Doña Rosa's English helped her dabble in the export business, buying farm products and selling them abroad. Old friends of Don Juan Bautista discreetly loaned them money. Somehow the Casanovas got by without losing their pride or aristocratic connections. The three children were sent to a well-known private school in La Coruña, where, as Casanova reminisced in her nineties, "aprendí más que hoy se enseña en las modernas" (Bugallal *Siglo* 6) 'I learned more than what is taught today in modern schools'. Despite their financial pinch, the Casanovas strained to keep up appearances and their society connections.

These difficult early years helped shape Casanova's personality. By nature she was shy, solemn and introverted. Her family's reduced circumstances, when compared to the affluence and ease enjoyed by their social circle, were a source of great embarrassment. Her father's mysterious absence was also troubling: for years her family did not reveal to her the full details but she knew there were unpleasant implications and avoided asking direct questions about the subject. To the end of her life she glossed over his disappearance: "Mi padre...político poeta...marchó a América, no volvió..." (Bugallal *Siglo* 6) 'My father...a politician who was also a poet...went to America, didn't return.' She was sickly and withdrawn. Her family took her to doctors, worried about her health, melancholy nature, and delayed growth. The doctors recommended sunshine, fresh air, exercise, a settled routine and cutting down on her constant reading (Niklewicz; *Idilio* 75).

Along with a liking for politics, Casanova also inherited her grandfather's and father's taste for literature. She took full advantage of the family library and began to read at an early age. Immersed in books, she developed a heightened sensitivity to words and language (Pitollet 134). At home, the family library included the popular Núñez de Arce, Gustavo Adolfo Bécquer, and other post-Romantic Spanish poets. She was familiar with Gertrudis Gómez de Avellaneda and Carolina Coronado, but her literary idol was fellow Galician Rosalía de Castro. Unlike others, Rosalía wrote both in Galician and Spanish. Along with Gómez de Avellaneda, she was one of Spain's truly great poets.

It was through Casanova's readings in the *pazo*'s library, and in the many general magazines and women's publications that flourished during that period, that she discovered the lives of heroines Isabella of Spain, Teresa of Ávila and Joan of Arc, who had gone out in the world and achieved spectacular feats. Her romantic nature craved epic events like those she read about in French novels and Spanish Golden Age drama.

Provincial La Coruña provided no support or even sympathy for non-conformist women. Although Galicia was the only region of Spain to have a history of great women, theirs was a lonely and difficult tradition. Celebrated *gallegas* such as Concepción Arenal, Rosalía de Castro, and Emilia Pardo Bazán discovered before Sofía Casanova's time that it was difficult, if not impossible, for a woman to aspire to anything beyond family and religion without receiving public and private condemnation.

Clearly, from childhood on Casanova loved Galicia and its beautiful countryside. But in her later writings, beneath the traditional longing and *saudade* of an uprooted Galician, there is an undercurrent of discontent. Someone as exceptional as Casanova was stifled by its traditions. As she observed in a semi-autobiographical novel written many years later, Galicia was reactionary and hostile to spontaneity and creativity, especially in women (*Vida* 43). No matter what her gifts and ambitions, Casanova encountered envy in her peers, and ridicule and condescension from elders outside the family. In a country where only ten percent of all women knew how to read and write, her literary and personal ambitions were considered absurd.

But Sofía Casanova's mother had been forced by circumstances to work and to seek her family's fortune, and Casanova had an unusual female model to follow. Her family encouraged her writing during periods when her health improved. Around her twelfth birthday, the Casanovas decided that she and her two young brothers deserved a better education than could be found in Galicia. The family sold their holdings in La Coruña and moved to Madrid in 1873. That same year, a coup had placed sixteen-year old Alfonso XII on the Spanish throne. Ironically, the Bourbon restoration would have a powerful impact on the liberal Casanovas' future. An old friend of Don Juan Bautista from La Coruña, Patricio Aguirre de Tejeda, Count of Andino, held high office in Court and had the Royal family's confidence. He helped them resettle in Madrid (Bugallal *Siglo* 6; *PSB* 148-149; *EG*).

Madrid flourished during the Bourbon Restoration, relatively free of political strife. The city had an active cultural life, although the art of this period reflects the conservative taste of its prosperous middle class. But the intellectual atmosphere was lively enough for Casanova to satisfy long-held dreams. School records at the Madrid Conservatory show that she studied drama, literature, music and *declamación*, the reciting of poetry. Her brothers were also enrolled in good schools: "en Madrid...nuestra educación fue lo esmerada de entonces" (Bugallal *Siglo* 6) 'in Madrid...our education had the polish of that time.'

Afternoon social calls, trips to the parks of La Moncloa, El Retiro and La Granja, hours spent at El Prado museum or at the theater made Madrid infinitely more interesting than provincial La Coruña. Casanova loved high culture and the pleasures of the city. She waited impatiently to be allowed to wear long dresses, go out at night and attend plays (Niklewicz, K. interview).

Although Casanova was completely fluent in Galician and knew much about its poetic tradition, she chose Spanish as her literary language and was well acquainted with Spanish classics. She also read and spoke Portuguese fluently, and knew many Portuguese poems by heart.

French, which she studied at school, was another of her passions. Alfred de Musset was her favorite French poet. Musset was the poet "des grands douleurs" 'of great sorrows,' and she identified with his romanticism. But she was also attracted to the Parnassist ideal of a serene and remote poetry combining emotional feeling with philosophical content. She appreciated the Parnassist tradition of delicately chiseled poetry and devotion to art as a religion. From all accounts, including her own, at that time she was quiet, sensitive, devoted to her mother and brothers, sociable and well-behaved but given to melancholy. One of those periods of despair came after her grandparents' deaths, and her first poem was reportedly published soon afterwards (her grandparents apparently died shortly after the move to Madrid). At around seventeen, she underwent a sudden surge of growth, matured physically and began to enjoy the good health and looks that would characterize her adult life.

14

Her poetry was melancholy and pessimistic, reminiscent of Núñez de Arce and Bécquer, but individual enough to show her own talent. Some of these early poems reflected the Romantic *mal de siècle* in vogue in Europe. There is no trace of the abnegated, bourgeois *ángel de la casa* myth. Even when she handled conventional post-Romantic images (swallows or mountains), her earnest quest for truth and justice was noticeable. She combined concrete images (such as cliffs, rocks, even stalactites and stalagmites) with stately diction, and played out her verse in Parnassist and traditional Spanish rhyme. Readers and listeners must have been surprised by "serious" poetry coming from a woman. As a critic wrote, "...la lira de Sofía posee todas las cuerdas. Siente como una mujer, y medita como un hombre" (*Poesías* xv) 'Sofía's lyre possesses all the strings. Her feelings are those of a woman, and she ponders like a man.'

Despite its somber topics, her poetry was well received at readings. Her poems, first published in children's magazines, then in small Galician newspapers, began to appear in Madrid and in national literary magazines. The Count of Andino introduced her to the Royal Family, and she was invited to read her poems in Court.

Aside from her talent, Casanova's blonde hair, green eyes and fair complexion were unanimously praised at her Court debut. At that age, Casanova was described by an admirer as being of average height, having a delicate bone structure, elegant features, and best of all, abundant and aristocratically blonde hair (both her grandmothers had Dutch blood, from the days when the Spanish Empire extended to the Netherlands). All these traits added cachet to the image of a young poet (Pitollet 134).

Chaperoned by her mother and the Count, she recited her poems before the king and queen, who were reportedly moved by her performance. According to family legend, Casanova was declaiming her verses to the king and queen when an usher announced the arrival of an important minister. Imperiously the usher was told: "Let the minister wait!" Even if this anecdote were only family legend, what is certain is that Sofía Casanova impressed Alfonso XII and Queen María Cristina enough that they agreed to subsidize her work. Despite the successes of Gómez de Avellaneda, Coronado and Rosalía de Castro, it would have been difficult for Casanova, a penniless young woman and an unknown writer, to take her work directly to a publisher. Her first book, simply titled *Poesías,* was published in 1885 and dedicated to the royal family. Royal patronage had made all the difference (Niklewicz, K. interview; Meissner, H. interview).

The Marquis of Valmar and his wife ran a well-known literary *tertulia* 'gathering', and welcomed Casanova to soirees at their home on

Calle Cervantes (Velasco Zazo 159). Casanova dedicated one of her first published poems to the Marquise (*Poesías* 92). Don Ramón de Campoamor (then considered Spain's leading poet) was impressed by her talent, became her official mentor and introduced her to other poets and artists. She met her long-admired playwrights, José de Zorrilla and José Echegaray, and attended performances of their plays. She struck up a life-long friendship with another young woman, Blanca de los Ríos, who had also published her first book of poems in 1881 (Bugallal *Siglo* 20). In addition, she met Emilio Ferrari, Núñez de Arce's leading disciple, who was to have some influence on her style. Accompanied by her mother or another chaperon, she enjoyed the company of other now-forgotten literary figures such as Liberal playwright Joaquín Dicenta, poet Salvador Rueda, and many others (*Wolski* 83).

Slowly, Casanova began to be recognized as a new talent in Restoration Madrid. Through her royal connections, the family fortunes continued to rise. Doña Rosa and her children were received everywhere. Vicente Casanova entered the Navy and found a position in its Ministry, although now he, too, wanted to be a poet and was to have some success. The future looked bright. Later in life, in an interview printed in the Polish magazine *Świat*, Casanova remembered that those years of attention and success in Madrid, after her sad childhood, seemed "like a dream or a fairytale" (Świat 31 May 1913).

Wincenty Lutosławski

Although she never wrote about it directly, Sofía Casanova's unusual courtship and marriage loomed large in her life and works. The events preceding and following her marriage were profusely documented by the two protagonists. Most of the account that follows is drawn from their own accounts, particularly from Wincenty Lutosławski's autobiography *Jeden Łatwy Żywot* and from family memories.

At twenty-four "Sofitina," as she was called by her family, had reached the age when most Spanish girls were married. She had several admirers, but her pessimism made her think that in this world, happiness in love was impossible. Several of her poems hint at one disappointing romance, if not more.

Casanova knew that none of the Spanish men who admired and encouraged her writing would marry a woman who wanted to be a writer. Even the urbane Campoamor cloistered his wife from Madrid's *salons*. Marrying an ordinary Spanish man and having a family would put an end to her writing and what limited freedom she enjoyed. Casanova's mother had escaped that fate, having a "progressive" father and no husband, and Casanova herself had so far gone through her life with a minimum of masculine interference.

Still, some of Casanova's early poems show a yearning for an all-powerful, all-wise "soulmate." Several speak of this ideal man, a lover of beauty, "a haughty genius" (*Poesías* 75). Her intuition also told her that if she ever married, her husband would not be Spanish.

Along with many Spanish intellectuals of the time, Casanova was an admirer of the "genius of the North." Even before Madame de Staël wrote *De l'Allemagne*, many European artists and intellectuals agreed with Voltaire: "C'est du nord d'où nous vient la lumière" 'Light comes to us from the North.' For Casanova, as for many Spanish intellectuals and artists, Wagner, Ibsen, Strindberg and many others fell into a broad "northern" category.

In the 1880s, Spanish writers were interested in Ibsen, and read him in translation. Some of her ideas about the man she would marry came from reading Ibsen's plays with an unsuccessful suitor, a theater critic. From his works she learned about strong-willed men who were dissatisfied with the limitations that society and custom imposed upon them, men such as Brandt in the play by that name that had premiered in 1866.

At that time the family lived on the Travesía Conde Duque, #6, near the Atocha railroad station, then the terminal for trains coming in from France. At night, they could hear the mournful sound of whistles as trains arrived from and departed to the North. Casanova would tell her skeptical family, "Someday my husband is going to come from the North in one of those trains" (Niklewicz, K. interview; Meissner, K. interview).

On June 6, 1886, Wincenty Lutosławski, a young Polish philosophy student visiting Madrid, was told by his host, Don Ramón de Campoamor, to visit Sofía Casanova, the poet. Lutosławski, then studying Romance Languages at the École des Hautes Études, had taken the train from Paris to Madrid, and was staying in Madrid as Campoamor's house guest. Gaston Paris, the French medievalist, had sent Don Ramón a letter introducing the young Polish student as one of the most brilliant scholars he had ever taught. Lutosławski was intrigued by the allusion to Casanova's pessimistic poetry, and decided to visit her that very afternoon (Lutosławski, Żywot 137; Niklewicz, K. interview).

Lutosławski was tall and handsome, a polymath and the scion of a distinguished Polish family wealthy enough to support his vigorous program of study and travel. He had wide scholarly interests and worked in many disciplines. He had originally received scientific training, and held degrees in chemistry and philosophy. But he also read Latin and Classical Greek with ease, and was fluent in Polish, Russian, German,

French, English, and now Spanish. At the moment, he was doing research for a book on European pessimism, and wanted to explore Spanish literature. Don Ramón's poetry did not fall within his topic, but he gave Lutosławski a letter of introduction to Casanova. Her poetry, he assured Lutosławki, "simply radiated pessimism (Lutosławski, Żywot 136)."

When Lutosławski arrived at Casanova's modest home and asked for her in halting Spanish, he was told by the servant girl answering the door that she was out. However, her mother, Doña Rosa Casanova, received him. After a pleasant conversation in English with her guest, Doña Rosita ordered a servant to summon her daughter home. Sofía Casanova had been visiting friends nearby and grudgingly cut short her visit. She returned to find an imposing foreigner by the outlandish name of Wincenty Lutosławski in her family drawing room. Eight years later, she wrote a novel, *El doctor Wolski*, whose main character was based on Lutosławski. She described him thus:

> Era el polaco un hombre como de veinticinco años, elevada
> estatura y sana conformación. Tenía los ojos oscuros, la frente despejada y altiva, como Byron, el pelo cortado al rape, y en todo su ser un algo que se imponía, que era el reflejo de su carácter, de su entusiasmo por la ciencia, de su alma...Era un hermoso tipo de hombre eslavo (25).

> The Pole was a man of about twenty-five, of great height and healthy physique. He had dark eyes, a clear and haughty brow like Byron's, his hair cut short... (there was) in... his manner something imposing, that was the reflection of his character, of his enthusiasm for knowledge... of his soul... He was a handsome example of Slavic manhood...

She surprised him in turn. Casanova was blonde and green-eyed, which he thought unusual in a Spaniard. Her fragile, fine-boned beauty and her high, feminine voice strangely affected him. As they chatted in Spanish he found that she had a lively intellect and a sensitive nature. He told her of his affinity for ancient Greece and its philosophy, particularly of his passion for Plato, which he read in the original Greek. He wanted to make his life's work out of the *Dialogues* and their quest for ultimate reality. Reincarnation and spiritualism also interested him (*Lutosławski, Żywot* 136).

Lutosławski told Casanova that in his native Poland (now divided into three by Russians, Germans and Austrians) Poles were not allowed to teach other Poles, or even to speak Polish in the classroom. He planned to remain abroad indefinitely, get a doctorate in philosophy and find a teaching post somewhere in Europe.

They talked until Doña Rosita reminded them that it was past

18

midnight. To their amazement, they had talked for five hours. The sixth of June had been Lutosławski's twenty-fourth birthday. He promised to return later and continue their conversation.

The following afternoon, she inscribed a copy of her book for him. As he glanced through it, he had an extraordinary experience which he related many years later in his autobiography, *Jeden Łatwy Żywot 'An Easy Life'*:

Then something took place, which I cannot explain without referring to our past lives, and the relations that had existed between us then. Looking at the inscription I told her I would write something in Polish, something that I would not translate as yet, but which she would witness. Half-consciously I wrote: "ta kobieta będzie moją żoną." 'this woman will be my wife.' This was not an act of the will, or of desire. It was almost a prophecy, expressed automatically, without involving the will or the senses. (137-138)

This incident made a profound impression on Lutosławski, but he did not mention it to anyone, including Casanova, for some time. He stayed for a few more hours, and the following day left for Paris as planned. But before crossing the French border at Irún, he sent Casanova the first of a series of extraordinary letters that took their marriage for granted.

In his letters, Lutosławski wrote about the "sign" he had received as he leafed through her book. He had read deeply in Polish literature, particularly in the "Messianist" school (Juliusz Słowacki, Zygmunt Krasiński, and above all, Adam Mickiewicz, Poland's greatest poet). The Messianists held that Poland's Christ-like sacrifice at the hands of her enemies would redeem the world. In one of Mickiewicz's visionary poems, Lutosławski found a foreshadowing of his relationship with Casanova. In 1823, Mickiewicz's famous *Dziady (Forefathers' Eve)* predicted that a great leader, the "Polish Messiah," would have a foreign mother and a Polish father:

Behold! A child has emerged
It grows -- it is a defender,
The resurrector of our nation.
His mother is an alien:
His blood, of ancient heroes,
And his name will be forty and four. (Mickiewicz 76-77)

Several generations of Polish Messianists had pondered these lines, trying to interpret the prophecy and identify the protagonists. Lutosławski believed that he and Casanova had been fated to meet, marry and bear the redeemer of Poland (He assured her that the allusion to "forty and four" would become clear later on). By marrying her, he would fulfill the voice's command and Poland's national destiny. She, in turn, would be instrumental in changing world history.

Her reaction was mixed. At first Casanova wouldn't consider the idea of marriage. Lutosławski's good looks and magnetic personality both attracted and intimidated her. She admitted that part of her was falling in love with him through the power of his letters. But she did not share his certainty about their "destiny" and his bizarre mixture of political and mystical ideas. She was attracted to the man, not to his beliefs. In a semi-autobiographical novel written in 1931, she described a similar courtship (*Idilio* 117-121).

Casanova sympathized with Poland's plight. And she was moved by Lutosławski's family dilemmas, some of which reminded her of her own. Like her, he had lost a parent when very young. Lutosławski's mother had died when he was six. Soon afterwards, while he and his brother were still grieving, they were deeply distressed when their father asked them, as "involved parties," to decide for him whether he should marry their mother's sister, Paulina Szczygielska. They told him to go ahead and marry her, but secretly resented the responsibility of having to make that decision (and the constant presence of their stepmother, who bore their father four more sons). In his autobiography, written many decades later, Lutosławski recalls the enormous feeling of responsibility he felt about deciding to "replace" their mother. It was too much to ask of children at such an early age. After a while they became resigned, although inwardly troubled and resentful. Lutosławski swore never to mention his mother again, and never to anger his stepmother (Żywot 22). As many children do when they lose a parent early in childhood, he developed an active inner life, and a sensitive, restless nature, always slightly dissatisfied with himself and the here and now, seeking something that he vaguely sensed was missing from the natural order of things.

Although Lutosławski wrote confident and persuasive letters, he was secretly uncertain. There was a darker side to his personality, a burden that came with the gift of high intelligence. He suffered from alternating periods of high, manic energy, and then of lethargic depression. He was vacationing in Spain to recover from exhaustion after finishing his university examinations. A near-breakdown had driven him to the brink of suicide. He was researching pessimism to purge himself of his own morbid preoccupations.

It was the irrational "force," not his own desire, that urged him to marry Casanova. As he admitted in his autobiography many years later, aside from the "force's" command he was really ambivalent. He was unsure about marriage between such different nationalities and temperaments. A woman would disrupt his Spartan scholarly life.

He also knew that the idea of having a son was much more exciting than the reality of a wife. Lutosławski was an early believer in eugenics. He firmly believed that the human race would be improved by allowing marriage only among healthy partners, and banning it for the diseased. In his letters to "Sofitina," as he too now called her, he quizzed her about her family's medical history. He reviewed his own, and came to the conclusion that their son would have optimal health. He also sketched the "hygienic" way in which their son would be raised, and the conditions that would bring out his best characteristics.

He had already planned a curriculum beginning with their child's earliest years. Even if they lived abroad, Polish would be the family language. Tutors would educate him (and the other sons to follow) in the thoughts of the greatest philosophers. The children would be brought up rationally, and become Poland's leaders. Their first son's name would be Henryk, after Goethe's *Faust* (actually Heinrich in German), and also after the main character in Zygmunt Krasiński's "Nieboska Komedia" 'The Undivine Comedy,' (1835) one of his favorite Polish plays and one of the great achievements of Poland's Romantic drama. He assured Casanova that she would enjoy the play someday, after she learned Polish.

This intense correspondence went on for four months. By fall, her resolve was weakening, but she still agonized about leaving her family and friends. Quite unconsciously, Casanova felt the weight of centuries of Spain's self-imposed isolation from Europe. Study abroad had been banned since the sixteenth century. She knew almost nothing of life beyond the Pyrenees except what she had read in French novels and literary journals. Lutosławski truthfully described Poland as an unhappy nation torn apart by foreign occupation. To Casanova it sounded like Poland was a harsh land of long, dark winters, a difficult language and a tense political situation -- far different from Madrid's lively and cheerful atmosphere.

Sometimes she felt inadequate to the challenge of sharing such an unusual life. In Casanova's novel *El doctor Wolski*, Mara (the brilliant young physician's fiancee), echoes her thoughts: "Enrique es un hombre superior. Su vida tiene una noble misión que cumplir. ¿Podré ayudarle? ¿No me encontraré inferior a él?" (*Wolski* 58-59) 'Enrique is a superior man: his life has a noble mission to fulfill. Will I be able to help him? Will I not find myself inferior to him?'

At other times she secretly exulted at having been chosen by Lutosławski. Being totally secure in his intellectual superiority, he was not threatened by her talent, but rather pleased at the thought of having a poet as a wife. His attitude toward her work encouraged her. With him she could travel far away from narrow-minded Spain and its self-imposed isolation. She would learn about Lutosławski's work in order to help him, and pursue her own writing and study. Together they would live on the

21

highest intellectual plane and strive for perfection. There would be nothing ordinary about them: as she told a confidante, it would be like marrying Plato! (Niklewicz, K. interview)

While long, impassioned letters flew back and forth between Paris and Madrid, the two families mobilized against the marriage. Although Doña Rosita was more-or-less sympathetic to Lutosławski on a personal level, she and her sons weren't aware of the crucial role in world history that he envisioned for her daughter, and argued against the marriage on personal, "selfish" grounds.

From the family's manor in Poland came a stern letter from Lutosławski's father, expressing his concern about admitting a foreign "artiste" to their hard-working Polish family. How could his son marry someone whose background was so different from theirs, whom they had never met and who knew nothing about their family's commitment to Polish independence? The match was obviously unsuitable.

Even his mentor, Professor Paris, to whom he confessed his "supernatural" experience (and with whom he was editing an Old French manuscript of *Tristan et Iseut*), thought that marriage between these unlikely partners was a doomed affair, "just like Tristan's," he joked (*Żywot* 139).

Still, the "mysterious necessity" that impelled Lutosławski was inexorable, and eventually overrode Casanova's doubts. He was an extraordinary man, in her eyes a genius. Perhaps it was the thought of being the helpmate to a genius that finally seduced her. What if she let this opportunity pass, and never had another? She had always longed for adventure, and here it was, beckoning her.

In October 1886, she agreed to marry him the following spring, and live abroad for the indefinite future, perhaps for the rest of her life. In the fall of 1887 Lutosławski planned to study in Estonia with one of his mentors, Gustav Teichmuller, a celebrated German philosopher. They would have to move to Estonia for at least the duration of the academic year. In terms of Spanish nineteenth-century society and her sheltered upbringing, this was a bold, almost heroic step toward the unknown (Niklewicz, K. interview).

The understandings that Casanova and Lutosławski reached in their letters would have shocked their families. They were secretly non-believers, but planned to marry in the Church for the sake of their families. However, they vowed to remain "spiritually free," so that either could regain his or her freedom if the marriage proved unsuitable. Casanova also solemnly agreed that their children would be brought up as Polish citizens, and that Polish would be the language of their home, no matter where they lived.

22

The Casanovas were still reluctant to consent to the marriage. Her mother wrote to the Spanish Embassy in Russia, with the help of the Marquis of Valmar (at one time Spain's ambassador to St. Petersburg), to investigate the young man's background. A letter arrived after a few weeks, informing them of the Lutosławskis' landed wealth, high-minded political pursuits and intellectual accomplishments.

In turn, at his father's bidding, Lutosławski visited Madrid for a week, and met confidentially with Campoamor. The worldly man of letters assured him that Casanova, although not rich, had good character and an exemplary reputation, and would make him an excellent wife. Lutosławski wrote to his father that he was satisfied, and that he would marry her (Lutosławski, Żywot 152). After Lutosławski departed for Paris, Casanova began to plan their wedding for the following March.

Faced with this turn of events, both families resigned themselves to the union. However, friends of the Casanova family expressed consternation when the engagement was announced. The young man was rumored to be "a bear from the North," and Casanova was criticized for being overly romantic and warned that she would regret her rashness (Idilio 238).

On March 19, 1887, Sofía Pérez Eguía Casanova and Wincenty Lutosławski were married in Madrid's Church of San Marcos. Lutosławski's brother Stanisław came from Poland to be best man and represent the family. As Casanova had no older male relatives, the Count of Andino walked her to the altar and gave her away, while her brother Vicente Casanova was one of the witnesses (Marriage Certificate).

After the reception, the bride said heart-breaking but brave good-byes to family and friends. That evening, her new husband at her side, Casanova left for Portugal by train, stepping out of her old life into the new.

Chapter 2

Marriage and Motherhood

During the summer of 1887, Casanova and Lutosławski travelled through Europe on a scholar's honeymoon. They spent a few weeks in Portugal, visiting philosopher Teófilo Braga, Cristóbal Ayres, the poet, and other notables. Then they stayed three months in London while Lutosławski did research at the British Museum Library. Finally, they spent six weeks in Paris while he finished his scholarly work under the guidance of Gaston Paris.

The British Museum Library impressed Casanova with its artistic riches, but, when she described her first visit there in an essay published many years later, it also intimidated her with its dazzling variety of scholarship and intellectual achievement (*Pecado* 131). Despite her accomplishments, on this first visit she felt an acute sense of her deficient educational background. She realized that outside of Spain, women enjoyed far better education and status. But she loved Paris and enjoyed her stay in France.

As they travelled together, they spent many hours discussing their lives and matters they had not touched upon in their letters. Casanova realized from her husband's thorough but impassioned recollections, that he believed that his life's mission was tied to Poland's re-emergence as a nation. Their marriage was but a small matter within the larger context of Poland's deliverance from foreign oppression. The more she learned about Polish history from her husband, the more her generous and enthusiastic nature sympathized with the sufferings of the Polish people. She was astonished as her husband's intellectual accomplishments and highly disciplined life revealed themselves before her. He was a truly superior man, an outstanding spirit who needed an outstanding woman to support him in his life work. She listened carefully as he described the uncertain status of his academic future, and the nomadic life they could expect until he was assigned a permanent professorial post.

And still another factor, which Lutosławski called "instinct," drew their dissimilar lives together. As he noted dryly in his autobiography, "It is easier to submit to the charm of a beautiful body than to plumb such a different soul (Żywot 173)". Casanova became pregnant a month after the wedding. In Lutosławski's mind, this child would be "Henryk," the redeemer of Poland. To prepare Casanova for her future role, while still honeymooning in Portugal, he began to teach her Polish. Without a grammar book or dictionary they went over the Polish national epic, Mickiewicz's *Pan Tadeusz*, stanza by stanza, translating it into Spanish as they read. By the end of their honeymoon, they both had translated *Pan Tadeusz* from Polish to Spanish twelve times. The results varied: his Spanish improved to the point where he was soon able to write scholarly articles on philosophical matters for the *Revista de España*, but her Polish still faltered and was heavily accented to the end of her life (Niklewicz, K. interview).

Later that summer, the couple reached the manor of Drozdowo, the Lutosławski estate located sixty miles northeast of Warsaw. Casanova was warmly received by the large Lutosławski clan, whose high-mindedness and political activism she quickly grew to admire. Lutosławski's father, Franciszek, stepmother Paulina and five brothers (Stanisław, 23; Marian, 17; Jan, 13; Kazimierz, 8; Józef, 7) were all fervent Polish nationalists. The father and oldest son ran the family estate and managed several prosperous businesses, including a brewery. They enjoyed substantial wealth, and had no worries about their financial future. The elder Lutosławski, who prized rationality and self-control, ran the estate like a benevolent patriarch, managing his large staff, supporting an *Ochronka* or primary school, a church and a small clinic for the peasant families. He scheduled a daily regimen of work, exercise, study and recreation for his large family. Thanks to their affluence and discipline, the Lutosławskis dedicated their professional lives to the reestablishment of a Polish nation. Their nationalism and ardent Catholicism were driving forces behind the family's involvement in social issues and education. Casanova, who was exempted from work and did not have to help her mother-in-law run the household, admired their version of "plain living and high thinking."

Lutosławski and his family epitomized a political and philosophical tendency that pervaded all three Polands at that time. As a reaction to Poland's romantic but ultimately catastrophic history, Polish "Positivists" replaced the revolutionary spirit of the past with a conservative reaction. Within a broad framework that embraced everything from politics and literature to daily life, Positivism encouraged optimism, hard work and above all positive and rational activity in every field. The Lutosławski's earnestness and dedication made an enormous impression on Casanova. She wanted to imitate their rational lifestyle and orderly good works. She described their ideals and her reaction to them in an article written later and published in a collection of her essays:

Todos han cumplido sus obligaciones del día, y en todos se nota la satisfacción honrada y discreta de quienes van por la vida sabiendo lo que tienen que hacer y lo hacen... se me entra en el alma un deseo ardiente, un ansia, que es impulso febril de hacer algo por mi patria... Algo... No sé que... Una obra de humildad y de amor por mi patria. (*Exóticas* 179-181)

They all have carried out their daily responsibilities, and in all of them one can notice the honest and discreet satisfaction of those who go through life knowing what they have to do, and doing it... a burning desire enters my soul, an aspiration, a feverish impulse to do something for my country... Something... I don't know what... A work of humility and love for my country.

During that first idyllic summer, she studied Polish with the children's tutors, played *gallego* songs on the piano for her new relatives while they taught her to play their Polish favorites, visited neighboring estates and enjoyed the high regard of her new family and friends. She wrote long letters to family and friends in Spain describing Poland and its politics, and remained in touch with Spanish happenings through newspapers, magazines and books sent to her almost every day by her brother Vicente.

Conditions in Poland outside the oasis of Drozdowo were much less to her liking. Although temporarily erased from the map of Europe, Poland clung tenaciously to its Catholic religion, language and identity in the face of brutal occupation. Although a strong supporter of Spanish military intervention in Cuba and other colonies, Casanova was outraged by the abuses of the Russian military, whole-heartedly siding with Poland in its struggle against foreign rulers. The partitioned Polish nation might not have been entirely blameless (Polish anti-Semitism disturbed her greatly), but she considered Poland the injured party.

By the time she first arrived in 1888, the corrupt Russian military bureaucracy had begun to slacken its hold on Poland's intellectual life, but backward censors still dominated the press and the publishing industry. Newspapers were closed, magazine articles suppressed, unauthorized books denied publication. Heavy fines were imposed on publishers, newspapers or writers who printed or wrote any item contrary to the authority of the Czar. Unlike most authoritarian states, which have a list or index of *proscribed* works, czarist Russia banned so many books that they simply developed a list of *authorized* works. For the book-loving Lutosławski couple, who travelled with many boxes of books in several languages, getting the necessary permission to bring their books into the country required months of humiliating red tape and bribes (*Exóticas* 49).

Other violations of Polish rights angered Casanova's generous nature. She found the obligatory prayers in Polish for the health of Nicholas II and the Royal family, at the end of the Latin mass, to be a refined form of cruelty. Orthodox Russia had always suspected Roman Catholic, western-oriented Poland of betraying the Slavonic tradition, and the czarist government tried to force Roman Catholics into submission. Polish worshippers were admonished in their own language to thank the Czar for the kindness he had shown Poland. Casanova reacted:

¿Dar gracias al zar por su bondad y su protección? Imposible, jamás, gritan las conciencias de los asistentes al templo, en un momento de rebelión... Pero el sacerdote, volviéndose a ellos desde el altar, les ordena prosternarse a todos, que recen con sublime obediencia, y las plegarias y los llantos llenan la católica iglesia de rumores tristes.
(*Volga* 10-11)

To thank the Czar for his kindness and protection? Imposible, never, cry the consciences of those attending worship in the temple, in a moment of rebellion... But the priest, turning to them from the altar, orders them to kneel and bow their heads (to pray) with sublime obedience, and prayers and weeping fill the Catholic church with sad murmurs.

Casanova was also disturbed by new insights into Spanish politics. From her new, Eastern European perspective, she wrote that Spain's lax atmosphere and rotating Liberal-Conservative governments kept the nation in a state of ignorance and apathy (*Volga* 9). These concerns were reflected in her intense correspondence with friends and relatives in Spain, and in articles about Poland that she wrote for Spanish newspapers. Her husband was pleased by her growing political interests, sensing that her detailed descriptions of Polish life and Russian oppression filled a vacuum in Spanish public opinion (Lutosławski Żywot 144-145).

In September 1889, the couple moved to Dorpat, Estonia, where Lutosławski began a rigorous academic program at the University of Dorpat. As the elation of marriage, meeting her new family and exploring new cultures faded, Casanova was overwhelmed by the brutal winter, new language barriers, and the enormous distance between Estonia and Spain. She suffered the *saudade* of exile, and her poems reflect this condition (*Fugaces* 76). As the birth of their child approached, Lutosławski talked to her about the future and about the children they were going to have. In her novel, *El doctor Wolski* (which appeared several years later in 1894) the eponymous main character describes the ideal family which he and his fiancée would have someday:

Realizaré el sueño de mi existencia... tendré hijos, los cuidaré desde antes que nazcan, desarrollaré sus fuerzas físicas y morales en el medio adecuado... que nos indiquen la razón y la ciencia. Mis hijos serán inteligentes y sanos, servirán a mi oprimida patria, y los hijos de ellos continuarán mi obra de regeneración... (65)

I will fulfill my life's ambition... I will have children, and nurture them even before they are born, I will develop their physical and moral force in an adequate environment... shown to us by reason and science. My children will be intelligent and healthy, they will serve my oppressed country, and their children will continue my work of regeneration.

Lutosławski's belief in eugenics was documented in his memoirs, family recollections, and his wife's account of "hygienic" ideas in *El doctor Wolski*. He believed that one could improve the human race by researching the health of the two families involved in a marriage, and by matching individuals of acceptable histories.

He envisioned his future son being brought up according to the latest theories of health and child care. The family home would have a large garden, running water and a northern exposure. The boy would take in plenty of fresh air and exercise, avoid eating meat (following Teichmuller's example, Lutosławski had become a vegetarian), and eschew coffee, tea and alcohol. Tutors would educate him and other sons to follow in the tradition of great philosophers. They would be trained as exceptional leaders for their country. Even when abroad, Polish would be the only language spoken at home. They would be like Plato's "philosopher-kings," and bring light to Poland and the world. Dr. Wolski spoke for Lutosławski:

¡Nuestros hijos! Tu no sabes con que ardiente afan estudié pensando en ellos... serán polacos... y para que sirvan a nuestra Polonia les daremos la salud, la instrucción y la fuerza de voluntad necesarias a los hombres que tienen el santo fin de ayudar a la salvación de su patria...ese manantial de salud y energías que nuestros hijos y nuestros nietos aportarán a la vida, no se perderá en el flujo y reflujo de las generaciones. (*Wolski* 65)

Our children! You don't know how eagerly I studied with them in mind... they will be Polish... and to help them serve our Poland we will give them health, education and the willpower needed by those men whose holy goal is to help redeem our country.. this stream of health and energies that our children and our grandchildren will bring to life, will not be lost in the ebb and flow of generations.

Lutosławski waited for "Henryk"'s birth with confidence. Casanova went into labor on January 19, appropriately enough the eve of Saint Henryk's Day. It was a great disappointment to Lutosławski that "not the longed-for son Henryk, only a daughter" was born on St. Henryk's Day (Lutosławski, Żywot 158-159).

At first, Lutosławski was taken aback by the birth of a girl. But, as he noted in his autobiography, "I soon forgave my daughter for not being a boy" (Żywot 159). There would be other children, and for a philosopher, the experience of fatherhood was "interesting." He candidly admitted that Marie (or "Mania", as his family called her) made more of an impression in his life in a few weeks than his wife had in a year (159).

Casanova did not mind at all that the baby was a female, and dubbed her "Mañita" (her version of the Polish nickname and the Spanish diminutive -ita, which soon became the child's permanent name). She noticed that the Lutosławski family made much of the first female child born in a generation. As Casanova became fluent in Polish, she realized that her husband's ideas about Messianism, and about the "son of a foreign mother and the blood of ancient heroes" were not shared by his family, nor by the great majority of the Polish people she met. Although he was held in almost universal high esteem thanks to his high intelligence, outstanding educational achievements and strong character, he was also generally considered idealistic and impractical. Some detractors actually derided his more esoteric ideas (reincarnation, eugenics, the Polish Messiah) as downright peculiar. But his intellectual superiority and self-confidence (somewhat tinged with arrogance) gave him an added edge of magnetism that attracted many others.

By the end of the academic year, Lutosławski had received other unpleasant surprises. His mentor at the University died unexpectedly in May, leaving him without support or the possibility of an academic job. That summer, Lutosławski fruitlessly tried to find a position teaching philosophy in the Russian university system. Although Lutosławski did not need to earn a living, he was anxious to embark on his teaching career. In 1889, in a desperate effort to find a job, he and Casanova, who was again pregnant, traveled to Moscow via carriage, train and sled. The search proved fruitless, with the consolation that he was able to do research at the Rumiantsev Museum Library (now Lenin State Library) (Lutosławski, Żywot 160).

Casanova found Russia unbearable. She loathed the bitter winter weather, and saw her worst suspicions about czarist rule confirmed. She had been predisposed to dislike the Czar, given his treatment of Poland.

But the poverty and degradation in which the Czar's rule kept the Russian masses astonished her. Everything seemed grossly out of balance. There was both enormous wealth and enormous poverty, great religious faith but almost total illiteracy, social chaos compounded by rigid totalitarian rule. Her first experience of Russia was negative:

El clima de Rusia, inclemente enemigo, hace a los hombres duros, ineptos, bestiales. (*De Rusia* 129)

Russia's climate, an inclement enemy, makes men harsh, inept, brutal.

Along with the harsh weather and language difficulties came another reversal. To Lutosławski's dismay, "another daughter," Izabela, was born in Moscow during the winter of 1889 (Lutosławski, Żywot 161). Casanova, although again surprised that the promised male child had not arrived, was once more delighted with the new baby.

The long, harsh winter in Moscow had taken its toll. When they packed their many belongings and books in spring, and returned to Drozdowo in June of 1890, Casanova fell into a state of exhaustion. Depressed and tired of moving, she was desperate to return to Spain and to her family. Lutosławski, however, thought that even a few weeks in Spain would be a frivolous waste of time. His academic future stood at a crossroads: his failure to find a position had convinced him that the sooner he finished research at the British Museum and wrote his book, the sooner he would find an academic job and begin his life's work. Lutosławski actually wanted the rest of the family to stay in Drozdowo with his relatives for a year, giving him total freedom to conduct his research. But Casanova insisted passionately that she had a right to go home, even if it were only for a few days on the way to London. Finally he gave in, and without enthusiasm prepared for a trip to Spain.

Among Lutosławski's many deeply-held theories was one that affected the family's travel. Lutosławski was of the opinion that one could only get to know a country and its people by travelling third-class or even less expensively (James *Essays* 230). For someone with his linguistic abilities and Spartan habits, this was perhaps true. But it was certainly difficult for the rest of the family. Loaded with luggage and books, accompanied by a maid and two babies (one nursing), they took a long and trying trip over the plains of Eastern Europe, from Warsaw to the German border, through Cologne and Berlin, through France via Paris, and across the Pyrenees through Irún to Madrid.

Lutosławski's lack of sympathy pointed to the sharp difference between his and Casanova's natures. He dedicated himself completely to an intellectual career, and could not understand her emotional attachments to family and place. As long as he was doing satisfying scholarly work, he was impervious to weather, place and emotions. Unconsciously, he was pushing her away with his self-absorption, emotional detachment, and relentless idealism (Lutosławski, Żywot 162).

El bárbaro del Norte

While Casanova rejoiced at being reunited with her family, her husband resigned himself to a few weeks wasted in what he perceived as a cultural backwater. This time Lutosławski found much to dislike in Madrid, as recorded in his autobiography. The quality of intellectual discourse appalled him; his earlier, more favorable impressions vanished. The literary and philosophical life of Madrid was a "Vanity Fair." He viewed Spain as a strange combination of wretchedness and progress, and dismissed his wife's aristocratic and literary acquaintances as amateurs and intellectual lightweights. To someone of Lutosławski's rigorous training, the few in Madrid who called themselves *filósofos* were contemptible. Their knowledge was superficial, their ideas vapid, their teaching methods deplorable. Lutosławski did not want to teach philosophy, he wanted to *be* a philosopher, unlike those he viewed as Madrid's readers of translations. Lutosławski felt what the Generation of '98 expressed a few years later, but at the time his views were heretical. In response to their visitor's contempt, his Spanish acquaintances found Lutosławski's ideas on reality, and particularly on Messianism, to be "madness". They nicknamed him "el bárbaro del Norte" (Lutosławski, Żywot 163-164) 'the savage from the north.'

However, there was one Spanish intellectual Lutosławski admired, and who, in turn, considered his ideas with interest. Don Francisco Giner de los Ríos, "the Spanish Socrates", had founded the *Institución Libre de Enseñanza*, a free, independent university that aimed to improve Spanish education and culture. As Lutosławski realized, the *Institución's* pedagogical methods were decades ahead those of other European universities. The Polish philosopher was able to contribute articles to de los Ríos' *Boletín de la Institución de Libre Enseñanza*, so he felt the trip to Madrid was not a total waste. The family went on to spend a year in London (1889-1890), where Lutosławski continued to work on his book on Plato's *Dialogues*.

Central Asia   (1890-1893)

After a summer spent in Drozdowo, Lutosławski received his first teaching appointment in the fall of 1890. He was named *privatdozent* at the University of Kazan, in the Tatar region of Eastern Russia. Kazan, a river city situated on the Volga, was more Tatar and Muslim than Russian in culture and architecture. With its mosques and church spires, it proved to be a mixed blessing. Lutosławski finally had an academic position, but he chafed under the provincial Russian university system whose meager resources limited his research.

For Casanova, life in an "oriental" Russian city, with bitter winters, a provincial cultural life and an oppressive political atmosphere was stifling. She kept detailed notes on daily life in Kazan, explored the *Stara Tatarska* (the old Tartar quarter), and documented its exotic atmosphere. She was repelled by the brutal attitude of the czarist authorities and the suffering of the peasants and nomads living outside Kazan. Two narratives, the short story "El Intruso" 'The intruder'[3] and her first novel, *El doctor Wolski* (begun in 1890 and published in 1893), date from this period. In Kazan she was cut off from a normal social life and unable to share her husband's interests, and she suffered acutely from *saudade* and alienation. These feelings are reflected in her few poems from this period, some of them published in Spain by the prestigious *La Ilustración Ibérica*.

Lutosławski spent his days teaching, doing research, and following a strenuous regimen of exercise and vegetarian diet to fight his alternating manic and depressive states. His brooding deepened with the birth of the couple's third daughter, Jadwiga, in 1891.

The idea of breeding and educating a genius was a popular one during the nineteenth and even twentieth century. Writers as diverse as Flaubert and George Bernard Shaw have approached the topic, some quite seriously and others humorously (particularly Unamuno in *Amor y pedagogía*, 1902). But for Lutosławski, who had a strong awareness of his intellectual gifts coupled with an overwhelming sense of obligation to Poland's future, bearing the "Messiah" became an obsession. Casanova's "failure" to bear him a male child was at first inexplicable, then increasingly irksome, and finally inexcusable.

That same year, when his father died, Lutosławski, Casanova and the children returned to the family manor in Poland. After the estate was settled, Lutosławski had even more money and leisure for his travels and writing. Teaching in Kazan had become monotonous and, to Lutosławski's mind, irrelevant. The Lutosławskis returned to Kazan for one final semester in January, 1892. Leaving the children in Drozdowo, they took a train to St. Petersburg, on to Nizny Novgorod, and then rode a horse-driven sled on the frozen Volga. Casanova kept a journal of the expedition, which covered one hundred leagues in forty hours. The journal later on became her first travel book, *Sobre el Volga helado* (1902).

Word of Lutosławski's growing reputation as a philosopher reached America, and he was invited to the Parliament of Religions at the World's Fair in Chicago, in September 1893. He went to the United States alone, leaving Casanova and the children in Drozdowo. En route to the Midwest, he stopped in Boston with a letter of introduction to William James (1842-1910), the American psychologist and philosopher. The two men felt an instant rapport. Their friendship would be sustained by a voluminous correspondence that lasted until James' death in 1910. James found Lutosławski somewhat impractical, but glowingly described him thus:

[He is]...the author of philosophical writings in
seven languages...knower of several more, handsome,
and to the last degree genial. He has a singular
philosophy -- that of friendship. He takes in dead
seriousness what most people admit, but only half-
believe, viz., that we are souls...that souls are
immortal, and that the chief concern of a soul is to
get ahead by the help of other souls with whom it can
establish confidential relations. (Allen 401)

James, a family-oriented man, was puzzled by Lutosławski's silence on the subject of his family. He knew that Lutosławski had a wife and several children, and found it curious that his friend never alluded to them either in conversation or letter. James' repeated inquiries as to their health and well-being were never answered.

After his United States tour, Lutosławski returned to London for another year of research and writing. Casanova and the children joined him there. Lutosławski was now working on a new chronology for Plato's *Dialogues*, based on an exhaustive analysis of Plato's style and vocabulary and involving the listing of thousands of words in ancient Greek. The work took up an enormous amount of time and required his total concentration.

El doctor Wolski (1894)

Sometime during this year, Casanova finished *El doctor Wolski*, which was published in Madrid in 1894 (reportedly, Polish and Dutch translations appeared soon thereafter). The novel was dedicated to Don Ramón de Campoamor, who had introduced her to "a compatriot of Dr. Wolski" (i.e. Lutosławski). It claimed to be a portrayal of life in Poland and Russia, "dos curiosos pueblos del Norte" (*Wolski* Intro) 'two unusual nations of the North', but was a thinly-disguised account of her husband's calamitous idealism.

"Wolski" is a portrait of Lutosławski, who acknowledges the parallel in his autobiography:

> As an artist, despite outstanding intelligence she was incapable of developing an interest in philosophy, and her view of theory was later expressed in her novel *Dr. Wolski*: in which she represented me as a fanatic of the will, frustrated in his aspirations to creative omnipotence. (Lutosławski, Żywot 173)

Perhaps the two unforgivable feminine imperfections that shatter Wolski's idealistic plans (Mara's consumption and Gelcha's sterility) were, in Casanova's mind, associated with her own "failure" to bear her husband a male child. In any case, as the years went by, Lutosławski and Casanova first grew distant and then antagonistic. She still considered him superior, and followed his instructions on diet, child-rearing and education to the letter. But secretly she began to detest the ideas by which he lived: eugenics, vegetarianism, reincarnation, Swedenborgianism, yoga and spirituality. She felt a constant sense of inadequacy, of falling beneath his exacting standards, combined with the growing knowledge that he did not love her.

According to one of Lutosławski's students, the Polish translation of *El doctor Wolski* by "Hajota" (a well-known translator and literary figure whose pseudonym contained the initials of her given name, Helena Janina Pajzderska), created a stir. Possibly reacting to Casanova's candid observations on Polish customs and attitudes, some critics recommended that the author should not bother writing any more novels, but limit herself to disseminating her husband's "hygienic" ideas. These critics, who admired Lutosławski, could not see that the book was a rebuttal, not an endorsement, of his theories on eugenics, love and marriage (Jedrzejewski, C. interview; Porębowicz).

At best, Lutosławski acted indifferent to her, at worst he was resentful of her "failure" to bear a son. As the gap between them widened, he grew increasingly insensitive to her interests and talents, resenting her creative life. At home, he spent most of his time closeted in his study. Outside of the home, he felt free to meet other, more congenial women who shared his esoteric interests. These were potential "soulmates," with whom he pursued intense relationships, mostly by correspondence.

As Casanova reflected on the past, she realized that their marriage might have been one of Lutosławski's passing eccentricities. He had uprooted her from her country, separated her from her family, changed the path of her career and taken her to live in some of the most remote and inhospitable corners of Europe on account of a "voice" which she now perceived as a symptom of his recurring nervous disorders.

Life with an almost Nietzschean *übermensch* was cold and uncomfortable. Casanova concentrated her affections on the children, watching them grow with satisfaction. In 1894 Mañita was seven, Bela six, and Jadwiga four. Blonde, dark-eyed and energetic, the girls were healthy although they blithely ignored their father's exhortations to follow his "hygienic" system of sunbaths that scandalized the Polish peasantry, a vegetarian diet, and strenuous hikes and calisthenics.

Disenchantment and Despair (1895)

In 1895, the family settled in the manor of Drozdowo, since Lutosławski needed seclusion and leisure to finish his book on Plato. When Jadwiga developed some stomach disorders on September 17, 1895, Lutosławski examined her, and was convinced that she was not seriously ill. Despite his wife's pleas, and confident that his scientific training was adequate, he refused to let her call a doctor.

Four-year-old Jadwiga had dysentery. When she died after hours of intense suffering, her parents were overwhelmed with grief and guilt. In his autobiography, otherwise crowded with details and reminiscence, Lutosławski notes Jadwiga's death and his grief without comment (Lutosławski 205-207).

For Casanova, the fault was not her husband's alone. How could she have allowed this to happen? How could she have believed her husband to be infallible? Her frustrated love became resentment and loathing. She never recovered her confidence in his authority and from that moment removed their children from his ideas and influence. His grief-stricken brothers and other family members were equally unforgiving (Niklewicz,

K. interview).

Jadwiga's death, combined with other tensions and memories, made life in Drozdowo unbearable. It occurred to Lutosławski that since he had finished the research for his book and only needed seclusion to write it, a few years in Spain would be ideal. Perhaps his wife would emerge from despair in her native Galicia.

Chapter 3

In Galicia

Late in 1895, the Lutosławski family settled in Playa de Mera, a little fishing village aptly described as a "lonely hamlet" across the bay from La Coruña (Mollenhauer 145-151). It was there that Lutosławski's hopes for a male heir were given a final blow, after Casanova became pregnant for a fourth time. Convinced that the unwanted child would be a girl, Casanova went into seclusion, refusing to see even a midwife. The couple's fourth and last child, "another daughter" (Lutosławski 209), was born in 1897, and christened Halina. She was nicknamed "Halita" by the family, but also affectionately known as "la Meracha," a unique amalgamation of her Spanish birthplace and the Polish -cz ending). Vivacious and energetic, Halita became her mother's and everybody's favorite (Niklewicz, K. interview; Meissner, H. interview).

After Halita's birth, Lutosławski went into a severe depression, which as he revealed in his autobiography, lasted almost seven years (209-227). Noted Polish critic Stanisław Pigoń, in his youth Lutosławski's student, described this period glossed over by Lutosławski in his autobiography:

Lutosławski's foreign wife Zofia Casanova had just given birth to a fourth daughter which had exasperated him as he wanted a son. This was due to Lutosławski's desire to fulfill [Mickiewicz's prophecy]... about a national savior to be born of a foreign mother into a long line of heroes. Lutosławski was also of the belief that it is a man's duty to search for his soul-mate or kindred soul. If he errs in making a choice, as he seemed to feel he had in marrying Zofia Casanova, he is free to continue his search... at approximately (this time) Wincenty Lutosławski entered into a relationship with an Irish woman named Caroline Fitzgerald, still hoping to father the son of Brother Peter's prophecy. (Fines 37-38)

The woman who we have now identified as the likely correspondent, Lady Caroline Fitzgerald (an Irishwoman who was a published poet in her own right and who later married to Lord Edmund Fitzmaurice) is only described in passing in Lutosławski's autobiography as "a well-born lady of refined culture." It appears that the two corresponded extensively. They discussed immortality and other lofty topics in correspondence that Lutosławski frankly described as "love-letters" and which were the basis of his book, *The Progress of Souls* (*Souls*, Introduction 14-20).[4]

Since Casanova never spoke or wrote directly about her marital problems, she left no record of her reaction to this liaison, or to others. The irony that she was in the same situation her mother had faced many years before -- abandoned by her husband and raising three young children in La Coruña -- did not escape Casanova. Unlike Vicente Pérez Eguía, Lutosławski had not disappeared completely: he had begun to take lengthy spiritual pilgrimages to remote places such as Greece, Constantinople and Palestine and frequent study trips to the University of Helsinki to complete his doctoral dissertation. These travels kept him away for months at a time.

Like her mother, although Casanova may have felt forsaken, she was not alone. Doña Rosita lived with her, happy to be with her grandchildren and help run the household. And their family circle widened with the addition of Josefa López, "Pepa," a Galician peasant woman who became Halita's nursemaid in 1897. Pepa had borne an illegitimate child and had to leave her home village in disgrace. She became close to Casanova and her daughters, and eventually emigrated to Poland with them, only occasionally returning to visit Spain.

On the positive side, Lutosławski's absence freed Casanova to read and write, to go by boat or carriage to La Coruña and other towns to visit acquaintances (such as Emilia Pardo Bazán, or Galician fellow poets Fanny Garrido and Filomena Dato Muruais), and to receive visitors at home (Bugallal *Siglo* 11).

Casanova had returned home at a fateful point in Spanish history. Like many other Spaniards, she followed the development of the Cuban insurrection and Spanish-Cuban-American war with growing anger and disenchantment. By 1898, the collapse of the Spanish Empire had left her demoralized and bitter. Casanova took almost as personal offenses Spain's excruciating defeat by the despised United States, and the loss of Cuba and the Philippines.

Lutosławski had to import his companions from abroad. Some, like English Hispanist James Fitzmaurice Kelly, were academic acquaintances who came to discuss philosophical or scholarly matters (Lutosławski, Żywot 220). Others came to visit because of Lutosławski's growing reputation in Polish emigre circles. Attracted by his theories on progressive reincarnation, Messianism and spiritualism, rising talents such as poet Tadeusz Miciński (1873-1918), and controversial literary figure Stanisław Przybyszewski (1868-1927), came to Mera to sit at his feet.

Casanova forbade Lutosławski to spend time alone with their daughters during his scant free time. She was afraid that they would absorb his theories, grow up to be eccentrics, and distance themselves from her. An icy formality fell between them, broken occasionally by angry exchanges. Lutosławski wrote to Caroline Fitzgerald:

...no judge can ever learn all the sufferings which may be mutually inflicted by an ill-assorted pair... adultery is only the last stage of a process begun much earlier, and adds nothing to the already existing estrangement between husband and wife. (*Souls* 170)

For Casanova, her husband's recurring bouts of manic-depressive behavior expressed themselves in many forms, one of them being his intense idealism. By nature and background unable to understand his ideas, she later wrote her private opinion of the Messianists and their obsession with Mickiewicz's prophecy of Brother Peter:

Gentes sensatas y espíritus enclenques se han chiflado buscando la raíz de esa genealogía... el secreto de la profecía... (*ABC* 11-1-1921)

Both sensible people and fragile spirits have lost their minds looking for the source of the genealogy... the secret of the prophecy...

Elsewhere in her work she describes the Slavic "Don Juan" to a Spanish audience:

Ha vuelto a ser el enamorado de todas... Dice que el hombre que se sabe superior tiene el deber de prodigar la ciencia y sus sentimientos para bien de la especie y de la humanidad... No me era desconocido el tipo del Don Juan eslavo, que justifica su libertinaje para procrear dioses... (*Rusia* 213)

He has again become the lover of all women... He says that the man who knows himself to be superior has the duty to lavish his knowledge and his feelings for the good of the species and of mankind... the Slavic Don Juan type was not unknown to me, trying to justify his licentiousness to beget gods...

Lutosławski had become deeply involved in a new interpretation of the Eleusinian mysteries. Increasingly drawn to the pre-Platonists, he shared their concern with the immortality of the soul, believing that a revival of Eleusinian spirit with emphasis on spiritual purification and asceticism (and on misogyny, said some critics), would lead to the redemption of Poland. A number of young Poles, like the brilliant and intense Miciński, yearned for personal sacrifice and meaning in the midst of their own country's suffering. Lutosławski's esoteric theories struck a chord.

Miciński arrived in Mera in fall of 1897 and stayed until the following spring. His enthusiastic reports on Lutosławski's ideas brought to Mera two even more extraordinary visitors, Stanisław Przybyszewski and his lover, the Norwegian beauty Dagny Juel. They had become the focus of a well-publicized international scandal when Przybyszewski took Juel away from her lover, August Strindberg. Since then, they had been enmeshed in a cult of passion and eroticism. Their bohemian attire, drinking and flamboyant behavior rocked Mera to its foundations and infuriated the high-minded, teetotalling Lutosławski.

This interlude in Mera inspired in Miciński a new interest in Spanish literature. Miciński's mystical and philosophical sensibility made him feel close to Casanova, whom he admired. She helped him learn Spanish and while he studied Teresa of Ávila and Calderón, he also read her poems. He translated "Quejas" into Polish and included it in his first volume of poetry, *W mroku gwiazd 'In the Twilight of the Stars,'* which was published in 1902 (The autobiographical "Quejas" describes Casanova carrying her cross and praying to be released by death from her sufferings). Miciński's comparative study of Słowacki's translation of Calderón's "El Príncipe constante" was another result (Miciński, *Słowacki i Calderón w Księciu Niezłomnym* 62-76).

On a more polemic level, the three Polish writers produced works denouncing one another. Przybyszewski's portrait of Lutosławski and Miciński in his interesting (if self-serving) memoirs *Moi Współcześni* 'My Contemporaries' (Vol. 1 1926, Vol. 2 1930), is decidedly unfavorable (Vol. 1, 273-287). Miciński's novel *Nietota* has a "Luciferic" main character based on Lutosławski, the Baron de Mangro, whose supposedly spiritual quest conceals selfish material desires. In print and in person, Lutosławski led an all-out campaign against his former guests. His autobiography's disdainful account of Miciński's scholarship is mild when compared to his anti-Przybyszewski pamphlet, "Soap bubbles, a critical look at the so-called Satanism of naked and drunken souls" 'Bańki mydlane...' (Krzyżanowski 457).

Considering the frankness of the works produced by the others as a result of this period, Casanova's restraint is remarkable. After her novel *El doctor Wolski* (1894), she never wrote directly or indirectly about her husband, his eccentricities or their married life. She broke her silence only once, when she was in her sixties. In a short autobiographical sketch donated to the Royal Academy of Galicia, she describes her marriage as twenty years of being "enfermera de un marido enfermo...(Bugallal *Siglo* 9) 'nurse to a sick husband'.

After Jadwiga's death, Casanova became despondent and at times wished for her own death. Her poems from this period contain many references to suffering and pain. But they were gripping, inspired and appealing: they appeared in Madrid publications (*España Artística, La Gran Vía, El Álbum Ibero-Americano*) and in *Revista Gallega* (La Coruña) and other regional publications.

Many of them were collected in Casanova's second book of poetry, *Fugaces*, which was published in late 1898. *Fugaces* captured the bitter realizations of a soul at the lowest ebb of its struggle against despair. It also reflected the universal human experience with sorrow, and the uneasy spirit of an age and a nation mired in disillusion.

Although her husband had approved earlier of the idea of a wife having her own interests, at this point (perhaps due to the impact of *El doctor Wolski*) Lutosławski abhorred the thought of a wife having her own career. As he wrote to Caroline Fitzgerald, the ideal female spirit was one who "dreams of helping (her mate) with his labours, and would rather undertake the humblest anonymous task at his side... than earn the applause of the world" (*Souls* 169).

By writing again and producing a body of work independent of her husband's influence, Casanova began her escape from his overwhelming shadow. As she came to terms with the mistaken premises of her marriage and its inevitable end, she faced the failure of her youthful quest for a "soulmate." Writing helped her to recover a sense of self.

During this time, her spiritual feelings and religious practice deepened. She found in her relationship to God and in daily religious life the solace and structure that she needed to face her strange destiny. This was manifested first in her more structured life of prayer and contemplation. On the more practical side, the poor and sick of Mera and villages farther away benefited from her gentle care and from small gifts of clothing or money. Word spread among the local peasant families that she had what they called "the healing touch," and to her bemusement, they begged her to nurse them during her illnesses and to place her hands on their bodies (Meissner, H. interview).

As she recovered her equilibrium, Casanova's pessimism evolved into a philosophy of hope. If she could not trust in humankind, then she would put her confidence on the mysterious workings of God. Through her surviving children, her creative work and her fervent return to the Catholicism of her childhood, life seemed to offer meaning and direction after all (Niklewicz, K. interview).

In 1897, Lutosławski's book on Plato, *The Origin and Growth of Plato's logic, with an Account of Plato's Style and the Chronology of his Writings,* was published to universal academic praise, an acclaim that lasts to this day (the book has stayed in print most of these years). After finishing a doctorate in philosophy at the University of Helsinki in 1899, he was offered a teaching position at the University of Cracow. Cracow was under the relatively more lenient rule of the Austrian-Hungarian Empire; Polish was allowed in the classrooms, and its curriculum was far superior to that of the Russian academic system. He eagerly accepted the position.

Despite the couple's estrangement, Casanova honored her early promise to raise the children as Polish citizens. She admitted that it was now time for them to receive a better Polish education than they were getting from tutors and governesses in Spain. But she worried that Poland's political atmosphere would exacerbate Lutosławski's nervous disorders. In Cracow, away from the isolation and protection of the family manor, they would be subjected to the political indignities that ordinary Polish people had to endure. She also worried that young people eager to follow her husband's ideas would create problems with the authorities.

Finally, Casanova was distressed at leaving her family and country once more, particularly after her career had begun to prosper again. The Liga Gallega, a civic and literary circle, held a gala event on April 24, 1899 to mark her departure, and presented her with a parchment scroll in her honor (Simón Palmer, *Escritoras* 177). As she wrote years later in the introduction to her play "La madeja," every time she left Spain she felt the excruciating "desgarramiento íntimo" 'intimate pain' of not knowing when she would return to her homeland and family. Stoically she prepared for the trip abroad.

Chapter 4

Cracow, 1899

The Lutosławskis moved to Cracow in October 1899. At the turn of the twentieth century, Poland's "museum city" still had old cobblestone streets. Its walls and towers reflected its medieval past and presided over the city, as though defeat of the "free city" of Cracow by Austria in 1846 had not broken its spirit. At the heart of the city stood Jagellonian University, founded in 1346. Cracow offered a lively intellectual and political life, and stirrings of independence. It was cultured and cosmopolitan, open to foreign influences and fashions. During those years, Cracow's great tradition of theater, music and art was in the midst of a revival.

Casanova and Lutosławski, their children and nursemaid Pepa moved into a sunny and spacious flat near the renaissance palace of Wawel. In her memoirs, Mañita remembers the family sitting around the table, listening to the city bells usher in a New Year and century (Gicgier 7).

Thanks to Lutosławski's family ties and scholarly reputation, and to Casanova's allure as an exotic foreigner with a literary career of her own, the couple enjoyed a vogue in Cracow society. They were welcomed everywhere. Count Stanisław Tarnowski, one of Poland's wealthiest and most cultured men, received them in his palace (Lutosławski, Żywot 241).

Soon they began holding a weekly *salon* of their own. Lutosławski attracted writers, students, politicians and a number of idealistic, high-minded youths, while his wife, having a "poetic temperament", drew a more literary and artistic set. The day of their "at-home," Wednesday afternoon was printed on their Polish calling cards. They were amused when Spanish friends included it as part of their address on cards and envelopes.

Casanova took a small room in their flat, filled it with Spanish paintings, engravings, books and objets d'art, and called it *Hiszpania* 'Spain.' This was her study, her private drawing room, and her domain. Her poetic aura intrigued many admirers. Photographs taken during this period show a deepening of her beauty and a growing dignity in her bearing. As Polish politician Stanisław Kozicki wrote in his memoirs:

[Zofia Casanova Lutosławska] was a person of unusual spirit and charm. She was a woman of much wisdom and an extraordinarily artistic temperament. (Kulakowski 235)

Her own country's defeat in 1898 had made Casanova sensitive to her role as a Spanish citizen abroad. Foreign news services disseminated biased and hostile information about Spain, about the loss of Cuba and other colonies, and about the end of the Spanish Empire. As one of a handful of Spaniards in Eastern Europe, Casanova often had to defend her country's positions before her Polish circle. One consolation if holding dual citizenship was that, protected by her Spanish pen name, her articles criticizing Russian policies could be printed in Madrid without repercussions to her Polish family (Niklewicz, K. interview).

As was the case in other European countries, Poland's artistic life was in the high-tide of Modernism, epitomized by a group now called *Młoda Polska* 'Young Poland.' "Młoda Polska" was a heterogeneous group of writers, artists and followers who were restless after years of oppression. They were attracted to foreign art and ideas, and, after decades of isolation, eager to open Poland to European influence. This period's art is particularly brilliant and anguished, well represented by Norwegian artist Edvard Munch (1863-1944), whose *angst* captured the mood of the period. Munch painted many portraits of Cracow celebrities, Przybyszewski and Dagny Juel among them.

Major and minor figures of the *Młoda Polska* movement visited the Lutosławskis' salon for tea and inspiration. As Casanova wrote to her Madrid correspondents, there were many interesting literary figures among this motley band of academics, painters, poets, peasants, politicians and members of the intelligentsia -- and some truly great ones.

In this general revival of Polish culture and nationalism there stood out one extraordinary artist and personality: Stanisław Wyspiański. Like the English William Morris, Wyspiański was talented in arts and crafts. Born in Cracow, he lived and worked as if submerged in its medieval past, although he was also interested in the heroic times of Greece and Rome. Some of his plays are based on medieval themes, others draw on classical or contemporary topics. In addition, Wyspiański was a gifted illustrator, painter and stained-glass artist. Today he is considered the father of modern Polish theater, not only as a writer of plays, but also as a creator of sets, decorations and the like, aiming at enhancing the total effect of a theatrical production.

At first the tall, blond Wyspiański did not appeal to Casanova. Stern, ascetic and aloof, he would come to their Wednesday afternoon receptions and sit alone in a corner. The next day she would hear from others what an interesting time he had enjoyed at her *salon* (Niklewicz, K. interview).

Soon he began to visit *Hiszpania* to explore Spanish literature: "Hábleme usted de España"... Hablé... Él... del pasado sabía mucho. El Príncipe Constante... traducido por Słowacki... le encantaba... Sta.

Teresa...(el) Cid Campeador... (*Exóticas* 167)
"Speak to me of Spain"... I spoke... He... knew a great deal about the past. He adored "The Constant Prince"...translated by Słowacki... St. Teresa...the Cid...

Wyspiański took careful notes on the Cid, the Spanish Middle Ages, and the *Romancero*. Years later, he would base one of his dramatic works on the Cid, drawing on Corneille's version of the Spanish poem and legends. (Less evident were the surreptitious notes he was taking about Professor Lutosławski, later represented in Wyspiański's play "Wyzwolenie" 'Deliverance,' by *two* characters).

Recognizing his great talent, Casanova and Lutosłavski made sure that the family was present at a historic moment in Polish drama, the premiere of Wyspiański's play, "Wesele" 'The Wedding,' on March 16, 1901. "Wesele" is a vast, symbolic panorama of Poland's history. In her memoirs, Mañita recalls learning by heart many of the play's stanzas, at her parents' urging (Gicgier 7). Casanova held an enduring affection for Wyspiański, and wrote a sensitive memoir for a Spanish publication after his death (*Exóticas* 163).

Poland was then in the throes of *chłopomania* 'peasant mania'. Intellectuals and artists admired the Tatra Mountains in the south of Poland near the Slovak border for their natural beauty, and admired the folk art and the freedom-loving nature of the mountain peasants. Polish intellectuals turned to the Tatras for inspiration and guidance, and it became the fashion to associate with peasants. In the autumn of 1900, a young poet and writer who frequented the Lutosławski salon, Lucjan Rydel, married a pretty peasant girl from the Cracovian region (It was their unusual and widely publicized village wedding, attended by intellectuals, peasants, bourgeois and government officials, that sparked Wyspiański's writing of "Wesele"). After a morning of selling eggs in the open air market, Pani Rydlowa would visit the Lutosławski's salon, adding "local color" to the gathering with her sumptuous peasant costume (Niklewicz, K. interview; Meissner, H. interview; Gicgier 6-7).

Any Wednesday afternoon at their salon, one could also meet the novelist Stanisław Reymont (1867-1925), then writing his enormous novel, *Chłopi* (*The Peasants*, 1902-1909) excerpts of which Casanova translated into Spanish. In 1924 he would receive the Nobel Prize for Literature for this monumental work. Reymont became a close friend of Casanova and her daughters. He later visited them in Spain, and became a passionate follower of the *corrida*, 'bullfight' writing articles on bullfighting for Polish publications (Gicguier 7).

Jan Kasprowicz (1860-1926) was another of Casanova's favorites: she considered him a true poet. Kasprowicz, of peasant origins, also worshipped the Tatras. At the time he was working on a book of verse hymns, *Ginacemu światu* (*To a Perishing World*). Casanova described him thus:

> Jan Kasprowicz era un poseso de los montes Tatras, un místico de lo que consideraba su divinidad... [era] humilde...sublime, bárbaro, independiente como los huracanes, desigual y gigante... ("Desde los Cárpatos," *ABC*, 1 October 1933)
> Jan Kasprowicz was possessed by the Tatra mountains, a mystic of what he considered their divinity... [he was] humble, sublime, barbaric, as independent as hurricanes, uneven and gigantic...

Casanova devoured the new Polish novels, many written as the nation recovered from the disaster of 1863. Sienkiewicz's *Quo Vadis?* (1896), a historical novel, purportedly took place during Nero's reign, but had subtle allusions to Poland's frustrated desire for freedom. Nationalist intentions aside, it enjoyed a huge international success at the turn of the century, as millions of copies were sold in French, English, Russian, Italian and German translations. Casanova translated it into Spanish (her version was the first drawn directly from the Polish original), and the translation was published in Madrid in 1906, a year after Sienkiewicz received the Nobel Prize.

As she translated excerpts of other Polish writers into Spanish, Sofía Casanova became a regular conduit of information, fostering understanding between Spain and Poland. Even as she grew to love Poland, her identification with Spain strengthened. For example, she could not describe Poland's efforts to end illiteracy without reproaching Spain for its indifference towards its own problems in this area.

Bartek el vencedor (1902)

This new concern for Spain is evident in the preface to her translation of *Bartek el vencedor*, ('Bartek zwycięzca', 'Bartek the Victor') a short story by Sienkiewicz (1882, tr. 1902). Far from her country, but constantly connected to it through her writing, she addressed her Spanish readers:

> ...permíteme que retrase el placer... de hacer conocimiento con Bartek... hablándote confidencialmente un instante... Entre las obras de escritores polacos que me propongo traducir... [Bartek] me ha hecho pensar en tristezas análogas y en peores malaventuras [españo-

las] soportadas heróicamente por nuestros soldados en los recientes días de los desastres. ("Bartek" Introduction)

...allow me to delay the pleasure... of getting to know Bartek... by talking confidentially to you for a minute... Among the works of Polish writers that I propose to translate... [Bartek] has made me think of similar sorrows and worse [Spanish] mishaps heroically endured by our soldiers in the recent days of disasters.

She went on to deplore how Ibsen, Tolstoy and Gorky were enjoying a vogue in Spain, while Polish literature was still virtually unknown, or represented by partial or misleading translations.

On one level, Casanova hoped that the novels of Reymont and the works of Wyspiański would become known in Spain, and that Spanish youth would get to know their Polish counterparts. Her implied hope was that her politically apathetic Spanish readers would learn to be better citizens from the Polish example:

...la literatura polaca... [es] la más bella de todas las del Norte, la más completa, la mas floreciente, y la más interesante, pues refleja en sus múltiples manifestaciones la lucha titánica de un pueblo que va marcando las etapas todas de su largo camino hacia la libertad, con obras de arte complejas y grandiosas, con la radiante luz que todo esfuerzo humano hacia el bien --la belleza y la justicia -- proyecta en las tinieblas. ("Bartek" Introduction)

Polish literature [is] the most beautiful of the northern literatures, the most complete, the most flourishing, and the most interesting, because it reflects in its many manifestations the titanic struggle of a nation that is tracing all stages of a long journey to freedom, with complex and grandiose works of art, with the radiant light that all human effort towards what is good -- beauty and justice -- projects against darkness.

And finally, Casanova hoped that once Spanish readers had sampled the best of foreign literatures, they would return to the Spanish classics:

Conocer lo ajeno es indispensable a la cultura individual; pero para orientarnos en nuestro propio destino, para aprender a cultivar, en provecho de la patria nuestras aptitudes de raza, tenemos que... descubrirnos a nosotros mismos... haciendo triunfar cuanto de genuinamente hermoso, grande y creador tiene el alma humana. (Bartek, Introduction)

To know other literatures is indispensable for personal culture; but to find our way towards our own destiny, to learn to cultivate our racial aptitudes for the benefit of our fatherland, we have to...discover ourselves... helping suceed all that is genuinely beautiful, great, and creative in the human soul.

Casanova does well by Sienkiewicz's original: her translation's rendition of the novel's description and dialogue rings true, and lets the story moves forward with energy. Her transparent, almost minimalist rendering of the Polish into Spanish allows the stark dramatic contours of the novel to appear, without falling into exaggeration or melodrama.

Sobre el Volga helado (1903)

The following year Casanova published an original travel book, *Sobre el Volga helado*, based on her adventures with Lutosławski ("Victor") on the trip to Kazan they had taken by train to St. Petersburg and Nizny Novgorod, and then by *kibitka* or horse-drawn carriage on the frozen Volga. Casanova kept a journal of the expedition, which covered one hundred leagues in forty hours. *Sobre el Volga helado* is part travel journal, part social and political commentary, filled with discerning observations on Russian daily life and character, and on the negative effect of Russia's domination of smaller nations.

The account of their three-day-long sled ride amidst raging blizzards can also be seen as a comment on their marriage. Following a whim of her husband's, who, as noted before, liked to experience the life of a country by travelling in the cheapest mode of transportation, Casanova spent endless hours inside the primitive carriage, shut off from the world (*kibitkas* were considered so unpleasant that they were used by the Russians to send Polish political prisoners to Siberia). Inside its unheated and damp enclosure, the couple was swathed head to foot in furs so they could not move, and time seemed to stand still. For entertainment, Lutosławski asked her to recite Spanish poems: she recited stanza after stanza of Bécquer, Núñez de Arce and Ferrari, Mediterranean poetry strangely out of place in the glacial atmosphere of the *kibitka* (83).

Volga introduces several concerns of the author's, such as Polish anti-Semitism, which would become her lifetime obsessions. Casanova's haunting initial contact with anti-Semitism took place in the summer of 1886, the day she arrived in the city of Łomza on her way to Drozdowo for the first time. The city had a large Jewish population, and as she descended from the train, she had a first glimpse of how Jews lived in Poland:

Al entrar por primera vez en Polonia...me sobrecogió el horrible aspecto del poblacho, de su plaza, cercada por míseras casucas de madera y en sus puertas aquellos hombres imprevistos, torvos los ojos, y la negra hopalanda, hasta el suelo, alargando sombras funerarias las figuras. Una angustia de soledad, de presentimiento, me hizo llorar secretamente (*Guerra* 169-170).

On entering Poland for the first time...I was overcome by the town's horrible appearance, by its square, fenced in by miserable wooden shacks, and at their doors those unexpected men, with sullen eyes and black cassocks all the way to the ground, dragging funeral shadows behind them. An anxiety of solitude, of foreboding, made me cry secretly.

From the moment she set foot in Poland as a one-of-a-kind, unassimilated alien, she identified with the Jews. Casanova, like the Jewish people were unwilling outsiders within a nation that was fiercely trying to preserve its cultural homogeneity. In turn-of-the-century Polish Russia, few Jews had been assimilated into either Polish or Russian society. She was appalled by the restrictions that bound their daily lives, and by the great and small indignities imposed upon them by the Russian bureaucracy. For example, on their Sabbath, Jews were not allowed to walk in public parks. She witnessed a Cossack violently kicking a Jew to the ground, and then beating him with his rifle-butt for violating this rule.

She could not understand how Jews withstood such treatment so passively, while she was ready to attack the Cossack herself. One of her relatives explained to her that perfect self-control was needed to wait out Russian oppression. To this Casanova could only respond that to live like Jews or Poles, in perpetual hope, would be for her worse than death (*Exoticas* 28-29)

Beyond the institutionalized racism of the Russians, lay the virulent and spontaneous anti-Semitism of nationalistic Poles. She could not understand how devoutly Catholic Poland could harbor such un-Christian feelings against the Jews.

¿Por que en nuestro tiempo, que se precia de liberal, tan solo los judíos opulentos viven respetados en las mas intransigentes sociedades, en tanto que los judios pobres, arrojados de todos los pueblos, proscriptos de todo bien, no saben donde asentar su planta sin que la hieran, no encuentran en el mundo un hospitalario rincón donde edificar sus cabañas sin que la maldición y el escarnio en ellas entren? (*Volga* 14)

Why in our time, that prides itself of being liberal, only wealthy Jews can live with dignity within the most intransigent societies, while poor Jews, cast away from all nations, deprived of all good things, don't know where to settle without being hurt, can't find a welcoming corner in this world where they can build their humble cottages, without having curses and scorn enter them?

49

She called on Christian charity to welcome them back into the family of man:

…no olvidemos que Cristo, el divino Maestro, los perdonó al morir, y que, para templar la fiereza de los hombres, dijo con divina palabra, nacida del mas grande amor a la humanidad: todos los hombres son hermanos (*Volga* 15)

…Let us not forget that Christ, our divine Master, forgave them as he died, and that, to temper the fierceness of men, said with divine Word, born of the greatest love for humanity: all men are brothers.

Among other observations, she uncannily predicted how a general European war would affect Poland, a land bridge between several great powers (16-17). Yet despite these serious reflections, the general tone of *Sobre el Volga helado* is one of curiosity, discovery and description. Along with many perceptive observations about the Russians, she admitted the attractions of the Northern landscape and of the sheer size, variety and richness of Russian life.

Within Poland, Casanova's reputation as a literary figure grew. Following Miciński's example, some of her literary colleagues translated her work. Antoni Lange (1861-1929), well known for both his poetry and his interest in Western European literatures, translated her signature poem, "Gotas de agua," into Polish. The muted inflections of "Krople Wody" reflect the original poem's elegiac mood (Łączyńska).

Narodowa Demokracja

On a different plane, Lutosławski's growing reputation as a public figure attracted several members of the *Liga Narodowa* 'Nationalist League' (*LN*), a clandestine nationalist group which would later become the *Narodowa Demokracja* or National Democratic Party (*ND*). He soon became involved in the right-wing, nationalistic organization, and *LN* leaders visited the Lutosławski home for political meetings. Some of them became Casanova's lifelong friends.

Zygmunt Balicki (1858-1916) was the author of the National Democrats' bible, *National Egoism* (1902). His wife Elżbieta (Ela) Balicka had studied science at the University of Freiburg, and was one of the first women in Europe to receive a doctorate in science. Tall and blonde, with large blue eyes and an engaging personality, Dr. Balicka was a feminist, campaigned against capital punishment, and took moral and political stands far ahead of her times. She and Casanova struck up an immediate friendship. Ela Balicka became her confidante, and Casanova wrote

50

several poems about her as "la Princesa de las nieves 'Princess of the Snows'. One of her poems, "Rebelión," tells how through the Balickis' friendship and counsel, Casanova gained the detachment and perspective needed to assert herself as an individual (*Cancionero* 11).

Roman Dmowski, a friend and political collaborator of the Balickis, also paid daily visits to *Hiszpania*. This up-and-coming *LN* politician had become the leader of the party and a representative of Poland to the Russian *Duma* or Parliament. Dmowski shared Lutosławski's ultra-nationalistic ideas, but expressed them in a very different manner. His pragmatic philosophy of co-existing with and manipulating the Russians to the maximum advantage for Poland's future (very much like Balicki's "national egoism") was the thesis of his best-selling book, *Thoughts of a Modern Pole* (1906). Lutosławski's lofty political ideas, based on the poetry of the three Polish bards or "*wieszcze*" (Mickiewicz, Słowacki and Krasiński), were too romantic, even utopian, for a politician like Dmowski. He teased Lutosławski: "Wicek [a diminutive of Wincenty]... the trouble with you is that you think you are the *boss* of the three bards" (Kulakowski 235).

The two men had conflicting styles, and inevitably clashed. Lutosławski writes unfavorably about the pragmatic Dmowski in his autobiography (Lutosławski, Żywot 242). Still, Dmowski visited their home daily to plan political strategy with Lutosławski, and to converse with Casanova and her circle of friends about art, literature, and politics. He was fascinated by Spain, and spent hours discussing Spanish poetry and politics with Casanova. Although very gallant, he was decidedly anti-feminist, and argued good-naturedly with his hostess and Dr. Balicka against the emancipation of women (Kulakowski 265).

Roman Dmowski's charismatic presence brought in a new factor the Lutosławski family drama. For years Casanova had steadfastedly prevented her daughters from falling under their father's influence. Lutosławski was away much of the time, doing academic and political work. His three daughters were strongly drawn, as to a father figure, to the charismatic and much older Dmowski, a confirmed bachelor committed to Polish independence. They called Zygmunt Balicki "Uncle," but over the years, particularly for Mañita, Roman Dmowski became a substitute father. He exerted enormous influence over all three daughters' personal and spiritual lives, a power that Lutosławski must have resented, but never mentioned (Meissner, H. interview; Niklewicz, K. interview).

Although Dmowski became a lifelong friend and confidante, Casanova saw him as a peer and was never swayed by his political ideas. She found "conciliationism" with the Russians alien to her character, and his virulent anti-Semitic ideas unacceptable to her humane way of thinking. Still the three girls became Dmowski's devout followers, and two of them married *ND* partisans.

Indeed, some of his peculiar ideas were turning Lutosławski's popularity into a public scandal. Besides being admired for his impeccable academic reputation and for his expertise as an expert on Greek philosophy, many of his contemporaries took Lutosławski seriously as a teacher of absolute truth. Within the university's student body he found "a community of souls" that shared his ideas, his love for the Polish messianist poets, and his patriotic zeal (*Lutosławski, Żywot* 237-258).

Stories were told about his unorthodox lecturing methods: he lectured best in the evenings, from eight to two in the morning, speaking without notes, and stopping once an hour to remind his rapt audience that they were free to leave at any time. Most listeners stayed until the end. Seven decades later, Clément Jedrzejewski, a student of Lutosławski's at that time, vividly remembered his brilliant lectures. Despite her doubts, Casanova tried to dispel the gossip that swirled around her husband. Lutosławski's student remembered how she would approach her husband's exhausted listeners and gently try to justify his unusual lecturing habits (Jedrzejewski, C. interview).

He also participated in many public polemics, including a widely publicized exchange with an ultra-nationalistic woman writer in the magazine *Kraj* 'The Land' who denounced Joseph Conrad (and all Polish expatriates) for living abroad. A lively polemic followed, with other writers joining in the chorus of her condemnation, and making snide remarks about the "Polish Plato" (Lutosławski, *Żywot* 214, 215-216). Lutosławski also engaged in some skirmishes against his former acquaintance Przybyszewski, who was now living in Cracow. He edited the influential journal *Życie* 'Life,' had become an avowed Satanist, and was "everybody's Lucifer," much to Lutosławski's disgust.

Outside the university, Lutosławski had started a Nationalist philosophy seminary, and a secret temperance society for young men, "Eleusis," intended to further their education and promote their spiritual welfare, and perhaps to counter the excesses promoted by Bohemians such as Przybyszewski (Krzyżanowski 458). Dozens of young men flocked to their meetings.

Eleusis centered around Lutosławski's charismatic personality as a cult around its master. The small band of young men took a vow to avoid wine, tobacco, "impure relations," dancing and card games. Although the group furthered the education of some worthy young men who otherwise would not have the opportunity (among them Stanisław Pigoń, later a well-known writer and critic), its secret nature gave rise to damaging rumors. It was whispered that Lutosławski's followers thought him to be the re-incarnation of Master Andrzej Towiański, whose theosophical and messianic teachings had ruined Mickiewicz's academic career in 1844. When they issued a pamphlet, *Eleusis* (mostly written by Lutosławski under several pseudonyms), its misogynistic and messianic ideas caused a furor (Jedrzejewski, C. interview; Cywiński).

These polemics were mild when compared to the controversy that grew around Lutosławski in university and government circles, eventually leading to his dismissal. The Austrian authorities were alarmed by his popularity as a lecturer who preached ultra-nationalistic theories to packed lecture halls. Rumors circulated about his unconventional theories on love, reincarnation, marriage and Messianism, which were heretical in Catholic, nineteenth century Poland. Despite his return to the Church in 1900, Lutosławski's ideas were too advanced to be contenanced by general Polish society (*Żywot* 239).

As his political and intellectual life grew more complicated, Lutosławski went into a frenzy of activity that worried friends and relatives. He kept a strenuous writing schedule and published several books, pamphlets and articles while maintaining a rigorous regime of exercise and diet. As his long-time friend William James warned him in an unpublished letter dated December 1, 1900:

Dear Lutosławski... you are having a *stürm und drang* period with a vengeance! I cannot read the experiences you write about without anxiety for you... no man who risks his life for a patriotic ideal can rightfully be disapproved by anyone else... those things are the freedom of individuals and their vocations. But it is that you seem to have no definite practical movement in view...the great man acts so as to succeed, no matter how long it takes; and you seem to have been consuming yourself in a fire of prophecy, etc. Do slow down; let this be enough for this year; recommence lecturing prosaically on abstract subjects; keep clear of such exciting situations...you ought to save your gifts for life-long use as a professor...My best wishes and prayers go with you -- but do sober yourself down. Don't think I am a hopeless Philistine writing you these words.

Alarmed by Lutosławski's activities and popularity, the authorities called him to task several times, trying to force him to leave Cracow. Lutosławski, near total nervous collapse, entered a sanatorium in Switzerland for a few weeks. But soon he was back in Cracow, immersed in controversial activities in and out of the classroom.

For Casanova these brilliant and turbulent years in turn-of-the-century Cracow were a turning point. She had arrived in Cracow filled with uncertainty and pessimism, but because of its intellectual ferment, grew involved with Polish politics -- quite apart from her husband's mystical and overwhelming theories. In Cracow she initiated life-long friendships, concerns and connections which marked her writing as more political. It was there that she finally carved out a unique role for herself as a conduit between two disparate cultures (*PBS* 138).

By 1905, when the Lutosławskis left Cracow, their years of cohabitation were over. Casanova and her daughters (aged seventeen, sixteen, and eight) went to Madrid, planning to visit for an extended period. Casanova and Halita lived there more or less continuously for the next eight years. The older girls shuttled happily between the two countries, but spent a great deal of time studying in Drozdowo, or staying with friends in different Polish cities.

In a new, more spiritually-inclined cycle of his life, Lutosławski moved in even broader circles and farther away from Poland and his family. He lectured for several semesters at the University of London, then travelled to Egypt, Constantinople, Rumania, Greece, the United States, Tunisia and Algeria. He studied yoga with the famous Swami Vivekananda in England, experiences which are recorded (along with a description of how Hatha Yoga finally cured him of his manic episodes) in William James' famous essay "Energies of Men" (James *Essays* 230-231). Only occasionally he did he visit his family in Madrid.

Lutosławski never spoke of his wife or children to his large international circle of colleagues and acquaintances. Even those who did not know the story behind his reticence sensed that something was deeply wrong in his relationship to his family. In an unpublished letter dated August 31, 1900, Willian James chided him:

> I have been anxious all this time about your pecuniary affairs, as well as about your relations to your wife and children, of whom you have never written a word for two years. Men of your temperament should not marry, but they can't help it and hence tragedy!

Great political forces were taking shape in Poland while the girls were in Spain. After the Russian defeat in the Japanese War in 1904, and the rebellion of 1905, the czarist empire showed the first signs of strain. Russia's hold on Poland loosened, and the political situation changed dramatically.

While their father was travelling and lecturing all over the world, the three Lutosławski girls became increasingly closer to Roman Dmowski.

Dmowski, a Polish member of the Russian *Duma* or Parliament, wrote long letters to the girls from Poland and Russia, noting the changing events, and giving them fatherly advice. One letter to Mañita and Halita encouraged them to return to their homeland after they finished school, to commit themselves to Polish independence. His suggestions were given in a tone and manner diametrically opposed to their father's romantic, idealistic approach: "Life means movement, activity, work, and not meditation, reflection, or psychological analysis." (Kulakowski 274) The girls treasured his advice and followed it throughout their long and active lives.

Sometime in 1906, Lutosławski had a decisive talk with Halita, then a child of eight. Did she think that he should continue to visit the family now and then, causing them all great unhappiness? Or should he go away forever and start anew, without them? Lutosławski was unconsciously repeating his father's pattern of asking his children's permission to marry another woman (Niklewicz, K. interview).

Halita gently agreed that it would be best for all if he broke off the pretense of a normal family life, and started anew with somebody else. Lutosławski rushed to the nearest post office and joyfully wired his young disciple and future wife, Wanda Peszyńska, in Cracow: "Halita says it is all right!" A child's consent gave him the freedom to start a new life and family, free from a hopeless misalliance (Meissner, H. interview).

Casanova chose not to leave any record of her reaction to his departure, but began to sign herself "Viuda de Lutosławski" 'Widow of Lutosławski', the standard Spanish usage. According to family testimony, despite her earlier agreement to give each other "spiritual freedom," now that she was a devout Catholic, Casanova was appalled by what she considered Lutosławski's flouting of their sacred marriage vows when he started a second family. Her own public and private behavior remained that of a decorous married woman. Although she might have had some temptations, there is no indication that she ever broke her side of the marriage contract. Even after the death of love, she considered herself bound by their marriage vows (Niklewicz, K. interview).

Her works also reflect that during those years in Madrid (1905-1914), finally unburdened of her husband's overwhelming presence, and surrounded by admiration and support from her peers (including her brother Vicente Casanova, by now a published poet and journalist), she enjoyed some of the happiest and most productive years of her career.

Chapter 5

Literary Success in Madrid

As Casanova returned to Madrid in 1905 with her two younger daughters, the capital's literary and artistic life began to expand. Spain was catching up with the rest of the continent in literature, politics and journalism. These advances helped Casanova reestablish herself artistically and professionally. Before her expatriation, she had been known only for her poetry. She still considered herself a poet, but now her international experience broadened the scope of her work.

At this time in her life, Casanova enjoyed more leisure than before. Her older daughters were often abroad, and Halita attended an aristocratic school run by Irish nuns. Since she now received her husband's share of the family estate, Casanova had the leisure to explore different genres, while her financial independence helped her maintain her aristocratic connections and artistic integrity.

During this period, she produced two different types of work. Her journalism focused on Eastern Europe. But her creative poetry and fiction were deeply personal expressions, and resonated with the nationalism that had emerged in Spanish literature as a reaction to the crises and bitter realizations of 1898.

Casanova became even more visible in Madrid's social and literary circles. A fellow writer recalled his impressions of Casanova:

Cuando conocí a Sofía, hará unos cuatro años, acababa de llegar a Madrid después de una ausencia larga en Polonia. Su nombre, harto de rodar en mis oídos, hablábame no sé por qué, con insistencia llena de misterio, de un trozo de leyenda.... En el otoño de aquel año (1905) nos reuníamos en su casa varios amigos... Desde entonces ha vuelto a asentarse y a vuelto a tornar. En todo ese tiempo sus triunfos han sido mayores, sus libros mas elogiados, y lo mismo sus prosas que sus versos... (*Cancionero* 12-13)

When I first met Sofía, some four years ago, she had just arrived in Madrid after a long absence in Poland. Her name, which had been mentioned to me many times, sounded to me, I don't know why, with mysterious persistence, as if it were part of a legend... During the autumn of that year (1905) some of us who were friends would meet in her home... Since then she has reestablished herself and has returned. During this time her triumphs have become greater, her books more highly praised, her prose as well as her poetry....

Buoyed by her newly-found independence, self-confident and and happy to be in Madrid, Casanova received social, political and literary figures in her home. Blanca de los Ríos remained a close friend, and Doña Emilia Pardo Bazán visited her often. Don Antonio Maura was one of her great admirers and supporters. Jacinto Benavente, scientist Don Ramón Plá y Cajal, and even General Valeriano Weyler (famous for to his notorious attempt to subdue the Cuban insurrectionists), enjoyed Casanova's *salon*. Her home was a haven for the *Modernistas*, whom she affectionately called "mis poetas," and whose cause she championed.

Casanova's writing career was assisted by the enormous growth of Spanish journalism in the first decade of the twentieth century. She was acquainted with Don Torcuato Luca de Tena, who had founded the weekly *Blanco y Negro* in 1891. The son of wealthy industrialists, Luca de Tena was a Monarchist with literary inclinations. He loved journalism, had traveled abroad and was a fierce patriot. After succeeding with the popular, family-oriented weekly *Blanco y Negro*, illustrated with photographs and *art nouveau* drawings, he founded *ABC in 1905*, a modern illustrated daily in the tradition of the great European newspapers he admired.

From its inception, *ABC* reflected the interests of its founder. It was more literary, more internationally-minded, yet remained as political as its competition. Articles and columns by many of Spain's leading intellectual and artistic figures graced its pages. Like *Blanco y Negro*, its literary section often featured works by both classical and iconoclastic Spanish writers. Even the *Modernistas* had no qualms about having their work published by Luca de Tena, and relished his generous fees. *ABC*'s excellent graphics, vigorous editorial slant and lively style set the pace for the rest of Madrid's dailies.

Casanova had reportedly contributed poems for *Blanco y Negro* during the early part of the century.[5] Luca de Tena was now pleased to have her write occasional articles for *ABC* on Polish history and culture in a column entitled "Desde Polonia." Her work was also published in the Catholic *El debate* (thanks to her warm friendship with Don Antonio Maura), *El mundo*, and in Court journals and periodicals. She wrote on eclectic topics ranging from history and politics to art, and produced a notable series on tuberculosis and public hygiene for *El mundo*. In addition she wrote a few articles and short stories featuring *gallego* themes for other publications.

57

The development of a broader reading public had created new outlets for Spanish fiction. Heralded by the birth of *El Cuento Semanal* in 1907, more than thirty new fiction magazines published a total of over five thousand short novels that flooded Spanish bookstores and supported a new class of writers (Saínz de Robles 13). They were a boon to Casanova, who had nine short novels and many translations and stories appear in these magazines. For example, her translation of Sienkiewicz's *¿Quo Vadis?* was published in 1908 by *La Novela de Ahora*, in a hybrid book/magazine format printed in two columns, with sumptuous color illustrations.

Her contacts in the journalistic world were aided by her brother Vicente Casanova's own growing career. By 1912 he had collaborated in two newspapers and edited a journal. He also had to his credit two books of poetry, four *zarzuelas*, two plays and several books. He and Casanova must have collaborated on at least one of his zarzuelas, "El pino del Norte," which has a Polish setting and theme (Casanova, V., "Pino").

Más que amor

That same year, Casanova also published *Más que amor: Cartas*, an epistolary novel chronicling the rise, decline and fall of a long-distance idyll between "María Cruz" a Spanish widow living in Warsaw, and "Carlos de Vargas," a Madrid politician. This novel, with its engaging characters, swiftly-moving plot and psychological insights into Carlos's jealousy and María's ambivalence, is perhaps Casanova's best work of fiction. The novel's captivating tone, and the lovers' zest for writing - and for describing their lives - makes it one of Casanova's most intimate and individual creations. It was well received in Madrid and described as having "éxito ruidoso y legítimo" 'noisy and legitimate success,' (by writer Prudencio Canitrot in his Prologue to Casanova's collection of short stories, *El pecado*, 1908)

Perhaps part of *Más que amor*'s inner-circle appeal was the knowledge that the star-crossed lovers were none other than Casanova herself and Madrid editor Alfredo Vicenti. Protected by distance, Casanova freely told her family in Warsaw that the book being published in Madrid was her correspondence with Vicenti, but she never showed the book to them. As of 1983 they were unaware of the letters' romantic focus. Vicenti, like Casanova, was interested in poetry and politics, and supported the *Modernistas*. His writings had enjoyed a vogue some years before, but as his journalistic production grew, his literary reputation declined (*EUIEA*). "María" and "Carlos" corresponded in an intense, romantic style, idealistic lovers whose love was bound to pall when brought to the light of reality.

When a translation of *Más que Amor: Cartas* (*Więcej niż miłość: powieść wspolczesna*), was published in Cracow and excerpted in the Warsaw Daily, *Gazeta Codzienna*, it caused a different kind of stir. In the novel, Carlos de Vargas makes a passing comment about the Czar's authoritarian rule. Russian military censors abruptly suppressed the daily and forced the *Gazeta* to close down (later reopened under a different name). Casanova was personally fined 500 rubles, and detailed her outraged reaction in an article, "Novela española castigada en Rusia," that appeared in a Madrid newspaper and was later collected in *Exóticas (16)*.

Lo eterno

Casanova's short novel, *Lo eterno*, was also published in 1908. In the Preface, written by the author, she describes the book as a "narración española" 'a Spanish narrative,' and wonders whether her many years abroad have made her Spanish outlook change. This short novel narrates the dilemma of a young priest torn between the sincerity of his religious vows and his attraction to a young woman.

Lo eterno is a curious blend of *novela rosa* 'romance novel' and psychological study. In its parallel love stories involving Father Juan and Consuelo, it is full of clichés and heads towards the inevitable happy ending. Part of the plot also addresses a thoughtful man's soul searchings about Christianity, the rules of the Church, and his personal vocation. In addition, it has some fine descriptive passages on Madrid's urban life. It is permeated throughout by the unique ambiance of Spanish catholicism, which Casanova at one point describes as "la atmósfera especialísima del templo, húmeda, cálida, perfumada por los incensarios y los cirios olorosos, atmósfera peculiar de las iglesias españolas que penetra las almas...' (N. pag.) 'the very special atmosphere of a temple, humid, warm, perfumed by censers and fragrant tapers, an atmosphere unique to Spanish churches that pierces one's soul'.

Una nihilista

In 1909, Casanova's translation of *Una nihilista*, a novel by the Russian woman academic and author Zofja Kowalewska, brought to the Spanish public's attention the burning topic of nihilism and its spread among the Russian intelligentsia. Casanova dedicated her translation to her friend, Alberto Ínsua. In a letter which also served as introduction, she discussed Spain's lack of interest in feminism, which Casanova found to be "movimiento...hondo y curiosísimo." 'a deep and extremely curious movement.'

Adhering to her feminist ideals, Kowalewska, an "egalitarian," had earned a doctorate in mathematics and a distinguished teaching post, but lost the happiness and "poetry" that was the birthright of her more feminine counterparts (7). According to Casanova, she was too interested in "lo que la mujer *quiere ser*, olvidada de *lo que es*" (8) 'what woman *wants to be*, forgetting *what she is*.' Her turbulent life ("una novela trágica" 'a tragic novel'), summarized by Casanova in the Introduction to her translation, could serve as a warning to women who, like Kowaleska and her protagonist Weira Barankow, neglect love and family for theories and movements that will not bring them personal fulfillment.

"La mujer española en el extranjero"

At this time, Casanova was also giving successful public lectures. On April 9, 1910, she spoke on "La mujer española en el extranjero" at the Ateneo de Madrid. Her fiery statements about stereotypes of Spanish women in European literature (the jealous mistress, Carmen the seductress, etc.) strongly criticized hackneyed images of Spanish women. But at the same time, Casanova deplored the lack of education and traditional passivity of Spanish womanhood. She went as far as to say that she believed that instead of being subservient to men, women should be their friends and colleagues.

Although diplomatic, Casanova found it difficult to stifle her true convictions. Anyone who reads her "La mujer española en el extranjero" is struck by her identification of Queen Isabella and St. Teresa of Ávila as true examples of Spanish womanhood (7). They had been active and courageous women who took an important role in bettering the world. In her speech, Casanova pleaded for and end to the "quietism" that had shackled the spirits of Spanish women, and for education that would liberate them from inertia, from what she called "medieval habits," and incidentally from the "insulting obsesssions" of Spanish men (37).

In addition, she mentioned that Spain's image abroad was in general a negative one, based on outdated stereotypes. Even the great novelist Leo Tolstoy, (to whom she had been introduced in a Moscow *salon* during a trip to Russia) hearing that she was a Spaniard, had scowled and described Catholic Spain's reputation to everyone present as backward and not truly Christian. Casanova boldly objected to his comment, which had visibly increased the Count's irascibility. In total agreement with her ideas, Don

Antonio Maura sat in the front row of the packed audience, clapping and loudly cheering her presentation (*ABC,* 6 April 1958). The lecture was widely reviewed in the press, and translated into French at the request of several members of the audience.

El Pecado

In 1911, Casanova's writings addressed her Galician tradition, for the first and only time. She published a collection of eleven short stories dealing with *gallego* themes, most of which had been previously published elsewhere. *El Pecado* was printed as the tenth volume of the *Biblioteca de autores gallegos* - and, as noted recently, it was the only volume written by a woman (Galerstein 71).

Despite her enjoyment of fame and commercial success, Casanova at heart remained a poet who wrote for a small and highly select public. She had managed to produce a small body of work while living abroad, raising a family and coping with her difficult marital situation. Now, without these obstacles, her poetic career developed further, aided by opportunities for readings, review by her peers, and publication in magazines and journals.

Casanova had become close to Manuel Machado and to his brother Antonio (at the time, Manuel's poetic reputation far outran his younger sibling's). Manuel was a devoted fan of her poetry, and introduced her to Francisco Villaespesa, Ramón Goy de Silva and several other poets of the *Modernista* circle. Their support led to a coveted appointment to another literary society: when Machado and Villaespesa founded the *Academia de la Poesía Española* in 1910, they inducted her into the elite organization. On the evening she was admitted, Casanova read her poems to a distinguished literary audience at a soiree hosted by one of the Infantas 'royal princesses', Princess Paz.

El Cancionero de la dicha

By the time Casanova published *El Cancionero de la dicha* (1911), her third and last book of poetry, she had developed a following. *Cancionero* was prefaced by an *ofrenda de poetas*, eight poems by *Modernistas* (including Manuel Machado) extravagantly praising her art. The poems described her as goddess-like, treading the lyrical realm with haughty pride, as if leading lions. Highly flattering reviews by Ramón

Pérez de Ayala and others ensured the book's success, and *Cancionero* went into a second printing in 1912.

In addition to her literary and journalistic work, Casanova carried on a parallel career as a social activist. As is obvious in *El doctor Wolski*, Casanova had learned a great deal about public health and preventive medicine during her time abroad. Dismayed by Spain's backward public health system, she now did a great deal of social work with the help of her aristocratic connections. With the support of the queen mother, in 1910 she created the *Comité Femenino de Higiene Popular* 'Women's Committee for Popular Hygiene', which she led as president until her departure from Spain in June 1914. She also participated in a congress on tuberculosis, wrote articles on its prevention, joined the Spanish Red Cross, and was involved in the creation of a dispensary for the poor.

By 1913, Sofía Casanova was a well-known social, literary and public figure in Madrid. Her photograph often appeared in the daily press and in court and society publications. The lengthy entry under her name in the *Espasa Calpe* encyclopedia is a gauge of her celebrity, since the encyclopedia had few other articles on contemporary Spanish women. The description of journalist Carmen de Burgos barely filled a page. A literary figure of the stature of Pardo Bazán was allotted two pages. Casanova's two-page entry featured her photograph, listed her books and articles, described her poetic and linguistic achievements and noted the honors she had received, including membership in both literary academies.

Casanova had long admired Don Benito Pérez Galdós (She read some of his *Episodios nacionales* during a visit to Siberia many years before), and now received him in her home. After Don Benito listened to her read her play, "La madeja" 'The Web,' he was instrumental in bringing it to the *Teatro Español* for its premiere on March 11, 1913. Although due to casting and other problems the production did not go well, and did not run for more than one evening, the play itself was critically admired and brought her even greater prestige (Simón Palmer, "Madeja" 569; *Świat 31 May 1913*).

By 1914 Casanova had achieved eminence in Madrid. If she remained in Spain, she would have the freedom, celebrity and financial rewards enjoyed by only a tiny minority of Spanish women. But her family ties to Poland were hard to break.

Roman Dmowski had become a powerful man, one of Poland's three leading politicians (the other two were Ignacy Paderewski and Marshal Józef Piłsudski). In 1909 Casanova's eldest daughter, Mañita, married one of Dmowski's closest collaborators, Mieczyslaw Niklewicz, a serious-minded and hard-working political journalist committed to the *ND*'s cause.

A political crisis in the young couple's life brought to light just how closely Casanova remained bound to Poland, despite her thriving life in Spain. As a teenager, Niklewicz had spent a year in a Russian prison, as punishment for circulating a petition demanding that Polish children be allowed to learn the Catholic catechism in their native language. When arrested again in 1910 for political activities, he faced a lengthy prison term under a law that ordered a minimum of five years in jail for anyone who had already served time for "subversive activities." Family and friends failed in their efforts to have him released, until it occurred to Casanova to write Queen María Cristina, her long-time protector, asking for her intercession. Niklewicz was pardoned, and when their first child (a daughter) was born in 1910, he and Mañita named her after the queen.

Casanova's two younger daughters were also being drawn back to Poland. First Bela and then Halita decided to live in Poland with the Niklewiczes, and to work for Polish independence. Casanova began to visit Poland at least once a year, for months at a time, despite the trip's difficulties and the financial burden. Slowly she was being pulled away from Spain and her place in its literary world.

Chapter 6

World War Preparations

On June 28, 1914, most of Europe was in turmoil over the assassi-
nation of Austrian Archduke Ferdinand by Serbian nationalists in
Sarajevo. Spain, insulated from these tensions by geographic distance and
political choice, resisted involvement. The nationalities of the two Spanish
Queens reflected part of the delicate balance of power that had maintained
European peace for almost one hundred years. Queen Victoria Eugenia,
Alfonso XIII's wife, was English, the granddaughter of Queen Victoria.
The Queen Mother, María Cristina (Casanova's long-time protector), was
Austrian. It was said that King Alfonso had promised to join forces with
France if Germany attacked, but at the time of the Archduke's assassina-
tion he did not seem inclined to lead Spain into the conflict.[6]

In June 1914, at the first signs of trouble, Casanova hastily said good-
bye to her mother, brothers and friends in Madrid, and headed for
Warsaw. As she travelled east, from Spain through France, Belgium and
then Germany, she realized that rumors of impending war might be
correct. There was an undercurrent of hysteria in other European capitals
that was not felt in Madrid. Casanova's distaste for violence, acquired
during years of Russian oppression, made it painful for her to watch
preparations for a technologically advanced "war of wars."

Her Polish friends idealistically backed the Entente, although Roman
Dmowski and the *ND* supported the Allies as a tactical part of their
pragmatic "conciliationism" with Russia. Many freedom-loving Poles were
not happy to see progressive England and France allied with the autocratic
Czar (Niklewicz, K. interview).

At the time, Spain was flooded with *germanófilo* 'pro-German'
propaganda. As is obvious from her writings, Casanova did not like the
Germans, but she also did not hate or fear them. And she resented the
annexation of Posnań and Germany's cultural imperialism against Poland
(*Exóticas* 10).

Casanova agreed with Dmowski that Germany was an enemy of Polish
independence. One of Dmowski's basic tenets was that Prussian Germany
(not Russia) was the main enemy of Polish nationality, since East Prussia
controlled Lithuania and other key regions of the Polish nation. If Poland's
heartland were "Germanized," the Polish nation would cease to exist.
Under Slavic Russia, he theorized, the unification (if not independence)
of all three Polands would take place in a more culturally compatible

atmosphere.

On the other hand, Casanova respected the cohesiveness of German society, and admired their orderly life ("Aclaración," *ABC*, 3 April 1917). She never fell into the blind hatred of Germany and "the Hun" that was prevalent in Europe before and during the World Wars.

Casanova did mistrust the czarist government, and suspected Russia's alleged good will. She knew that Dmowski's "conciliatory" ideas were criticized by many patriotic Poles, who held that Russians, not Germans, were the ancestral enemies of the Polish people. An alliance between the freedom-loving Poles and the tyrannical government of Germany offended her Liberal conscience. Still, she couldn't blame them too harshly for allying themselves with nations they despised. She believed that history and geography had forced this paradox on them: "¡Triste suerte de este pueblo! Entre enemigos tiene que asociarse a uno de ellos y pone su porvenir en cetros de tiranos" (*Guerra* 187) 'What a sad fate for this nation! Caught between enemies, it has to ally itself to one of them, and place its future on the scepters of tyrants'. Although slightly partial to the Entente, Casanova was mostly neutral in her political allegiance and steadfastly opposed to war.

By late 1914, Casanova's attitude towards the war had become that of a pacifist and realist. Two of the three partitioning powers were united in a struggle against the third. War would devastate the Polish nation, then divided among these three giants. Would an independent Poland be adequate compensation for the horrors of battle and occupation? The population in each partitioned area was torn between loyalty to the power that ruled them and the directive to fight their Polish brothers.

To her dismay, Casanova saw that some Poles actually looked forward to an all-European war. These citizens, who came from every social class, shared Adam Mickiewicz' hopes (expressed in *Księgi narodu i pielgrzymstwa polskiego*, *Books of the Polish Nation and Polish Pilgrim*, 1832), that an extended war, even world conflagration, might deliver Poland from her oppressors. Casanova thought it irresponsible not to consider the human suffering that such a conflict would bring. But in those early days, the idea of war seemed simple and inspiring to most idealistic Poles, who longed for independence after more than a century of foreign oppression.

Shortly before the mobilization of troops, slogans and rumors of war filled the papers. Disaster seemed imminent. On August 1, 1914, Germany declared war on Russia. Six days later, the Austro-Hungarian Empire followed Germany's lead. With dizzying speed, Austria invaded Serbia, Russia invaded East Prussia and Galitzia, France invaded Alsace. Germany invaded the Lorraine, devastated Belgium, and threatened

Russian Poland. Communications were severed between Poland and the rest of the world. Casanova was cut off from Spain for several months. Family and friends (including the Queen Mother) inquired at the Russian Embassy in Madrid about her whereabouts and safety, to no avail.

No sooner had the Poles in Russian Poland recovered from the shock of the declaration of war, when on August 14 the Grand Duke Nicholas, Commander-in-Chief of the Russian army, issued a proclamation hinting that Russia planned temporarily to give up its autocratic hold on Poland. Although similar statements were issued by the German and Austrian governments, Casanova noted that only the Grand Duke's manifesto had had the power to throw Russian Poland into unimaginable excitement. This was a personal triumph for Dmowski, and the Niklewicz side of the family rejoiced. The *ND* and other nationalist parties signed a political statement that echoed the mystical language of the proclamation, and agreed to cooperate with Russia in fighting the war.

Casanova did not take the Russian manifesto and its rhetoric at face value. She listened to ordinary, non-Russophile Poles, such as her mother-in-law and non-political members of the family, and recorded their reaction to this "perfidious" enticement: "Nos traicionarán siempre" 'They will always betray us' ("Impresiones" 6). After more than a hundred years of oppression, she reported, they were not convinced of Russia's sincerity.

She was in Drozdowo when the Russian army's mobilization began ("Impresiones" 5). She watched in fascination as the vast Russian administrative bureaucracy struggled to gear up its army, the largest in Europe, and send its forces towards the German border. Hundreds of thousands of professional soldiers and civilians drafted from every Russian ethnic group slowly made their way to the line of battle through Russian Poland, travelling over Poland's ill-kept road system that the Russian military had neglected for decades. It was clear to Casanova that the Russian bureaucracy that supported the war effort was outdated and inept, and would not hold up for long against the efficient German war machine.

Casanova was also surprised at how the traditional Polish hostility towards the Russians vanished overnight ("Impresiones" 6). She also wondered at the passivity with which the illiterate and ill-prepared Russian soldiers went into battle. They were enormous in number, but hampered by poor organization and cultural heterogeneity. Kalmuks, Caucasians, Letts, Jews, Poles and Muslims fought side by side, often without sharing a common language or ideal ("Impresiones" 8). The rigid discipline of the Russian army undermined the common soldiers' morale, and the ban on vodka for the duration of the war affected them deeply. Even to her inexperienced civilian eye, the Russian army was riddled by incompetence and corruption ("Impresiones" 8).

As early as 1903, in *Sobre el Volga helado*, Casanova had written about the unfortunate geographical location and characteristics of Poland as a land-bridge with few obstacles to deter enemies (16-17). She had predicted an easy invasion if war ever broke out. Eventually her prophesies came to pass, but she never imagined that the invasion would be so brutal in reality: "...los horrores de mi visión fantástica son humo, son sueño comparados a la realidad que vivimos" (*Guerra* 170) '...the horrors of my fantastic vision are smoke, a dream, compared to the reality we live'.

At first, the fortunes of war favored the Russians. The general population in Poland suffered greatly as the tides of battle flowed and ebbed over their land, and wrought appalling devastation. The Russian Military High Command decided to commandeer Drozdowo as Polish headquarters for the Grand Duke Boris, the Czar's uncle and one of the highest-ranking officers in the Russian army. Drozdowo was near Łomża, on the east to west railroad line. The estate was chosen because of its size, superior organization, and strategic location. The arrival of the Grand Duke, his retinue and several divisions threw the manor (and Casanova's daily life) into near-chaos. Thus began a slow decline for Drozdowo and the Lutosławski family fortune, which was never reversed. The days of leisure, reading and poetry-writing were over for Casanova, at least for the duration. The war had changed everything.

"Ángel de hospitales" - Warsaw, 1914-1915

Moving to Warsaw to live with her daughter Mañita Niklewicz and her family, Casanova found that everyone in her social circle had taken on a worthwhile task to contribute to Poland's war effort (and more or less directly, to Poland's eventual independence). Her son-in-law Mieczisław Niklewicz worked at Dmowski's side, edited the *ND* newspaper, and helped plan political strategy. Her brothers-in-law Marian and Józef Lutosławski organized a Dmowski-sponsored Civic Committee, the CKO, and feverishly carried out relief efforts to feed and shelter the thousands of displaced persons streaming into Warsaw. Every Polish woman Casanova knew joined some charitable or relief organization. She felt that, although a foreigner and an avowed pacifist, she should volunteer somewhere. Moved by the sight of trainloads of wounded soldiers that arrived in Warsaw daily, she decided to focus on helping the war casualties.

Dr. Ela Balicka had joined the Red Cross, and because of her scientific training, immediately found a post as a Sister of Charity nurse in an emergency hospital. This hospital was next to the railroad terminal where trains from Vienna and the west stopped (near the present-day location of Warsaw's Palace of Culture). With Dr. Balicka's help, Casanova was quickly accepted as nurse-in-training and was certified after a few weeks. In a Sister of Charity uniform, she waited with other medical personnel for each train to bring hundreds of wounded Russian and German soldiers in need of first aid and emergency surgery. She served at the hospital for almost a year, from September 1914 until the evacuation of Warsaw in August 1915. During that time approximately two hundred thousand emergency patients passed through the hospital (*Guerra* 15).

Casanova's life and career were being deeply affected by the German invasion and by the war. As has been noted elsewhere, the Great War offered European women tremendous opportunities for self-determination and for the release of suppressed talents and pent-up energies. At the age of fifty-two, with no previous experience of nursing or indeed of any other traditional job, Casanova threw herself into long hours of hospital duty, often staying around the clock. She performed not only nursing duties, but also back-breaking domestic chores she had ordinarily delegated to maids and laborers ("Prisioneros y heridos", *ABC*, 23 April 1915). Her Spanish "social work" had been enjoyable and inspirational, since it focused on children and the family. It took up at most a couple of pleasant afternoons per week. Now Casanova spent ten to twelve hours a day surrounded by horribly wounded men, gangrene and death.

Russian Poland lacked essential supplies. Casanova and her colleagues in the emergency hospital were inadequately equipped to cope with the number of wounded: there were not enough medications, anesthetics, or bandages. There were never enough hospital beds. And working in the hospital was not safe because of its nearness to the railroad lines. Casanova often rode in military trains to battle zones to bring in the wounded, and on at least one of those occasions her train was hit by the Germans fire (Pitollet 135-136).

With the outbreak of the war, the situation worsened for Jews as they were unanimously (and unfairly) branded as spies, and jailed or shot without a trial. Many Jewish civilians caught in the line of fire were sent to Casanova's hospital in Warsaw, where she tried to lighten their suffering:

Me dan mucha lástima los judíos; aborrecidos por todo el mundo, hastamuriendo y sufriendo como los demás son mal mirados. En cuanto losdescubro, y esto no es fácil mas que por el tipo, todo mi cuidado es para ellos.

I feel a great deal of pity for the Jews: despised by everyone, even dying and suffering like the others they are held in contempt. As soon as I pick them out, and this is not easy unless it's by their looks, I give them all my care.

During a trip to Drozdowo she discovered that the Jewish population of Lomza had been decimated. Two-thirds of the Jews had fled, or been killed.

¿Dónde están? Huidos, y en las cárceles. La acusación de espionaje los pierde...(*Guerra* 143)

Where are they? They have fled, or are in jail. Being accused of spying dooms them...

The War Correspondent: Warsaw (1914-1915)

There had been private and public concern in Madrid over Casanova's virtual disappearance behind enemy lines. She resurfaced in the Spanish press in December 1914, when *El debate* published a letter from Casanova telling of the war's beginning. More significantly, in April 1915, *ABC*, prominently featured the first of a series of articles under Casanova's byline, smuggled in from the Eastern Front. The articles described Casanova's daytime work with the Red Cross in a Warsaw emergency hospital which often received as many as five thousand soldiers a day. At night she would write her passionate anti-war articles, a mixture of factual reporting, political acumen and emotional appeals that goaded the guilty conscience of "neutral" Spain.

From the start of World War I to the time of the evacuation of Warsaw in September, 1915, Casanova sent twenty articles to *ABC*, most of which took several weeks or months to reach the paper. She did not know until February, 1915 that a letter she had sent to *El debate* the previous October wasn't published until that December. The few Spanish newspapers and magazines that she received (including *La correspondencia*) were months out of date, and she had no idea of public reaction to her articles. Despite the time lapse, her eyewitness accounts were widely read and reprinted throughout Spain and Latin America.

At the time *ABC* boasted the most modern newspaper plant in the country, and the largest circulation. Newly redesigned, and leading the Spanish press in a circulation war, *ABC* increased its sales by providing readers with the most technologically up-to-date and thorough coverage of war events. At this time *ABC* had some of Spain's best-known journalists and writers on its staff. Casanova's articles were published next to those of luminaries such as "Azorín" (Jose Martínez Ruiz, 1863-1967), Ramiro de Maeztú (1874-1936), Alberto Ínsua (1885-1934), Armando Palacio

Valdés (1853-1938), and other prominent writers.

Like Casanova, *ABC* was openly monarchist and committed to parliamentarianism and democracy. But unlike Casanova (and probably unknown to her at that time), during the Great War *ABC* was also *germanófilo*. Yet the newspaper published the uncensored work of columnists representing all points of view. *ABC*'s readers, the Catholic bourgeoisie, wanted to be guided as well as informed. They could keep up with world events through the wire service reports that appeared at the back of the paper. But from their feature columnists they expected in-depth analysis and personal opinions, no matter how uncommon (and even whimsical), as long as they stayed within the limits of a certain broad philosophical and political spectrum, limits that Casanova pushed at times. For the time being, ABC was happy to pay for the services of an experienced writer with background in Eastern European affairs who also demonstrated a highly developed political sense -- even if that writer was a woman. At that time, a female war correspondent was considered an absurdity. Spanish women were supposed to write articles only on literature, fashion, children, religion and the home, and perhaps sometimes on 'appropriate' literature. Journalism was considered an extension of politics, and politics an exclusively male pursuit. It appears that before Casanova, only Carmen de Burgos had broken this taboo, in 1909 when sent by her newspaper to cover the battle of Melilla (1909). Casanova's reporting career broke new ground, since she wrote from the center of the anti-feminist, conservative press. Perhaps the emotional anti-war content of her articles, in the best tradition of feminine empathy and humanitarianism, fell within the range of emotions expected from women. Pacifist and other views that would have been considered unconventional and minoritarian if evinced by a man, were considered very differently (perhaps dismissed) when they were expressed by a woman. Also, her status as a widow and as a mature woman (fifty-four) helped the positive reception of her work.

Of course, Casanova was not the only Spaniard reporting the war, or the only one at a front. Her old friend, Ricardo León, had been sent by *El imparcial* to France and Germany, and several lesser Spanish journalists were at Verdun and the Marne. Even her eminent literary reviewer, Pérez de Ayala, was covering the war from the Italian frontier. However, she was the only Spanish journalist in the Eastern front. Aside from communiqués from press services, Spain was out of touch with events in the area. Casanova's eyewitness letters and articles filled this void, aroused a great deal of public attention and inspired admiration for her womanly sensitivity and courage. Encouraged by newsstand sales, ABC overlooked the taboo against women correspondents and rather exploited

Casanova's image of an "*ángel de hospitales*," possibly to diffuse any criticism.

Typical of the adulation she received for her feminine "sacrifices" was an article published by journalist Nicasio Hernández Luquero in the evening newspaper *España nueva*:

De entre la tupida flora de literatura y de comentarios sin literatura puesta por nuestros escritores al margen de la hecatombe que enrojece a Europa, emerge como una abierta rosa de ternura y de amor... la prosa de Sofía Casanova... despues de (su) santa tarea escribe estas crónicas, las mas hondas, mas emotivas y mas calofriantes que han salido de plumas españolas para glosar la gran tragedia... es fuerte, a mas de delicada y lírica, el alma de Casanova. Es fuerte porque en ella no ha hecho nido el rencor. (*Guerra* Introduction)

From among the over-growth of literature and of non-literary commentaries created by our writers at the edge of the pyre that reddens Europe, Sofía Casanova's prose emerges like an open rose of tenderness and love...following [her] sacred duty she writes these chronicles, the deepest, the most moving, and the most chilling issued from Spanish pens to gloss the great tragedy... Sofía Casanova's soul is strong, besides being delicate and lyrical. It is strong because it does not harbor hatred.

Sofía Casanova, Anti-War Witness

In 1915, Casanova worked for six weeks in a blur of exhaustion. At the end of October, as Russian victories reduced the numbers of wounded entering the hospitals of Warsaw, she regained her bearings. From reading out-of-date Spanish newspapers and publications, she learned that her country was among the few European countries to declare neutrality (others were the Scandinavian countries, the Netherlands, Switzerland and Italy).

A strong pro-German faction had emerged in Spain, especially among the upper classes. The well-organized German propaganda machine produced reams of copy and hundreds of photographs aimed at swaying Spanish public opinion with its exaggerated image of Germany's vast war machinery and "invincible" forces. Many Spanish intellectuals, on the other hand, felt that Spain's neutrality was a flagrant betrayal of France, and a boon to Germany. Sharp public debate flared on the subject. When Madrid newspapers published the latest news sent over the telegraph wire, crowds gathered outside of their offices eagerly awaiting bulletins. Spanish businessmen and speculators began to trade with both sides in the conflict, and the Spanish economy enjoyed a boom period.

Casanova worried about the proliferation of *germanófilos* in Spain (*Guerra* 31). She loyally supported King Alfonso's neutrality, but was dismayed and disappointed by her country's pro-German bias. Somewhat consoled by news that the queen had joined the Spanish Red Cross, she was also glad when the king made a large contribution towards the purchase of medicine and books for soldiers in military hospitals.

Casanova was strongly motivated to write, despite the demands of her nursing job. Even though she received no confirmation that her writing was being read in Madrid, her strong moral position against the war made her feel that by chronicling its horrors she was fulfilling a duty to humanity. The enormity and inhumanity of the war shocked and revolted her. She said that she hoped, as a woman and a Sister of Charity, that her articles about the horrors of war would generate public compassion. As she repeatedly told her readers, she was not pursuing political aims, but recording the sufferings of Eastern Europe. She noted bitterly that her feminine objectivity and descriptions of the horrors of war were not as popular as "masculine heroics" ("Aclaración", *ABC*, 3 May 1917).

Casanova had lived in a highly politicized world for many years, and developed a distaste for propaganda. She read the foreign language press and had many foreign contacts, so she was aware of the equivocations and stereotypes used by all sides in the war. The hate-filled images of "the Hun" or "perfidious Albion" in the international press disturbed her, and she did her best to dispel them with facts.

Casanova believed *all* nations were equally capable of violence and injustice (*Guerra* 155-157). She considered it her duty to tell the truth as she saw it, and to bring "un soplo de aire respirable (al) infecto territorio de los combates y la política" ("Aclaración," *ABC*, 3 May 1917) 'a breath of fresh air to the infected territory of battles and politics'. The enormous volume of militant journalism disseminated daily by all sides would not disappear, but at least her *ABC* readers would get an alternative view.

After years of watching Roman Dmowski and the Russophiles temporizing with what she considered evil, Casanova finally took a stand. She quoted Quevedo's famous lines:

¿No ha de haber un espíritu valiente?
Siempre se ha de sentir lo que se dice.
¿Nunca se ha de decir lo que se siente?
("Aclaración," ABC, 3 May 1917)
Shouldn't there be one brave spirit?
One should always feel what one says.
Shouldn't one ever say what one feels?

Casanova was driven by the need to communicate her observations and judgments to like minds, to be reassured that her values were human and valid. Not one person among hundreds she knew in Poland shared her pacifist views, her neutrality, or her sympathy for the Jews and her distaste for anti-Semitism. Her closest relatives and friends, almost all anti-Semites, mocked her attempts to help Jews in the hospital, or to defend them against the blanket label of "spies." In 1914, nineteen years before Hitler's "Final Solution," there was general support for their extermination:

"Debían todos ser muertos, pues, sin excepción, sirven al enemigo." Es la voz general, pero no la creo justiciera... y mis amigos los nacionalistas polacos, ironizan amablemente mi defensa de los israelitas... creo que hay judíos entre los espías, pero no todos ellos lo son. (*Guerra* 99)

"They should all be killed, because, without exception, they serve the enemy." That's the public opinion, but I don't believe it a fair one... and my friends the Polish nationalists, cordially mock my defense of the Jews... I believe that there may be Jews among the spies, but not all of them are.

In Spain, however, there were many people who had no nationalistic interest in the conflict, and understood her views as a natural, human reaction to prejudice and bigotry.

When Casanova began to write her letters to the Spanish press, the atrocities of the Germans against the Belgians were still fresh in the minds of the general Spanish public. On the other hand, they knew nothing of Poland. Casanova's repeated comparisons of Poland to Belgium were intended to arouse sympathy for the long-neglected *question Polonaise*.

Casanova described the problems of a partitioned Poland, the nation's unfortunate history, the tragedy of fratricide, the seductiveness of the Grand Duke's manifesto, the sordid reality of the dead and wounded arriving by the thousands at Polish hospitals. She praised the Polish people, because of their refinement and culture, as "the Parisians of the North," and portrayed them as sympathetically as possible to her Spanish readers, who knew little about them. She held their patriotism and devotion up to Spain as an example of a united nation -- what Spain was not. She described the organizing efforts of the Civic Committee and a number of other organizations trying to set up shelters, orphanages, and schools to care for the flood of displaced persons (*Guerra* 120).

Casanova depicted modern war, random in its violence, as sacrilegious and anti-human. She constantly reported new horrors (the first aerial bombings in history, experiments with mustard gas, attacks upon the civilian population) with indignation and disbelief. She described how during a raid of Russian Poland on May 7, 1915, the Germans set a Red Cross hospital ablaze, killing all the patients and staff. She said that the reality of the incident was too awful for the spirit to accept, even during a war:

> Leo y releo estas atroces líneas, y me vuelvo a proprios y extraños indignada, incrédula, gritando que eso no puede ser. Matarse en el combate, en las emboscadas, en el aire y bajo los mares, es natural en la guerra; pero incendiar un hospital después de golpear a los heridos, que vivos aun, ardieron, eso no tiene nombre: es culpa, pecado, por inhumano, innominable. No puede ser, repito. ¡Imposible, imposible! (*Guerra* 157)

I read and reread these awful lines and I turn to those close to me and to strangers indignant, incredulous, crying that it cannot be. To kill one another in battle, in ambushes, in the air and under the seas, is natural in war; but to set a hospital on fire after beating the patients, who, still alive, burned to death, that is impossible: it is culpability, a sin, so inhuman, it is unnameable. It can't be, I repeat. It's impossible, impossible!

A new invention, mustard gas, was particularly vicious. Its victims suffered a slow and excruciating death by asphyxiation. The gas that saturated their clothes and was exuded by their bodies affected Casanova and other hospital personnel. A few months later some palliatives were discovered, but during those first weeks the hospital lost over six hundred patients without being able to relieve their suffering (*Guerra* 174). at times Casanova sank into utter despair:

> En las seis semanas que llevo en el hospital, he visto tales lástimas y tales horrores, que la guerra, todas las guerras habidas y por haber, son para mi prueba irrecusable de la bancarrota espiritual de la humanidad, y no comprendo como Dios...les da un día mas de vida en este planeta, que merece deshacerse en polvo sangriento como los campos y las aguas de Europa. (*Guerra* 15)

In my six weeks in the hospital, I have seen such sorrows and such horrors, that war, all the wars ever waged and yet to be fought, are for me irrefutable proof of the spiritual bankruptcy of humanity, and I do not understand how God...allows one more day of life on this planet, which deserves to dissolve into bloody dust like the fields and rivers of Europe.

As she reported, from the ninth to the twenty-first of October, zeppelins bombed Warsaw daily. Her hospital was hit several times, with several staff members and passersby killed. She and other Sisters of Charity had refused to leave their posts. At one point the civil authorities fled Warsaw, and it seemed that they were about to be invaded, but the

Germans were pushed back.

By January, 1915, the cities and villages of Poland were suffering severe food shortages. Casanova reported in detail to her readers in Spain what they had already read in brief agency news bulletins: that two of Poland's greatest artistic figures, novelist Henryk Sienkiewicz and pianist Ignacy Paderewski, had formed a Polish Relief Committee. She also reported with pride that in April 1915, following the Pope's example, the king of Spain had made a generous contribution towards Polish relief. She beseeched her readers to follow the king's and the Pope's example, and assist Poland's war victims (*Guerra* 123).

As a result of these international efforts -- and Casanova's articles -- Spanish public attention was directed to Poland more that ever before. In Spain (as in England, France, and the United States), the *Question Polonaise* 'Polish question' was resurrected overnight as a result of sympathetic press coverage. This renewed international interest had a far-reaching impact on Poland's future.

By Easter, 1915, Casanova had become acclimated to her new life of hard work and sacrifices. She had also undergone some striking changes in attitude. Months of nursing Russian soldiers had softened her dislike of the Russian invaders. Ironically, that Easter Sunday, the czarist Government chose to announce that "concessions" had been made to Poles for their efforts during the war -- the anti-climatic reissue of a few half-measures of municipal autonomy, originally drawn up in 1892 but even then rejected as irrelevant. Such was the "reward" granted to Russian Poland for its contribution of one million Polish soldiers and the many sacrifices of its civilians. An irate Casanova described Warsaw's disenchanted and bitter mood (*Guerra* 185).

The Evacuation of Warsaw

The tides of war turned again, this time against Russia. A last major battle had been won against the Germans in Przemysl, but Russia's defeat was in sight. The Germans began to prepare for an invasion of Poland from the east. Despite Dmowski's lobbying, anti-Polish elements within the Russian government tried to dissuade the Czar from granting any more political advantages to Russian Poland, now that it was about to fall into German hands. The Russian government's initiative for Polish autonomy finally collapsed.

By the summer of 1915, it was clear that Russia had suffered enormous losses. The Germans again prepared to invade Warsaw. Cannon fire rattled windows and shook Casanova's apartment building, which was near the Vistula and the edge of the city. At night, distant fires cast an ominous glow on the horizon as the enemy troops came closer, devastating the Polish countryside. (*Viajes* 43-44).

When the Russian army decided to pull out of the capital, a mass panic seized the city. Rumors that "the Huns" would inflict atrocities on the civilian population flew through every social class. Servants and aristocrats, laborers and professors all gave whispered examples of "proven crimes" that the Germans had committed against civilians in other invaded nations. Casanova tried to calm her friends and acquaintances, but between their obsessive terror at the thought of invasion, and the official Russian stance of bland optimism, she could not find a middle ground (*Guerra* 155).

Finally, Russian authorities ordered the evacuation of Warsaw and surrounding areas. During July, 1915, more than six hundred thousand people began an immense, poorly-planned and disorderly migration into the Ukraine and White Russia. Polish soldiers and peasants were ordered to burn lands and raze farms, to leave nothing behind for the Germans, or for those unfortunate Polish civilians who could not evacuate to the east.

Casanova and many others found the realities of this haphazard evacuation and destruction almost as brutal as any foreign invasion could have been. She wrote that the orders were heartless, the Russian leaders imbeciles, and the mass exodus of the Polish people comparable only to the wandering of the Biblical tribes in the desert, since both groups were not welcome abroad (*Guerra* 221).

Casanova, her two younger daughters Bela and Halita, along with nursemaid Pepa and the Niklewiczes, hastily packed a few trunks and shut down their flat. They left most of their possessions inside, praying that the flat would not be looted or destroyed. She recorded these anguished moments:

Dejé mi casa varsoviana cuando el cerco, el círculo de fuego cerníase, aprisionando la ciudad, y de nada hemos sabido después. Mis libros, mis cuadros, mis reliquias familiares ¿dónde estan? El día de la partida pasé la hora terrible de la selección de objetos queridos... ¿Qué tomar en una maletilla de mano? (*Guerra* 305)

I left my Warsaw home when the siege, the circle of fire was drawing close, imprisoning the city, and we have heard nothing since. My books, my paintings, my family relics -- where are they? On the day of departure I spent a terrible hour selecting beloved objects. What does one take in an overnight bag?

Casanova's choices were a change of clothes; the book that she kept at her bedside all her life, Thomas à Kempis' *The Imitation of Christ*; and a photograph of her mother.

Although Casanova and her family had money, exit permits and train tickets, they were not prepared for the Dantesque scene at the train station. Mobs of desperate people begged to be let on the train. The few fortunate ticket-holders were jammed into railway cars, which then slowly made their way east into Russia. The czarist government had made no provisions or preparations for the hundreds of thousands forced to flee Warsaw. Those without money ended up in squalid refugee camps and suffered from hunger and exposure, typhoid and pneumonia. Families were separated and dispersed by accident, and Casanova reported dozens of heart-breaking scenes involving lost children or disoriented old people who strayed from their families during the trek. Two articles movingly detailing the horrors of the evacuation were published by *ABC* in October 1915 (See also *Viajes* 46).

Insulated from this chaos by her family's money and position Casanova travelled safely on to the east with Mañita and Mañita's husband, her two grand-children, Krysia, aged four, and Romek (named after his godfather Roman Dmowski), aged one and a half, and the faithful Pepa. After fifteen hours on a train, they arrived in Minsk. There they rented a house about twenty kilometers from the city in the little village of Perezieka.

Through high-level connections, Casanova returned to Warsaw briefly to serve one final day at the hospital, and to report on the last few apocalyptic hours before the city fell to the Germans. As endless lines of carriages rolled through the streets towards the edge of town, and thousands of people loaded with bags and bundles streamed towards the east, she and Ela Balicka walked through Warsaw, saying goodbye to their favorite haunts. After walking through the elegant Nowy Świat district, they found a crowd clustered around the beautiful seventeenth-century statue of the Virgin on the Krakowskie Przedmiescie. They were weeping at the foot of the statue and saying the Rosary in final farewell to their city. Casanova and Dr. Balicka joined them and then said their own good-byes.

Alone, and with a heavy heart but still taking copious notes, Casanova rode a military train out of the city. A few hours later the German army entered Warsaw. Poland's one hundred and sixty-five years of hated Russian occupation ended with the arrival of an even more dreaded oppressor.

Chapter 7

1915 - Evacuation to the East

When Casanova arrived in Minsk in July 1915, she found the city in a frenzy of war activity. Situated on one of two main roads to Moscow, Minsk sheltered more than fifty thousand Polish and other refugees fleeing the Germans. Shaken by their narrow escape, Casanova and her party waited for news from relatives still in Poland. They heard constant rumors of "Hun atrocities" in the occupied sectors. To their horror, they read a report in a Polish émigré newspaper that Drozdowo had been razed, and most of the Lutosławski family killed. They waited for two agonizing weeks until, to their astonishment, the rest of the family (eventually twenty-eight people) began to arrive in Minsk. Those reports had been false and Drozdowo had escaped damage (*Viajes* 190-191).

Together they found a larger, more comfortable house twenty miles outside Minsk and began to work for war relief. Casanova volunteered at the Warsaw Red Cross's headquarters, now regrouped in exile. Just as they were settling down to a somewhat normal routine, Casanova's daughter Bela fell critically ill with dysentery.

Under Russian military rule, civilians had to follow complicated procedures to buy medicine. Casanova wrote an outraged article for *ABC* describing her struggles with indifferent officials and shopkeepers. In wartime, restrictions on medicine were one indignity among many imposed on civilians by the Russian military. Wherever she and Pepa went, their accented Russian gave them away as foreigners. They were constantly challenged to prove their identities and legal status by xenophobic Russian officials (*Guerra* 190-191).

By the end of August, it became clear that Minsk would also fall to the Germans, and that they would have to travel farther east into Russia. Unlike thousands of other Polish émigrés, the Lutosławskis still had access to family money, and this again made their emigration east relatively easy. Casanova and her daughters Bela (now recovering) and Halita, nursemaid Pepa, the Lutosławskis and the Niklewiczes travelled by train four hundred miles east to Moscow. There they rented two large old houses in a respectable neighborhood, and with money and effort, again made their new homes comfortable for their extended family. Among them the combined families had almost a dozen children, with Mañita expecting her third. The children took private lessons at home with Polish and Russian tutors, played in the large yard and later on when it snowed ice-skated and rode their sleds (*Viajes* 58-64).

In Moscow, Casanova's son-in-law, Mieczysław, resumed writing and editing for Roman Dmowski's newspaper, *Sprawa Polska* 'Polish Action', which had re-opened there. The ever-pragmatic Dmowski was again trying to negotiate concessions for Poland from the czarist government, now that its political position had been weakened by the war. Casanova's brothers-in-law Józef and Marian Lutosławski worked in Polish émigré circles, organizing relief and education services for the huge number of Polish refugees.

Casanova was tired of witnessing so much sorrow. After a heart-breaking year of nursing, and months of travel, she was relieved to turn her attention away from the war. In one of her first articles from Russia, she wrote that the chaos and panic on the road of evacuation to Minsk had vanished from her mind almost overnight, replaced by vivid impressions of life in Moscow. Removed from the disruption of war and with a settled daily routine, her spirits soared. At fifty-four, Casanova had energy, curiosity and resilience. Now she had time and leisure to reflect on what she was experiencing.

Moscow had much to offer a visiting journalist. At the time it had two million inhabitants and although it was not yet the administrative and business center of Russia, war made the city bustle. According to her way of thinking, Moscow might have had many of the institutions that make a great city (a university, medical schools, palaces and gardens) but she didn't consider Moscow to be even remotely a major city according to her "European" expectations. Still, every evening after dinner Casanova would jot down in notebooks the day's impressions and news.

In a few weeks, Casanova moved from war reportage to political writing. A few transitional articles in *ABC* described Moscow and its people, and gave some background information on Russian history for her Spanish readers, who knew little about Russia or its people. With this change of focus came a new openness towards Russian culture. For two decades, Casanova had written against czarism and against Russia from a narrow, pro-Polish point of view. Poles saw themselves as the champions of European, Roman Catholic culture, enslaved by "barbaric" Russian hordes. Anyone who read only Casanova's early books and articles would have concluded that Russia was a confederacy of bumpkins and brutes. By 1916 Casanova had read widely in Russian literature, and developed a more mature understanding of Russian culture. The war had brought a temporary thaw in previously strained relations between Russians and Dmowski's *Narodowa Demokracja* 'National Democracy' party, which was now able to lobby its ancestral enemy, the czarist government, even more intensely.

Her ties to the *ND* leader and rising political star, Roman Dmowski, opened the doors of Russian society to Casanova. As a Spaniard and a woman of letters, she was a welcome rarity in aristocratic salons. Almost against her better judgment, she was impressed by the country's noble mansions, the aristocracy's refined manners and dress, and the extravagant lifestyle they maintained even in wartime. She met countesses and generals, visited the Czarina's sister, the Grand Duchess Elizabeth, and spent hours chatting in French and exotically accented Russian with dozens of people from many social classes. Noting that foreigners enjoyed this rarefied atmosphere of luxury, she found herself to be no exception. Soon Casanova's initial distaste for exile in Russia vanished (Niklewicz, K. interview). An old proverb says that "Russia is not a country, it is a world". Casanova must have agreed: she told her readers that there was little in the Spanish or European experience to guide one in understanding the Russians.

Yet what she saw earned only qualified approval. Russia at the end of the Romanov era was a fascinating but corrupt political spectacle. Even an apologist, Count Witte, had described it as "this insane regime, this tangle of cowardice, blindness, craftiness and stupidity" (Tuchman 59). Casanova described the czarist regime to her readers as exotic, archaic, decadent and clearly doomed. The war was unanimously unpopular. The Czar and Czarina, influenced by the sinister Rasputin, were disliked and lacked credibility. Germanophiles riddled the government and fought against Russia's own interests.

Russia had never enjoyed a free press, even before the war. Military communiqués put on a false show of optimism that eroded public confidence. Casanova reported the forced closing of the *Duma* (Parliament), the shutting down by strikes of many sectors of the economy, and the day-by-day reality of a country seething with unrest. As early as September, 1915, she predicted the coming of "un paroxismo trágico" 'a tragic upheaval' (*Guerra* 250).

These candid observations got her into trouble with Russian authorities. Unknown to Casanova, her *ABC* articles had become an embarrassment to Count Kudacheff, the Russian ambassador to Spain. Her vivid reports of the evacuation of Warsaw, the closing of the *Duma*, and the demotion of Grand Duke Nicholas brought into question the optimistic official communiqués issued almost daily by the Russian embassy in Madrid. Count Kudacheff sent several protest notes to the Spanish king against *ABC*'s Russian correspondent.

His Majesty ignored the notes: the royal family had Casanova under its protection since 1885. In an unusual request, the king asked *ABC*'s editor-in-chief to provide him with a copy of Casanova's articles before they were published, as a "supplement" to his official information. In his book *La revolución rusa en el diario ABC de la época*, which analyzes *ABC*'s (and Casanova's) impact on Spanish public opinion during the Russian revolution, Professor Alfonso Lazo records that this was interpreted as a further insult by the Russians (18-19).

Irritated by the lack of official Spanish response, Kudacheff wired Russia several times, trying to find out who was "Sofía Casanova," *ABC*'s correspondent in Moscow. It was not until the winter of 1915 that authorities linked "Sofía Casanova" to "Zofia Lutosławska," the name on her Polish identity papers. Casanova was given a verbal reprimand by military censors, who also confiscated several articles and private letters. She had to contact a highly placed Spanish diplomat (probably the Count of Cartagena, Spain's Ambassador to the Czar in Petrograd) to have the articles released and forwarded to Madrid (Lazo 9).

As Casanova knew from her painful experiences in Warsaw, official reprimands could have serious consequences, from fines to a jail sentence. She still held Spanish citizenship, but was, by marriage, a subject of the Czar. Her new refugee status made Casanova even more vulnerable. In December, 1915, she travelled to Petrograd to visit the Spanish embassy.

The war had kept Casanova out of touch with Spain and the Spanish press for almost two years. She did not know how acclaimed she had become through her articles. When the Spanish ambassador personally called on her at her hotel and announced that she was the embassy's honored guest, Casanova was astonished. She was given a heroine's welcome at the Embassy, and offered an arrangement for getting her articles to Spain via diplomatic pouch. For the time being, she would be able to avoid direct confrontation with the censors (*Guerra* 286-288).

Christmas in Moscow was a great success. The family put up a Christmas tree, and celebrated a typically Polish Catholic Christmas eve, without what Casanova censoriously described as "pagan excesses" of the Russian Orthodox rite. They bought toys for the children and exchanged presents. Casanova recorded the celebration in detail in her notebooks and in an article to *ABC*. In retrospect her memorialization of that Christmas turned out be a blessing. The Lutosławskis and Niklewiczes had no inkling that this would be the last Christmas the entire family would share. Her careful note-taking recorded the happy moment for posterity (*Viajes* 58-59). The year 1916, as recorded in Casanova's articles and in Russian history was a year of escalating turbulence. Casanova noted that more than thirteen million Russians had died or been wounded since 1914. The Czar assumed command of the army and appointed a number of inept bureaucrats as "ministers." The *Duma* was outraged, and demanded the appointment of a government it could trust. The economy deteriorated, and foreign diplomats and businessmen reaped the harvest of Russian troubles. By 1916, conscription had undermined the country's agriculture and industry. Prices skyrocketed. There were constant shortages of food and other goods. The poor grew more restless and discontented with each passing month.

Casanova was astonished by the aristocracy's insensitivity to human misery. The upper classes flaunted their wealth next to people who lived in the most degrading poverty, and seemed to feel neither guilt nor even compassion. This lack of concern for their neighbors struck Casanova as monstrous.

Coming from a militantly Catholic milieu, Casanova had strong ideas about the responsibilities of those who enjoyed "privilegios de casta" (*Corte* 170) 'caste privileges' such as inherited wealth, social position and educational advantage. Those who had them had a duty to provide education, medical care, free religious instruction and fair treatment in general for the lower classes. According to Casanova, the Lutosławskis observed these responsibilities to the letter. Their social circle of Polish national friends and associates paid them at least lip service. Even this brand of Polish paternalism was absent in Russia (*Corte* 175). Casanova gave her Spanish readers a few examples of upper-class callousness: Mme. S., a socialite, complained to her that the war was curtailing parties and entertainment. Another socialite, a princess from the Caucasus, was infuriated when a train carrying wounded soldiers delayed the arrival of party favors she had ordered from abroad (*Corte* 177-178). The war had caused severe food shortages in Warsaw and White Russia, and thrown Russia's agricultural system into disarray. Casanova was appalled to see that as starving Ukrainian peasants were reduced to stripping bark from trees to feed themselves, in Moscow gourmet foods (an improbable cornucopia of delicacies ranging from Caspian Sea caviar to fresh Cuban guavas) were available to those with enough rubles. Floating above this social disorder, the Czar's family lived in what she described as an island of privilege (*Corte* 175).

Summer brought a new set of problems. Plague, spread by Moscow's abysmal public hygiene, swept the city. Despite the family's precautions, several of the children became ill, including Romek and Krysia. Romek died after a short agony. While the entire family grieved for their first-born, his mother (again pregnant), Pepa, who had been his nurse, and Casanova suffered the most. Painful memories of Jadwiga's death twenty-one years before rushed back as Casanova tried to console her daughter. They grieved for months, until the birth of Andrzej Niklewicz in 1917 helped their mourning (Niklewicz, K. interview).

As they recovered from this loss, the Niklewiczes decided to move once again. Health conditions were better in Petrograd, about 400 miles north of Moscow, and they had family and friends in the city. Mieczysław Niklewicz could continue to edit *Sprawa Polska* and coordinate the *ND*'s involvement with the Russian government in Petrograd's large Polish colony. In the fall of 1916 they migrated to Petrograd.

They found a large flat for rent on Fursterskaia Street, between the beautiful Tauride Gardens surrounding the *Duma and* Kirosnaia Street, which housed several military divisions. Police headquarters down the street added to the strategic importance of the area, a fact that did not seem important at the time, but would have consequences later. To her disgust, she discovered that the American Embassy was next door. Bela and Halita were much admired by the "Yanquis" and soon made friends among the younger diplomats. Casanova, who could not forgive the United States for the Spanish-American-Cuban war and other losses, shunned any contact with them.

Casanova enjoyed living in Petrograd (early in the war, in a fit of patriotism, its name had been changed from the Germanic-sounding "St. Petersburg"). With its sophisticated cultural life, wide avenues and luxurious palaces, it appealed to her aesthetic sense. She loved the romantic "white nights" of summer (*Revolución rusa* 193). Best of all, she was near the Spanish embassy. To Casanova's delight, a few months later the Spanish embassy moved its headquarters even closer to nearby Sergiezewska Street.

Casanova visited the embassy daily, attending diplomatic parties and receptions and catching the latest political news as she made her rounds. She knew the French, U.S. and British ambassadors, and discerned their role in Russian politics. She read the French newspapers, and probably had access to the excellent daily bulletins published by the French Information Bureau of Petrograd. All this contact vastly improved her grasp of world opinion and Russian politics. Now she had a much broader perspective, and could acquaint her Spanish readers with the welter of news and rumors that swept Petrograd and all of Russia (Niklewicz, K. interview).

Through Dmowski, who had been a Polish member of the *Duma*, and her own personal interest, Casanova was familiar with the few political parties that could operate openly. The Cadets (an acronym for Constitutional Democracy) were fairly liberal members of the upper classes, but pro-war. Casanova distrusted their leaders, Milyukov and Puriskiewicz. She also knew the political positions of leaders such as Prince Lwów, the President of the *Duma*, Rodzianko, and the "Octobrist" Alexander Guchkov (she had met him in Warsaw during his military service there two years earlier). She did not understand precisely how these and other political groups in Russia were plotting to overthrow the Czar. But by the end of 1916, she was as familiar with the apparent principal players in Russian politics as any of the other foreign journalists in Petrograd. Of the Social Democrats and their tiny Left wing, the Bolsheviks, she and the other foreign journalists knew almost nothing.

Casanova's mobility within Russian society added a new depth to her reporting. New sources included members of the Czar's household, who showed her letters written by the Czarina; members of the *Duma,* who provided her with excellent behind-the-scenes information; and the perpetually optimistic and fatuous "General Ivan Ivanovich," epitome of the Czarist military fossil, whose self-deluded ideas she gleefully reported.

One of Casanova's new contacts led her to an attempt to interview Rasputin that was foiled at the very end. She had heard rumors about the sinister monk who advised the Czarina on her son's illness and other matters, and met one of his followers, a devout widow at a party. This woman, who knew Casanova was a journalist for a foreign newspaper, tried to arrange an interview with Rasputin, to counteract the "black rumors" circulating about him abroad. Rasputin did not like the idea of an interview but one evening the widow convinced Casanova to hide in a house he was about to visit. Through a half-opened door, she got her first and only glimpse of the monk, a huge, unkempt, crass cleric. When Rasputin refused to be interviewed, the widow went into a panic and Casanova was rushed out of the house into a waiting coach. His alarming appearance and manner convinced her that he was an "hombre-diablo," (*Corte* 166-167) 'a man-devil' and a nefarious character.

Revolution in Russia

Rasputin's murder on December 16, 1916 was followed by public rejoicing. Censorship was lifted for two days, and Casanova reported versions and interpretations of his death in her article to *ABC* that week. That was the last straw for the Czarist censors: they refused to let her

send or receive mail from Spain. She was "absolutamente incomunicada" -
-- and furious -- for several weeks (*De la revolución* 115).

The Russian people hoped that Rasputin's death would improve the political situation. It soon became obvious that as long as the Czar was in power, there would be no change. Unrest increased as Petrograd's food supplies dwindled. In February, 1917, Casanova wrote to *ABC* that the struggle throughout Russia was intensifying. In political circles, among the working classes, and above all in the army, there was constant conflict. Early in March, a Russian baroness told Casanova that this situation could not go on much longer, and that "great events" were going to take place soon. She added in French, "Croyez-moi, nous sommes sur un volcan" (*ABC*, 9 June 1917) 'Believe me, we are standing on a volcano'. Casanova agreed, but wrote that she hoped change could be brought about without violence.

By the end of the first week of March, striking workers, noisy street demonstrations and shoppers waiting to buy food in long queues disrupted Petrograd. From army headquarters, the Czar ordered the *Duma* to close again, but his directive was ignored. The army (whose garrisons were near Casanova's flat) joined the proletarians. For once, the dreaded Cossacks refused to turn against the people.

Returning home from a visit on the afternoon of March 10, Casanova found streetcars blocked by striking workmen. The streets were crowded with workers bearing anti-war banners, singing, and demanding bread and peace from the government. The Army cut off the center of Petrograd from outlying working-class districts. Soldiers bearing whips stood guard at each bridge.

On March 11th, Casanova reported fighting in the streets. Since their flat was near police headquarters and military depots, she witnessed many violent incidents. Bullets flew over their home; the body of a soldier was brought to the house next door. Casanova wrote with shaking hand to *ABC* of being too close to these upheavals. While Russian newspapers were not allowed to report these incidents, by March 12, everyone knew that Petrograd was in the middle of a revolution.

Then came an abrupt change in the mood of the masses, and in the tone of Casanova's reporting. Huge crowds marched by her flat on their way to the *Duma*, joyfully singing the *Marseillaise* and bearing thousands of red banners and flags. Camaraderie was in the air. Startled by their joy, Casanova surrendered to their collective exuberance. Beginning with an article written early in March, 1917 (but not published in Spain until May 5th), Casanova reported the excitement and energy of the new revolution.

Proudly wearing a red bow on her lapel (a gesture for which she would be teased by family and friends to the end of her life), Casanova walked around the city basking in the euphoria of revolution. Before March, she had been war-weary, pessimistic, even cynical. Now she believed that Petrograd's happy and non-violent mood foreshadowed a new era for Russia and Poland and for humanity. She wrote that the people of Petrograd were living "una de esas horas misteriosas y fecundas, en que las almas de las multitudes se buscan y se funden en un sentimiento fraternal" 'one of those mysterious and fruitful times when the souls in a crowd seek each other and blend in fraternal feeling' ("El ejército y el pueblo," *ABC* 17 May 1917). Strangers now greeted one another easily. Meeting a group of elegant young ladies on the street, she asked them what was going to happen next. Smiling, they assured her that "ya somos libres, que nos hemos dignificado" 'we are free now, we have recovered our dignity' ("Los albores del nuevo regimen," *ABC* 6 June, 1917). That same day, she saw a soldier crying as the Rights of the Soldier were read aloud. He told Casanova that he was crying with joy because "Ya no hay oficiales y soldados: un general es lo mismo que yo, todos ciudadanos" 'There are no more soldiers and officers: a general is the same as I, we are all citizens' (*ABC*, 20 June, 1917). Casanova listened approvingly; she had resented the Russian Army's abuses for many years.

After years of alienation, euphoria overcame Casanova's pessimism: all her dreams seemed possible, even those of peace and social harmony. The Revolution had captured her imagination and her spirit.

Chapter 8

Disenchantment and Escape to the West

"Freedom," "Rights of Man," "Equality" -- these magic words were heard and read everywhere in Petrograd. With newspapers still closed, information was spread through leaflets tossed from cars and trucks. A young soldier, an elderly person, anyone who could read would pick one up and announce the latest events to the illiterate crowds. On March 14, Casanova sent *ABC* the translation of a broadside she found on the street, advising workers and soldiers to elect representatives for a meeting at the *Duma* that evening. Through Casanova's account, Spain learned of the first Petrograd *Soviet* (a Russian word that originally meant 'council' but now meant an assembly elected only by workers) .

News of the Russian revolution reached Spain and other European countries slowly and disjointedly, though communiques from news agencies. The street demonstrations that had taken place early in March were not reported in Spain until the sixteenth. On that day huge headlines about the revolution covered *ABC*'s front page but gave little factual information. The average European reader was confused by the sketchy wire service reports. A contemporary study acknowledges that Casanova's in-depth coverage lessened this confusion: *ABC* had "enorme suerte" ("enormous luck") in having an alert correspondent in Petrograd whose reporting illuminated unfolding events. One of the most interesting things about this correspondent was her gender:

Se trataba de una mujer: Sofía Casanova. Magnífica escritora con una fabulosa intuición, sus crónicas desde Rusia iban a dar a su periódico una extraordinaria popularidad entre los lectores españoles. (Lazo 18)
(The correspondent) was a woman: Sofía Casanova. An excellent writer of superb intuition, her chronicles from Russia gave her newspaper extraordinary popularity among Spanish readers.

Other foreign correspondents such as Philip Price of the *Manchester Guardian* wrote with a detachment that pales next to Casanova's vivid chronicles. Casanova not only reported the revolution, she lived it, to such an extent that the feelings of the Russian people in those days became her own. According to Professor Lazo, her partiality was noticeable:

Sofía, no solo cuenta la revolución sino que...la vive intensamente en cuanto que las alegrías, los deseos y los temores del pueblo ruso en

87

aquellos días, fueron sus proprias alegrías, sus proprios temores, y sus propios deseos...desde sus primeros artículos...la corresponsal de *ABC* no ocultó sus simpatías por el proletariado. (Lazo 18)

Sofía not only retells the revolution, she also lives it intensely, so that the joys, desires and fears of the Russian people during that time, were her own joys, her own fears, and her own desires...from her earliest articles, the *ABC* correspondent did not hide her sympathy for the proletariat.

A lifetime monarchist, Casanova was troubled by her own lack of support for the Czar. On analyzing her feelings, she found only a slight depression, which she attributed to her "spiritual complexity". She felt sorry for a ruler who failed to unify his people, and held up her beloved Spanish Bourbons as models of successful rulers (*ABC* 29 May 1917).

Casanova shared her Polish family and friends' joy at the fall of a regime that had tyrannized Poland for centuries. Dmowski had been abroad, lobbying England and France for Polish independence, and the revolution had almost caught him off guard. But he and other members of the *ND* instantly reversed their strategies: "the Poles warmly greeted the Revolution...as a victory of the idea of freedom...the Polish Right...saw that a pro-Polish declaration of the Provisional Government would enable Paris to support officially the cause of Polish independence" (Wandycz 35).

Casanova had leisure and mobility to roam the city, to interview a multitude of sources, and to write and revise her work. This was a change from the hasty writing she did while working as a nurse in Warsaw or while on the road to Minsk and Moscow. Despite her claims of "disarray," much of Casanova's writing during the revolutionary period is skillfully executed. She often wrote late into the night, pulling together notes from daytime conversations and experiences into accounts that convey the excitement of revolution. Her journalistic prose soared to new heights; she couldn't confine events of such tremendous importance to flat, news-agency prose. Stylistically, the Petrograd articles surpass even her best war reportage, combining the best features of professional journalism and Spanish literary style. They convey the excitement and significance of intensified history; there is emotional power in scenes of public rejoicing, tension and fear during times of danger.

Casanova's choice of powerful cosmic or natural metaphors reflect the importance she gave to the historical moment. For example, images of winter and light are used to describe civil disorder invading Petrograd like a frozen wind (*ABC* 15 May 1917): Russian democracy is portrayed as a rising tide, with Trotsky and Lenin steering the Russian ship into universal happiness and the promise of armistice is a star flashing on the Russian horizon (*Revolución bolchevista* 33). She often poses rhetorical questions, or dramatically intensifies nouns and verbs: "Escribir en tales condiciones de incertidumbre y aislamiento, oprime, desespera" 'Writing under such conditions of uncertainty and isolation oppresses, makes one desperate' (*ABC* 4 March 1917). She liked to end articles with a dramatic flourish: "Tendremos República, como Francia...¡República! claman todos" 'We will have a Republic, like France... a Republic! they all shout' (*ABC* 5 May 1917).

A year later, the anonymous introduction to her collection of articles on the Russian revolution called her new style "artismo" (a play on the Spanish words for "art" and "journalism"), and described her new journalistic style as intense literature, deep and full of truth. Her prose is characterized as inspired and translucent: cruel because revolution is cruel, but beautiful because of her art (*Rev.rus.*, Introduction). Readers responded accordingly. *ABC* headlined her columns on its front page, and sold many copies on the strength of her articles.

Casanova's personal involvement deprived her of the perspective that time and history have given modern analysts. She wasn't writing analysis, but reporting on a momentous historical event to which she was a sympathetic witness. She confused the joyous street scenes with the revolution itself. As weeks went by, and the initial euphoria subsided, Casanova's writing focused on new elements in Russia's political life. The Provisional Government meant well, but had not solved fundamental problems. Not far from Petrograd, the army half-heartedly still fought the Germans. The intelligentsia and the masses grew increasingly frustrated.

Casanova translated for *ABC* two important *Duma* speeches by members of the Provisional Government. One was by Guchkov, the Minister of War, the other by General Alexander Kornilov, who had given the Czarina the news of her husband's abdication. After summarizing their ideas, Casanova added that although she thought their reasons for opposing the government were understandable, they did not begin to address Russia's deeply rooted problems ("La revolución se consolida," *ABC*, 6 June 1917).

Despite the war's unpopularity, Foreign Affairs Minister Pavel Milyukov insisted on cooperation with England and France. On May 1, he sent a diplomatic note to both governments (reproduced by *ABC* on May 4, 1917) promising Russian solidarity. This was anathema to the Bolsheviks, the army and the workers, and touched off a series of bloody mass demonstrations called the "April Days" (it was April according to the

Old Calendar). Milyukov resigned on May 15, but it was clear that power in Russia was now divided between the Provisional Government and the more radical elements, led by the Bolsheviks.

Casanova witnessed daily clashes between officers and ordinary soldiers. In succeeding articles she described the abyss widening between the upper class elite that had ruled the army before the revolution and the suddenly socially-conscious proletarian soldiers. She also reported rumors of civil war that were sweeping through Petrograd. Hers were the first articles to inform Spain that the Russian revolution had become a class war.

Lacking power and moral authority, the Provisional Government lasted only two months. Lenin's dramatic arrival at the Finland Station on April 16, 1917, brought an entirely new element into the situation, and into Casanova's analysis ("Los hombres que vuelven," *ABC*, 29 June 1917).

Lenin and the other returning Bolsheviks (whom Casanova erroneously called "Anarchists" and even "Maximalists" for several months) were given the old Smolny Institute building as their political headquarters. There they began to organize their takeover of power. As Casanova studied these new contenders, she found G. V. Plekhanov's ideas and his cultivated, methodical personality easier to accept than Lenin's potent combination of pragmatism and fanaticism. Still, Lenin claimed to be against the war, and peace was as always the touchstone of Casanova's political sympathies. She found the Bolshevik concept of "democratic socialism" to her liking, and observed that members of the fallen Provisional Government had been opportunistic at best (*ABC*, 29 June, 1917).

Casanova still struggled against her restricted foreign status. In May 1917, she visited the *Duma* and asked for a pass as a visiting foreign journalist. A Polish officer let her in, but when they discovered that she was not affiliated with the Spanish Socialist press, she was coldly denied an official permit to visit the session. Overhearing her accented Russian, a vehement and very drunk proletarian soldier asked her origins. Hearing that she was Spanish, he knelt in front of her melodramatically, and exclaimed in Russian: "¡Española! ¡España! Yo conozco tu patria. Me llamo Smirnow. Y no hemos hecho la revolución para que no te dejen pasar al Soviet, hermanita (Pitollet 140-143). " 'A Spanish woman! Spain! I know your country. My name is Smirnow. And we haven't made the revolution for you to be refused access to the Soviet, little sister,'

Under Smirnow's protection, she entered the great hall where the Petrograd Soviet was in session. She noted that the room reeked with smoke and the stale odor of the unwashed masses. Peasants and heavily armed soldiers milled restlessly around the huge room. She met several Press Ministry representatives, but was repeatedly rebuffed as a reporter for a non-Socialist newspaper. The appearance of moderate Mikhail Sokolev, a recently appointed Minister, created an uproar. He could barely be heard above the din of the Bolsheviks. Casanova took notes and obviously enjoyed her foray, but found a terrible scene waiting for her at home. Her family and friends begged her not to take such a risk again. What if some Red Guards thought she was a foreign spy, and arrested her? What if she was raped or murdered, and never heard from again? She took to her bed with a headache, feeling guilty but also elated by her "scoop. "

Also in May, 1917, after a long hiatus, Casanova miraculously received some recent Spanish newspapers. They reported that there had been great public debate about Spanish intervention in the war. With the Czar deposed, and the U. S. willing to join the Allies in their fight against Germany, many liberal Spaniards now thought that Spain should go into the World War as well. *ABC*, however, remained anti-war. Casanova's indictment of Spanish involvement appeared in its pages a month later. She felt there were too many social problems facing Spain for the country to send its citizens to foreign wars (2 July 1917).

Public opinion in Petrograd was now overwhelmingly opposed to the war. Casanova sent translations of two articles, one by Leonid Andreiev, a well-known dramatist and writer who backed the war, and another by the famous author Maxim Gorki, who was a pacifist. By presenting their two different points of view, she summarized the debate that raged as the Russian social order disintegrated, and added depth to the polemic going on in Spain.

Tension increased between the Bolsheviks and the Provisional Government. Food shortages were just as severe as they had been before the revolution. There were no eggs, milk, meat or flour. Casanova reported that Petrograd lived on fish and coarse black bread, with straw often mixed in as a filler.

Social tensions escalated. Formerly pampered bourgeoises berated shopkeepers and servants for shortages and other hardships. The lower classes in turn were rapidly losing their traditional docility and snapping back at their former masters. Peasants wanted land, workers demanded higher wages. Antagonism grew between the Provisional Government and all other political groups. Street disorders became more common, and Casanova and other family members were caught in crossfire several times. The situation was ripe for the Bolsheviks' call for a "new revolution. "

For months, Casanova had been arguing about politics with her brothers-in-law and with Mieczyslaw Niklewicz. Being far to her Right, they had not been inclined to empathize with the Russian proletariat. As time went by, they challenged her pro-revolutionary ideas even more sharply. Marian and Józef were particularly opposed to the "new revolution", and became involved in clandestine pro-Polish activities. A Bolshevik coup would be fatal for them. By now the Polish émigré colony was acutely aware of their vulnerable status as refugees.

In late June Kerensky led a disastrous campaign against the Germans. His loss of Riga turned Russian politics upside down. During July and August, the Bolsheviks were outlawed, Trotsky was arrested, Lenin fled Petrograd. September maintained this turn to the Right. Then, in following months the tide began to turn in the Bolsheviks' favor.

Spontaneous protests of soldiers and workers erupted in the streets of Petrograd. Casanova was caught in one of these street riots. While trying to escape a sniper, she was struck by a coach also fleeing the melee. She lost consciousness, and when she awoke she found herself on a bank of snow at the side of the road, bleeding from a head wound. After struggling back to the flat, she discovered that her left eye was hemorrhaging internally. Her family, distressed by her injury and this latest show of recklessness, took her to a specialist who told them that Casanova's eyesight would be impaired for months. She could barely read, and her former stylized handwriting deteriorated into huge printed letters scrawled over the page. Not mentioning this setback to her readers, Casanova dictated her articles to daughters Halita and Bela, instead of writing them herself.

ABC published her analysis of Petrograd's political situation in August. Casanova refuted accounts disseminated by French news agencies that "these Bolsheviks" were German agents trying to stir anti-Allied feeling in the streets of Petrograd. Her articles confirmed that the street demonstrators were protesting an unpopular war and Petrograd's intolerable living conditions.

By October 1917, everyone in Petrograd knew that the Bolsheviks were preparing a coup, and that, if they succeeded, the situation would change for the worse. Casanova was still not wholly anti-Bolshevik. After all, she plaintively asked her readers (since no one around her was listening), wasn't the rise of Bolshevism an understandable reaction to czarism? She empathized with her Russian acquaintances' panic, but was convinced that the Bolsheviks would not unleash a general massacre.

Still, as early as August 1917, even while she was writing optimistic articles, Casanova began to plan her family's escape. She visited all of her

92

contacts in European embassies for safe-conducts passes out of Russia --
another personal situation not mentioned in her articles.

Leo Trotsky

In October 1917, Casanova's curiosity drove her to probably the
boldest event of her Petrograd reporting: an interview with Leo Trotsky.
A talented writer, stirring orator and brilliant personality, Trotsky was
more "European" in his thought than most Bolsheviks. He had formally
joined the Bolshevik Party in July, 1917, and began to give rousing
speeches at meetings, congresses and in the streets throughout Petrograd.
Casanova heard him speak at one of these events and decided that since
he was an intellectual and a rising star, he would be the most interesting
of Lenin's followers to interview. She began to do some research, to
prepare interview questions, and to plot her strategy.

The brash Trotsky, newly appointed Minister of Foreign Affairs, had
his offices in the Bolshevik headquarters at the old Smolny. Casanova
knew that if she had managed to slip into the heavily guarded *Duma*, she
could get into the smaller and more informal Smolny. She also knew that
as a member of the bourgeoisie and a foreigner, she was risking one of
those confrontations with Red Guards that were becoming daily ordeals.
She felt the risk worth taking, and secretly organized her visit.

Around five o'clock one icy afternoon in late October, as the fog
rolled into the city, she asked Pepa to hail a sled and accompany her on
a call (Pepa frequently escorted her on social visits now, since during
these hard times streets were dimly lit to save power, and the crime rate
had soared). Their *istwoschiki* or horse-sled driver was hesitant to drive
to the notorious Smolny, and Casanova had to pay a high fare. She did not
tell Pepa where they were going. Then, as they descended from the sled,
they saw dozens of armed Red Guards clustered around a bonfire in the
Institute's garden. It was then that Pepa realized the enormity of their
situation. They were in the "lion's den!"

Pepa babbled in *gallego,* clung to Casanova's arm and pulled her scarf
over her face. However nothing would stop Casanova, not even Pepa's
pleas to return home. She remained calm as she entered the building with
Pepa trailing behind, and was issued a foreign journalist pass to see the
tovarich ('comrade') with no complications. Led by a young secretary,
they made their way through crowds of soldiers and peasants who eyed
them with interest, passing by heaps of paper and stacks of propaganda
shoved against the walls. Room 67 was on the third floor, the "attic. "

After being checked yet again by the Red Guards who stood outside Trotsky's office, they were led to a small, sparsely furnished room where the Minister of Foreign Affairs waited behind a desk.

To Casanova's surprise, Trotsky had a pleasant voice and agreeable manners, and greeted them warmly. Although she did not find his long hair and goatee attractive, she did admire his "Mephistophelian" eyebrows and thought he could almost pass for a decadent French artist (a back-handed compliment). He invited Casanova to sit on the chair facing his desk, while Pepa perched nervously on a sofa. Trotsky's fond memories of Spain surprised and delighted Casanova as he spoke in French about his travels there: he remembered Spain as a beautiful country, although the police, "of course," had treated him badly. He had visited Madrid, Barcelona, Valencia and had regretted leaving Spain (Pitollet 141).

Then Casanova and Trotsky began to discuss serious matters. He insisted that the Bolsheviks' unilateral peace initiative was the only solution. The world hungered for peace, and he and his fellow Bolsheviks wanted not only a separate peace for Russia, but peace for all nations. With pride he showed her a telegram from Czernin, the Minister of Foreign Affairs of Austria-Hungary, supporting the peace initiative. He did not answer directly when Casanova questioned the Allies' refusal to let Russia relinquish her participation in the war. He must have realized that it was futile to argue with Casanova, since she considered pacifism a moral question, not a tactic. When the interview was finished, he shook her hand and added, "I am glad to have met you and through you send a greeting to Spain" (Pitollet 141).

By the time they got home, Pepa was drained and took to her bed. Casanova tempered her own elation to face her family and friends' horrified reaction. Her daring and informative interview with the man of the hour caused a sensation in Spain when it was finally published by *ABC* in March 1918 (Niklewicz; Meissner; Pitollet).

The Bolshevik Takeover

The night before the outbreak of the Bolshevik Revolution (the "ten days that shook the world" in October, 1917), a phone call from a friend high in the government warned Casanova that the Bolsheviks would seize power that night. Then came another call: Lenin had won, Kerensky had fled Petrograd. Episodically, Casanova related in an article how the Bolsheviks had seized the Petropavloska Fortress, taken the Winter Garden and captured other strategic points in the city. Kerensky had tried to reclaim the city, but failed. Lenin now openly called for a revolution by and for the proletariat.

Casanova spent those first few days in a state of wonder. This was the long-awaited resolution to the conflict. What was happening now was extraordinary: A new band of players, once banished from Russia or condemned to Siberia, had returned as their country's rulers. They represented millions of serfs and workers who had been powerless and forgotten until that moment.

Spain, like the rest of the world, stood in awe of the new events in Russia. News was scarce at first, and then contradictory. For once, ABC's excellent and timely coverage lapsed, since Casanova's reports arrived two months later (Lazo 146). Like newspapers in England and France, *ABC* printed erroneous reports of "Kerensky's victory" as late as November 19.

While the world press published exaggerated accounts of "slaughter" in Petrograd, Casanova recorded the events she witnessed. Right-wing friends and others could spread rumors about Bolshevik cruelty if they wished. But Casanova still believed that a comparison of the Russian revolutionary process with other revolutions would show that, with few exceptions, the Bolshevik Revolution was less violent. Hadn't Lenin pleaded for "moderation" for those deposed? In mid-November Casanova was still calling the Bolsheviks the most original and the most courageous element in Russian politics. Only bandits and army deserters were creating havoc. To *ABC*'s credit, despite their growing anti-Bolshevik editorial stand, they printed her articles without censorship or comment.

Casanova was familiar with a peculiarly Russian strain of radical Christianity that had devotees ranging from the most illiterate *starets* 'Old Believers' to Count Tolstoy and other intellectuals. She initially perceived Bolshevism as a variant of this religious idealism:

El radicalismo de los bolcheviques contiene latidos de humanidad, y su tiranía, lágrimas de idealismo... el credo de estos bárbaros, tiene algo del fuego que iluminó y elevó sobre el mundo pagano el mundo de los miserables, y una exaltación democrática de mentes jovenes atribuye significado de "nueva era" al cataclismo de Rusia.
(Lazo 173)
The Bolsheviks' radicalism throbs with a humanitarian beat, and their tyranny has tears of idealism...the creed of these barbarians has some of the fire that illumined and elevated the world of the poor over the world of the pagans, and a democratic exaltation of young minds attributes the cataclysm of Russia to a 'new era. '
(She was not alone in considering Bolshevism a religious phenomenon. Other observers misread the political nature of the revolution).

Another foreign writer, U. S. journalist John Reed, was sharing the excitement of this historic moment with his readers. There were many similarities in their approaches. Like Casanova, Reed was a published poet and had an enthusiastic, generous political nature. In *Ten Days that Shook the World* he too described the revolution with a series of powerful metaphors drawn from nature: the millions of men in Russia's armies were like the sea rising (27); the Congress of Soviets loomed "like a thundercloud" (35). He, too, loved to pose rhetorical questions: "And in the rain, the bitter chill, the great throbbing city under gray skies rushing faster and faster toward -- what?" (50). He, too, thought Trotsky's appearance "Mephistophelian" in *his* interview in Room 67, only a few days after Casanova's meeting (56-57).

Unlike Casanova, Reed, a committed Socialist, was far more familiar with the subtle political shadings of the Left. Armed with Socialist press credentials, he moved freely among Leftist strongholds. He loved romantic gestures, and rode the streets of Petrograd at night on a Bolshevik truck, tossing thousands of revolutionary pamphlets to the crowds.

As a witness to the revolution, Reed was handicapped by his lack of knowledge of Russian culture and history. His spoken Russian was minimal, and he could not read it at all, so he had to rely on friends and interpreters for second-hand information. At times his account is vitiated by inaccuracies and absurdities. Reed's over-eager presentation of the revolution often degenerates into propaganda. All members of the bourgeoisie could not have been "rat-faced" (86), "hard-eyed," "dissipated looking," "fat citizen(s) in expensive fur coat(s)" (239), etc. . On the other hand, could the masses have all been "great giants of men with the innocent clear eyes of children and the faces of epic warriors" (213)? Next to Reed's innocent enthusiasm for everything revolutionary, Casanova's equally favorable but better informed journalism is more balanced, even when she arrives at similar conclusions.

Casanova's enthusiasm for the Bolsheviks did not last as long as Reed's. In January, 1918, the arrest of the Rumanian ambassador as a hostage violated Casanova's sense of diplomatic process. By February, her pro-Bolshevism was cooling. Although she still admired the Bolsheviks' efforts to end the war, Casanova was increasingly disturbed by a series of radical measures that affected her family and her social class. With a stroke of the pen, private agricultural property was abolished. Banks and financial institutions were nationalized. Public labor (taking turns at sweeping snow off the street, cleaning sidewalks) became mandatory. Pepa and Casanova's three daughters were warned by their newly-created Building Committee to be ready for their share of hard work.

The courts and police system were also overhauled. People's Courts were empowered to order executions within twenty-four hours of sentencing, without right of appeal. Tension and fear made daily life excruciating.

Despite misgivings, Casanova still disagreed with the many around her who openly wished that the Germans would take Petrograd. In Spain, her growing disenchantment was noticed:

a partir de principios de mayo, el tono de sus crónicas cambia de una manera radical. Donde antes existía euforia, ahora aparece la decepción: donde antes había fe en el futuro, ahora se nota incluso miedo (Lazo 6)

...from the beginning of May, the tone of her chronicles changes radically. Where once there was euphoria, there now appears disillusionment: where there was faith in the future, now even fear is noticeable...

And her sympathy for Socialism finally came to an end:

El socialismo de Sofía Casanova era, a parte de moderado, puramente teórico, o mejor, utópico...su primera idea ante la revolución fue que Rusia acababa de comenzar un nuevo periodo montado sobre el orden y la convivencia de las clases...para el que diariamente compraba *ABC*, las cosas volvían a estar claras. Su corresponsal, digna de toda fe porque estaba presenciando en primera fila los acontecimientos, comenzaba a iluminar lo que...resultaba aun oscuro...la caida del zarismo fue aceptable; la revolución necesaria; pero no obstante, la avalancha de los bajos fondos y los irresponsables la estaban desvirtuando. (Lazo 6)

Sofía Casanova's socialism, besides being moderate, was purely theoretical, or more accurately, utopian...Her first idea concerning the revolution was that Russia was beginning a new phase based on order and co-existence between classes...for those who bought *ABC* every day, matters were again clear. Their correspondent, worthy of all trust because she was witnessing events from the front row, was beginning to illuminate what...was still shadowy...the fall of czarism was acceptable; the revolution, necessary; but nonetheless, an avalanche of low-lifes and irresponsible elements was tarnishing it.

Despite Trotsky's negotiations, by February the Germans threatened the city again. Petrograd came under siege. There was widespread famine. Factories closed. Life ground to a standstill.

Many of Casanova's Russian friends had been wealthy but unskilled. Dispossessed by the revolution, in order to survive they were now reduced to jobs such as cutting ice on the Neva, selling newspapers, selling their embroidery work, or performing menial tasks that, a few months before, their house servants would have refused. They cursed "ce sale peuple russe" (*Revolución* 111) 'these dirty Russian people,' as though they were not Russians themselves, and plotted escape as soon as possible. They would be part of a huge wave of Russian émigrés that would flood Western Europe, especially France. These members of the old regime considered the peace agreement of Brest-Litvosk a shameful defeat for Russia. The Bolsheviks had "lost" Poland, Finland and the Baltic states to Germany forever. Casanova wrote to her Spanish readers that the Russians had no awareness or regret of what centuries of their brutal occupation of Poland and other countries had meant to the oppressed nations. How could Russia "lose" what had never really belonged to them? (*Revolución* 111)

Casanova's fears for her family grew. The revolutionary government tightened control of Petrograd and suppressing the opposition became its highest priority. In December, 1917, the All Russian Extraordinary Commission for Combatting Counterrevolution and Sabotage (*Cheka*) was founded. The dreaded *Cheka* was led by Nicholas Krylenko and Felix Dzerzhinsky. The latter, a Pole by birth, was quoted as saying that the *Cheka* had to defend the revolution "even if its sword falls occasionally on the heads of the innocent" (Nettl 95). These policies would have tragic significance for the Lutosławskis, and for hundreds of thousands of others. The *Cheka*'s impact was sudden, sweeping and brutal. Throughout Russia the *Cheka* arrested and killed members of any group, such as the Cadets, that might challenge its control. Its terror and repression soon equaled that of the *Okhrana*, its predecessor under the Czar.

On April 18, 1918, Casanova reported that several Petrograd students, eating dinner at the home of friends of her family, were arrested by a group of Red Guards, driven to a nearby cemetery and shot (*Revolución* 105-106). Next, Casanova's son-in-law, Mieczysław Niklewicz, was arrested, but released and told to appear before a People's Tribunal. Then, during the night of April 25, 1918, the *Cheka* broke into the Lutosławskis' Moscow home, and took her brothers-in-law Marian and Józef Lutosławski to the Kremlin. They stood accused of engaging in counter-revolutionary activities, and of having forged diplomatic documents. Lawyers and friends tried to calm the family, claiming that because of Marian and Józef's prominence in the Polish émigré community, they would not be harmed. The two brothers' cell was next to the one where the sinister chief of the *Okhrana* (or czarist Secret Police) and other czarist ministers were being held, all of whom were sure to be executed (*Revolución* 143).

Into this already intolerably tense situation, the Bolsheviks unleashed the "Red Terror" of the autumn of 1918 to fight the anti-Bolshevik reaction in southern and central Russia. The "Red Terror" was heralded by an event so unthinkable that it eclipsed the worst that Casanova had heard or imagined before: On July 16, the Czar and the rest of the Royal Family were executed in Ekaterinburg.

For months there had been rumors of the Czar's inevitable execution, but Casanova had refused to believe that the Bolsheviks could commit regicide. In her mind, she identified the Russian royal family with her own beloved Spanish Bourbons. And although she had never thought much of the Czar, a weak man and ineffectual ruler, she had mixed feelings about the Czarina. Like Casanova, Empress Alexandra (formerly Alexis of Hessen) was a Westerner in a Slavic country, a devoted mother and a Sister of Charity. Although disapproving of her dependence on Rasputin, Casanova sometimes reported favorable anecdotes about the Czarina, learned from an elderly Countess who had been *grande maîtresse* (lady-in-waiting) to the Czar's family. In general, as a writer and journalist, she had been realistic about the Royal Family: the ineffectual and corrupt Romanov dynasty deserved to be removed. When the Czar abdicated, she reported the event without sentimentality.

Now news of the massacre made her ill, and she took to her bed. The Bolsheviks had not just executed an emperor: they had murdered a helpless woman and their four innocent children. Overwrought, she wept and prayed for all of them. Months later *Blanco y negro* reportedly published a poem she wrote for the dead Czarina: "He puesto tu retrato en un marco de oro" 'I have placed your portrait in a frame of gold' (Niklewicz, K. interview). More than any other single event, the murder of the Royal Family ended Casanova's briefly-held truce with Russia.

Around her, the situation worsened. Casanova reported that seventeen thousand people (ex-soldiers and members of the bourgeoisie) had been arrested in one day alone. Her Polish and Russian friends were trying to leave the country by any means. Some who could not find a way out committed suicide (*Revolución* 153). During this period, Casanova's articles became impressionistic and confused, reflecting the panic and chaos around her.

By the end of August, Casanova and the Niklewiczes knew that they must find a way to leave Russia, legally or illegally, or they too would die. Before they left, however, Casanova had to carry out a painful duty: she travelled to Moscow to visit Butirska Prison, then under the control of the ruthless Krylenko, to say goodbye to Marian and Józef.

Casanova had loved these handsome, idealistic and high-spirited brothers since she had first met them in Drozdowo in 1887, when Marian was seventeen and Józef seven. Now they were married men with seven children between them. Who would take care of their families? Casanova visited her cherished in-laws for the last time, taking up her allotted twelve minutes (among the worst moments of her life, she wrote later) and having to shout at them through her tears, since visitors had to stand three meters away from the cells' tiny, barred windows. For days, she was haunted by the constant wailing of women and children saying good-bye to loved ones already condemned to death. She was particularly shaken by the grief of a woman who, on coming to visit her husband, found out that he had been executed the night before (*Revolución* 143-145).

Casanova returned to Petrograd, and continued a series of desperate diplomatic appeals for safe-conduct passes for her family and Pepa. After many schemes and maneuvers, the new Spanish Ambassador, Polo de Bernabé, wrote to the German Ambassador, who in turn wrote a note to the German Consul. The German Consul signed papers allowing them into German-held Warsaw (Pitollet 147). Returning to German-dominated Poland would have been unthinkable even a few months before, but now it was their only hope.

Mañita, Bela and Halita rushed around Petrograd, returning ration books, filling out vaccination certificates and carrying out required formalities, while Mieczyslaw Niklewicz struggled to arrange his own release. They did not know if he would be excused from appearing before the People's Tribunal until an hour before departure. Casanova and Pepa stayed home with the children, packing the few possessions they could bring, trying to keep out a crowd of soldiers and neighbors who wanted to buy their belongings.

Just when they were ready to go, another problem arose. With tram workers on strike, they had no way to get to the train station. Halita ran over to the U. S. Embassy, where one of her American admirers commandeered a diplomatic vehicle. To Casanova's speechless astonishment, the despised "Yanquis" provided them a car, a U. S. flag and a military escort to their train. The family arrived in military splendor at the crowded station but with only a few minutes to spare.

Leaving Petrograd was the first in a series of long and arduous stages of their journey. The only train seats available to them and hundreds of other Polish nationals were in lice-infested, fourth-class cattle cars, into which they crowded with their luggage. Their fellow passengers were also trying to return to Poland, despite the Germans' reluctance to accept them. Some of them had safe-conducts, none of them knew if they would actually be admitted into the occupied zone. For two chaotic weeks, the

100

train crawled west through Russia, which was by then embroiled in civil war. They were slowed down by frequent and excruciating delays. Dirty, hungry, plagued by flies, lice and fleas, the family lay on coarse straw mattresses laid on the wagons' wooden floors. The adults read to the children (Krystina, Andrzej and their baby sister Maria, born earlier that year) and tried to console one another.

The train stopped at Toroszino for a few days, where they waited with thousands of other displaced persons, many sick with typhus or cholera. Then they were temporarily stranded in filthy, disease-ridden barracks outside the city of Pskov. One cold morning, after a nerve-racking wait, a German officer read out loud a short list of people allowed to proceed to Warsaw. Miraculously, all of their names were on the list (Niklewicz, K. interview).

They finally entered Warsaw on a sunny fall morning, exhausted, in a state of dazed unreality. Despite two years of absence, they found that their flat had remained sealed and intact. Everything looked exactly the same (Pitollet 147-149; *Viajes* 95-108).

Before they could adjust to these familiar surroundings, there came a final blow. A telegram from Moscow, printed in a Warsaw newspaper, informed them that Marian and Józef had been executed at dawn, on September 5, 1918, in a park in Moscow, "before a large crowd of spectators" (Niklewicz, K. interview).

Casanova's articles about Marian and Józef's deaths are among her most vivid and compelling. Like her friend Dr. Balicka, Casanova had always opposed capital punishment. Years before, one of her most moving articles about the Russian occupation of Poland was titled "Daily Executions," and vividly detailed the horror of political executions at the Warsaw Citadel (*Exóticas* 59). She had never imagined that her beloved Marian and Józef, privileged, law-abiding sons of a prominent family with connections in the highest places, would join the thousands of Polish patriots executed by the Russians over the past one hundred and fifty years. As many Poles before them, they had despised the Russians. But until the very end, they had limited themselves to participating in aboveground, legal political activities.

In retrospect, their deaths were inevitable. In Casanova's view, Marian and Józef were fated to become part of the human sacrifice that history demands from each Polish generation. For years the family tried to discover where they had been executed, under what charge, and where they had been buried. Many years later, Felix Dzerzhinsky's secretary, defecting from Russia after World War II, told them that the sinister Dzerzhinsky, himself a Polish national, had killed the two brothers by his own hand in his office at Butirska Prison after a violent argument about Polish politics (Niklewicz, P. interview). Most recent evidence confirms that they were indeed executed in a park, and that abbreviations of their names (and the names of dozens of others who died with them) were carved into the trunk of a tree (Letter, K. Niklewicz).

Friends, family, and thousands of those who had been helped by Marian and Józef's relief work organized a memorial at the Warsaw Cathedral. They tried to find comfort in the sermon's Biblical theme, "They were lovely and pleasant in their lives, and in their death they were not divided."

Among his many talents, Józef ("Jozio") had been an accomplished pianist, who loved to play *gallego* and Spanish melodies for Casanova, along with his standard repertory of Chopin and Liszt. His son, Witold Lutosławski (seven years old at the time of his father's death) inherited Jozio's gift for music, and grew up to be Poland's premier twentieth-century composer. Marian and Józef's deaths were still mourned, two generations later, by family members. Like little Romek, Casanova's grandson, their bodies were lost to Russia and are still "waiting for a return to their Polish land. "

Casanova was in Warsaw for the end of German rule in Poland, but she wrote about it without enthusiasm. Physically and mentally exhausted, she suffered from anemia, impaired eyesight, and a host of minor ailments. Her long blonde hair had finally begun to turn gray. She arranged to spend a few weeks in Paris with friends, to recover her health before returning to Spain in the spring of 1919. After four years of strain and self-discipline, Casanova had temporarily lost her zest for writing. Next to her personal tragedies, the end of the war was an anticlimax.

But then she learned from contacts in Paris that Spain was feeling the effects of the Russian Revolution. She reported met a Bolshevik just returned from Spain, who told her that the people of her country were full of enthusiasm for socialism and for the Russians. This news mobilized her. She had seen how easily Russia had been taken over. She felt it was her duty to warn Spain of the dangers of socialism, and to expose the Bolsheviks' plans to conquer Western Europe. Her truce with Russia had ended; her heart hardened against the seductiveness of revolution and social change.

All the anger and resentment she had felt against Russia for years, deserved or not, was magnified by these latest events. The *Cheka* was no better or worse than the Czar's *Okhrana* -- both were expressions of the same despotic Russian will. Casanova now believed that "barbaric Russia" was unredeemable. Whether ruled by the Right or by the Left, it would never be a civilized country (*Revolución* 165). This mission against Russia would drive her heart, her politics and her writing for the rest of her long career.

Chapter 9

1919: Return to Spain

Devitalized, penniless and worried about the future, Sofía Casanova returned to Madrid in April, 1919. She had said good-bye to her mother and brothers at the Estación del Norte in Madrid five years before. Now her mother was gone: she missed her nurturing presence, and bitterly regretted not having been at her deathbed. On a broader perspective, looking back on the intervening years of death and destruction, Casanova was disheartened. As historian Barbara Tuchman wrote in *The Guns of August*:

> The Great War of 1914 lies like a band of scorched earth dividing that time from ours. In wiping out so many lives...in destroying beliefs, changing ideas, and leaving incurable wounds of disillusion, it created a physical as well as psychological gulf between two epochs. (xiii)

But, as Casanova soon was to find out, a new factor had entered her life, magnifying her return home: she was now a national celebrity. Journalists hounded the entrance to her brother Vicente Casanova's home in the Calle de Urquijo. The Queen Mother sent greetings and a summons to visit. A steady stream of admirers left their cards, offered book contracts, sent flowers and mailed invitations to dinners, lectures, meetings and charitable functions. Besides her usual circle of literary friends, other people, military men and high governmental figures, came to pay their respects to the heroine of the Warsaw hospitals and the Russian revolution. Like George Sand, Lord Byron and other literary figures involved in politics, Sofía Casanova woke up one morning to find herself famous.

A Time for Glory

From spring through fall of 1919, Casanova was surrounded by a swirl of public adulation and activity. For the rest of her life, she would look back on this period with disbelief.

In the month of April alone, Casanova was constantly featured in the news, attending receptions, chairing meetings of the Anti-tuberculosis League and giving lectures. On the evening of April 19 she was honored by *ABC*: its editors, staff and workers, as well as a number of celebrities, were invited to her tribute. The head of the Council of Ministers, several ex-ministers, the Count of Romanones and his wife were there, along with the Countess of Pardo Bazán, Blanca de los Ríos, and the editors of *La Época, El Imparcial, El Debate, El Liberal,* and other dailies. Printers stopped the presses in Casanova's honor, and presented her with flowers. The editor of *ABC,* Torcuato Luca de Tena, assured the audience that Casanova was

> ...la mujer española cuyo nombre quedará en la historia del periodismo entre los magnos acontecimientos que ella refirió... *(ABC,* 20 April 1919)
> The Spanish woman whose name will remain in the history of journalism among the great events that she reported...

ABC featured the event the following day *(ABC,* 20 April 1919).

A similar affair was held at the editorial offices of *Blanco y negro.* Besides the usual photographs, a staff artist did a sketch of the guest of honor. Gaunt and unsmiling, Casanova's somber caricature captures the depression she was experiencing *(Blanco y negro,* 20 April 1919).

Later in the month, Casanova obviously looked and felt better. On April 25, she gave a lecture on her war experiences to a standing-room-only audience at the *Centro del Ejército y de la Armada* (Center for the Army and the Navy). Despite the interests of her audience, and although the lecture was titled "Impresiones de una mujer en el frente oriental de la guerra europea" 'A Woman's Impressions of the War in the Eastern Front of the European War,' the speech was an impassioned anti-war statement. Casanova openly stated her anti-war beliefs, described how war and social injustice had helped the development and spread of Communism, and warned that social reforms were needed within each country to avoid Bolshevism ("Impresiones" 4). The Center printed her short speech in pamphlet form, with the text punctuated by asides reporting the reactions of the audience. They ranged from "aplausos" 'applause,' to "asentimiento" 'agreement,' "emoción" 'emotion' and even "enorme sensación" 'enormous astonishment. ' Given the content of her speech, the reactions of the audience were remarkable, and attest to her credibility and the style of delivery.

Despite the applause and cheers, Casanova's words ultimately fell on deaf ears. The Spanish army, among the least progressive in Europe, had been willing to shoot rebelling workers in Catalonia and elsewhere. Furthermore, it had been involved in a muddled campaign in North Africa, suffered several humiliating defeats, and was on its way to total disaster at Annual in 1921. Frustrated and defensive, it was always ready to overreact with violence.

In general, Casanova's warnings about the dangers of Bolshevism went unheeded. In 1919, the Spanish Communist Party was not yet in existence, and until 1922 it was only a few thousand strong. Despite Lenin's and Trotsky's threats, the Party was a minor player in Spanish politics until just before the Civil War. The Spanish press of the Right may have called all their opponents "Bolsheviks," but direct Russian influence did not begin until the 1930s. Until then, like a modern-day Cassandra, Casanova foresaw the future but was largely ignored.

Nonetheless, in 1919 her celebrity status in high government and military circles made her spirits soar. She was the guest of honor at a meeting held at the *Casino Militar*. A more sedate reception in her honor was held by the *Comité Femenino de Higiene Popular* (Women's Committee for Popular Hygiene), which Casanova had helped found in 1910 under the auspices of the Queen Mother (*Blanco y negro*, 4 April 1919).

When Casanova arrived in her native La Coruña late in July, her home province outdid Madrid in its welcome. The city was festooned with flags and packed with cheering throngs, every balcony crowded with ladies waving handkerchiefs. Not since the Royal Family's last visit had there been such excitement. The entire population of the city crowded the streets to greet her. News stories described her homecoming as an apotheosis: she was greeted by cannons, military salutes, even a band (*Voz*, 30 September 1919). The mayor and local personalities received her with pride. Hundreds of well-wishers besieged her hotel window, imploring her to address them. With tears in her eyes she told the mayor, "Basta, basta: yo no merezco tanto" (*Martirio* 16) 'Enough, enough: I don't deserve so much'.

Serenaded by Galician choirs, toasted at an army banquet, celebrated by poems written in her honor, for a week Casanova was her hometown's guest of honor (*Voz* 29 July 1919; 30 July 1919; 31 July 1919). *Voz de Galicia* featured her day-to-day schedule on its front page, and recorded every celebrity or old friend's visit in the society columns. As an acknowledgement of her Galician forerunners, Casanova made a pilgrimage to Rosalía de Castro's grave (*Voz de Galicia*, 3 August 1919) and, following Concepción Arenal's example, visited the local jail (*Voz*, 1 August 1919).

Just as twenty years earlier Casanova had recovered from the death of her daughter in La Coruña, now she renewed herself after her war experiences. Like the mythical Antaeus, the touch of her native soil revived her. As Casanova wrote later, "Mi amada Coruña me resucitó"

106

(Bugallal *Siglo* 10) 'My beloved Coruña brought me back to life. ' She stayed in Galicia until October of that year, visiting Vigo, Caldas, Betanzos, and Orense, where she received similar honors and recognition.

That summer, Casanova tried to assimilate the changes that had taken place in Spain during her five-year absence. She was surprised to discover that, as in 1898, frivolity and a constant search for amusement had prevailed during the war. This euphoria persisted, despite the fact that by the end of the war "neutral" Spain had been seriously affected by the war's economic consequences.

As modern historian Tuñon de Lara notes, "En esta España donde los ricos se hacían mas ricos y los pobres mas pobres, prendieron las pasiones e intereses de la conflagración mundial" (29) 'In this Spain where the rich got richer, and the poor poorer, the passions and interests of the world conflagration flared up'. Spain had profited from the war, but it had also acquired a new set of problems. After the initial boom, serious financial problems arose. A new class of *nouveaux riches* and speculators became active and highly visible. As prices rose, workers demanded higher wages, and labor unrest spread across the country. In 1918 alone there were six hundred strikes. At the war's end, countries returned to their usual trading patterns and the Spanish economy slumped. The poorer classes suffered lay-offs and unemployment.

The changes were not only political. Casanova, having seen the demise of the Russian empire, could now assess the weakening of the Spanish aristocracy's traditional allegiance to the monarchy. Although they clung to outdated privileges and customs, the aristocracy did nothing to help the one institution that would ensure their survival.

Although Casanova, like most Spanish women of her rank, personally admired the King, she now admitted with regret that he was not popular with the people and seemed increasingly remote from the realities of Spanish life. The illustrated newspapers recorded Alfonso's avid interest in tennis, polo, and English-style hunting parties -- and his indifference to his Spanish subjects. The queen, although English, was a more sympathetic figure. Casanova admired her charitable efforts to help the poor and the sick. But the majority of Spain lived in poverty, and Casanova knew it would take far more than the queen and the queen mother's well-intentioned ladies' committees to solve the country's problems.

Spanish social life had changed, and not for the better. Other differences in the social atmosphere alarmed Casanova. The new middle classes were growing, and their brash secular customs were gradually replacing the genteel Catholic past Casanova had cherished. Contemporary society lacked the time and patience for the leisurely manners and courtesy of old pre-war Spain. Public behavior, in Casanova's view, was lax: women wore makeup, smoked openly and paraded on the beach in immodest bathing suits. Even *ABC*'s advertisements were more aggressive and vulgar. The urban masses followed the sports pages with more interest than they followed political events. The new world of night clubs and conspicuous consumption, coupled with the drastic decline of religion, troubled her greatly. For the rest of her life, Casanova alternated between Spain's centuries-old Catholic heritage of art and literature, and Poland's practical Catholicism when she wanted to describe true spirituality.

When she returned to Madrid in the fall of 1919, Casanova was still uneasy. In some respects, the Madrid of 1919 and the Madrid of her youth were the same. Madrileños still thought that the world centered on the *Puerta del Sol* and its surroundings. Some old friends, such Don José Echegaray (a Nobel Laureate) and Giner de los Ríos had died during her years away. Fellow Galicians Emilia Pardo Bazán and Ramón del Valle Inclán were still active. Casanova's old friends, Manuel and Antonio Machado, were writing poetry separately and still collaborating on plays. Vicente Blasco Ibáñez had published his hugely popular anti-war novel, *Los cuatro jinetes del Apocalípsis* 'The Four Horsemen of the Apocalypse' a few years before, and continued writing best-sellers. New names, such as José Ortega y Gasset and Ramón Pérez de Ayala, were bandied about in literary circles. The Rector of the University of Salamanca, Miguel de Unamuno, had just finished writing "El Cristo de Velazquez. "

Was there room for Sofía Casanova in the heart of literary Madrid, among the throngs that crowded the streets around the Prado, the Ateneo, and the Puerta del Sol? At the age of fifty-nine, an expatriate and a woman, Casanova was far removed from the intellectual centers of power. Younger students and academics looked to Europe to solve the problems of Spain. Although she disagreed with them on almost every issue, she knew that they were right in thinking Spain woefully neglected, and that the country had to be reformed from top to bottom. Although starting from an entirely different set of moral and political principles, she would have agreed with them that post-war Spain was devoid of any common ideals, goals or direction.

By age and social class, Casanova was part of another literary caste. It is clear from her writings of this period that she did not whole-heartedly agree with the Spanish Right. She had long been a friend of Blanca de los Ríos. They had been aspiring young poets during the eighties, but their marriages had led them to different paths. De los Ríos came from a well-known family of artists and writers, and married a man who shared her literary ideas and supported her career. The couple founded a new magazine, *Raza Española*, which she edited. *Raza Española*, as its title indicates, was a forum for "la otra España," that of aristocrats and ultra-nationalistic intellectuals who longed for a miraculous return to the *Siglo de Oro*, Spain's long-vanished moment of triumph.

Casanova had much sympathy for the feelings of the *casticistas* (traditionalists) who wrote for *Raza Española*. Its contributors, of which novelist Ricardo León was typical (he had written the enormously popular novel *Casta de hidalgos)* yearned for an eternal, completely Castilian Spain. In this utopia, free from the disruption of politics, only Spanish reality existed. Within its imaginary borders there reigned perfect order and harmony. Casanova agreed with *Raza Española* that Spanish art, literature and culture had reached an admirable peak during the seventeenth century, and that a "spiritual imperialism" based on the ideals of the seventeenth century would do the debased twentieth century world much good. But her contributions to the magazine (short stories or poems) were based on non-Spanish topics. Among other published contributions, her writings on Russia, Poland and the War stand out with anachronistic individuality. When compared with those of Casanova, most of the other articles in *Raza Española* seem irrelevant.

The writers and intellectuals of the Right were not only obsessed with Spain's past superiority, they refused to accept the present. They ignored the loss of the colonies in the nineteenth century, the squalor of provincial life, the dragging out of the war in Africa. *Raza Española* ignored the present and avoided thinking about the future. One article praised the marvels of the former Post Office Service of Catalonia; another castigated anyone who called *Hispano*-America, *Latin*-America; the "inexplicable" decline of the Spanish language in the post-colonial Philippine Islands was deplored. Sections dedicated to non-peninsular topics carried poems such as "Canto a la madre España" 'Hymn to Mother Spain. ' All too often, an entire issue would be a necrology: Dead writers were more interesting than those still alive.

Unlike other Spanish intellectuals, Casanova could not be completely aligned with either of the "two Spains." Although by birth and ties of friendship she belonged to the upper classes, she was too much of a humanitarian -- and a realist -- to follow the extreme factions of the Right. She knew that social injustice existed in Spain, felt that it should be corrected by those privileged with money or rank, and knew that ignoring injustice would bring revolution in the long run.

Casanova had a radically clear view of the Gospel message and took the social dimensions of the Gospels very seriously. She thought that a true Christian (read Catholic) should feel concern for the poor and the helpless. She was sorry to see that in Spain this aspect of the Church's teachings was not heeded. Casanova loved to say that she was "socialista, como lo fué Cristo, poniéndome al lado de los que sufren persecución y hambre" 'a socialist, like Christ was, on the side of those who suffer persecution and hunger' (*ABC*, 20 April 1919; Niklewicz).

After her experiences in Russia, Casanova knew that Spain faced similar problems, and that these had to be solved on a broad national level -- not by organizing a few more committees of well-meaning socialites. A Spanish proverb says, "No se usa aspirina para curar una apendicitis" 'You don't use aspirin to cure appendicitis.' Casanova's own personal circumstances and her lack of political allegiances kept her from pursuing global solutions or more activist methods.

In 1919, Casanova's vision for Spain was probably that of a constitutional monarchist. She would have liked to see the monarchy coupled with broad social welfare programs. The king of Spain and his allies seemed more interested in politics than in social issues. There is little indication that they would have progressed in this direction. Over the next few decades, similar monarchies developed in England, the Scandinavian countries, Holland and Belgium, but in Spain constitutional monarchy had to wait until 1975 to emerge.

Although Casanova believed that a country should have strong moral leaders, unlike her fellow *ABC*-writer Ramiro de Maeztú, she did not think that there had to be "monarchy and hierarchy" as in the Spanish Middle Ages. Casanova was still more democratic and progressive than her Spanish friends and collaborators. She even believed that women should be given the vote! It is clear that at this point, although she was a favorite of the establishment, her stance remained independent, her approach eclectic, and in her opinions in the minority.

November, 1919

Casanova returned to Madrid in the fall to receive her most brilliant honor. On November 9, the Minister of the Interior granted her the country's highest medal for service to humanity, "La Gran Cruz de Beneficencia" 'The Great Cross of Charity. ' This decoration was given to those who had served in others times of national crisis. It was given to Casanova largely because of her work as a Sister of Charity, but also in part for her charitable activities in Spain before the war. The event, attended by many political and literary figures, took place in the Ministry

110

of the Interior and was widely covered by the press. In a photograph taken shortly afterwards, Casanova is wearing the medal. She appears serene, satisfied, and fully recovered from her misfortunes abroad (Bugallal *Siglo* 25; *Blanco y negro* 9 November 1919).

To others, Casanova might have looked as though she had reached a pinnacle in her career as she bustled around Madrid, signing book contracts, collecting mementos of these glorious months, visiting old friends and making new ones. But over the summer she decided to return to Poland. As she got ready to leave Spain for Eastern Europe, where the political situation was still unstable, she was often asked her reasons for wanting to go back. If she stayed in Spain her life would be infinitely easier and more comfortable.

On the surface, the answer was simple. First, she wanted to be with her daughters: they were totally commmitted to living in the new Polish Republic. Other feelings were more complex. After five years of war and chaos, and over twenty years of living abroad, Casanova found Spanish daily life familiar, but incompatible. Spain was "España privilegiada" 'privileged Spain,' where life was too easy, and where political attitudes seemed frivolous and immature when compared to those of Eastern Europe.

111

Chapter 10

The 1920's -- Warsaw and Madrid

"Termina el año 1919 tan tristemente como empezó" '1919 has ended as sadly as it began' Casanova wrote in *ABC* at the end of the year. Drab, post-war Warsaw was the antithesis of Madrid. The glorious months spent in Spain suddenly seemed unreal and insubstantial next to the grim everyday life of war-torn Poland. As Casanova wrote to *ABC*: "Polonia no vive alegre...está triste. Ha sufrido demasiado" 'Poland's daily life is not happy...She has suffered too much' (9 March 1920).

Poland had little to celebrate at the end of 1919 except her independence. As historian Richard Watt notes:

...All of the many "new" nations that were born or reborn in the wake of World War I experienced considerable birth pains. But none of the so-called successor states was faced with the variety and enormity of problems that Poland encountered during its first months of existence. Here was a nation with no national boundaries...At least seven different currencies circulated in the area that would eventually be Poland. Four different legal systems operated...The Polish industrial plant had been looted or demolished...In 1918 only about 15 percent of the nation's industrial workers were employed. Devastation in the Polish countryside paralleled that of industry...Every aspect of Poland had been disrupted by the war...(79)

Poland was bracing for a long and difficult winter. Supplies and fuel were scarce, and although the new Polish government was feverishly trying to restore a working order to daily life, every day was a struggle for fundamental needs: shelter, food and work.

For Casanova, cultural adjustment was more difficult than usual. The brilliant months in Spain seemed like a dream. In Poland, she was a private citizen, another foreign resident in a city now crowded with thousands of émigrés and refugees from the war and the Russian revolution. The refugees' restless presence added to the sense of alienation and uprootedness that pervaded the country. To exacerbate matters, a severe epidemic of influenza struck Poland's ill-nourished masses. Racial tensions against Jews and other "ethnic minorities" ran high.

Marshall Józef K. Piłsudski was Poland's chief of state and the force who was to stabilize Poland for many years. Glum, dour, irascible, with drooping mustaches and an overbearing personality, Piłsudski tried to restore a semblance of order to Poland's daily life. Behind his brusque manners and rough language, this chief of state was an idealist, a lover of Słowacki's Romantic poetry, a patriot who placed Poland above everything (Watt 338).

From 1920 on, Casanova supported Piłsudski as the leader of Poland. Although she did not agree with all his decisions and policies, she considered him and his government's centralized powers the only answer to Poland's factionalized politics, and to the threat of Communism. She particularly approved of his fairness towards Jews and other ethnic minorities.

Readers of Casanova's columns in *ABC*, accustomed to her cerebral analyses of Piłsudski's, Paderewski's or Roman Dmowski's policies, would have been astonished to know of her personal living arrangements. As always, Roman Dmowski had retained the closest personal and political ties to Casanova's son-in-law, Mieczyslaw Niklewicz, to her daughter Mañita, and to their children. After Dmowski's greatest hour, on June 9, 1919, when as Poland's representative he signed the Treaty of Versailles, he returned to Warsaw in May 1920. He sold some family properties in Posnań and with the proceeds he helped the Niklewiczes (and with them Casanova and Pepa) move into a much larger and more stately flat, where he occupied a room and the drawing room. Thus Casanova lived in the most intimate family situation with the man who wielded the greatest measure of political power in Poland, next to Piłsudski and Paderewski.

In his late fifties, Dmowski was the live-in grandfather, resident sage, and authority figure for the Niklewicz children, as he had been a generation earlier for the Lutosławski girls. Since he was then the leader of the National Democratic party, a deputy to the *Sejm* (Parliament) from 1919 to 1922, and Minister of Foreign Affairs in 1923, his active political life constantly impinged on Casanova's consciousness. Day after day endless meetings, caucuses and interviews were held in the drawing room, which she would have preferred to use for entertaining or writing. Table conversation usually centered on the political topic of the day, and Casanova had access to political materials, information and rumors at the very source (Niklewicz, K. interview). Most foreign correspondents would have envied her insider's information on political affairs. Despite these intimate family ties, her connection to the prominent statesman and to his party was never mentioned in her *ABC* columns.

Cool, cultivated and dapper, Dmowski had been part of Casanova's inner circle since 1899. He was fascinated by Spain, read Spanish fluently and kept up a lively interest in Spanish literature and politics through his daily exchanges with Casanova, her friends and family. He particularly liked to read Manuel Machado, whose poem, "Adelfos," had captivated him.

Life at close quarters with Dmowski would have presented serious quandaries for any independent-minded person, much less a journalist. Casanova never accepted Dmowski's political theories, but the Niklewiczes and everyone else in their circle completely acquiesced to his views. Mañita and her husband deferred to him as their superior, and addressed him formally. The children considered him their grandfather, and in general the household and its activities centered around his schedule and needs more than around hers (Niklewicz, K. interview).

Dmowski's activities (and her son-in-law's work) kept the home buzzing with campaigns and strategies that Casanova did not approve of, and on which she passed sharp judgement in *ABC* columns. Dmowski's nationalistic bias made him take stands that were hard for his contemporaries to understand, even within the context of Poland's unfortunate history. His opponents (and some modern historians) found some of his views unforgivable.

One of the National Democratic slogans had been "Poland united, not independent."[7] Casanova never agreed with this reasoning, and was outraged (along with Polish public opinion) when the Russians passed a few irrelevant measures in 1915 as a sop to the Poles. These meaningless measures were no compensation for the enormous suffering brought to Poland by cooperating with Russia during the first year of World War I. Even independence alone did not make up for the price Poland had to pay.

Another difficult subject was Dmowski's "pragmatic" anti-Semitism. He raised the purging of the Jews to the level of a tenet of the *ND* (or *Endecja*, as it was referred to in Polish). According to Dmowski, Poland was too "heterogeneous," there had been "too much" religious tolerance in the past, and now he believed that the entire mercantile and other systems was in the hands of non-assimilated Polish Jews. He and the *ND* (and to be accurate, many other Poles) considered these Polish Jews, particularly those who were less assimilated and spoke Yiddish, to be aliens. In order to achieve national unity, Poland would have to "purge itself" of its large Jewish population.

Dmowski endorsed many successful anti-Semitic campaigns in the past, complete with anti-Jewish boycotts and slogans, and he would conduct others later on in his career. At times he was enough of a politician to put aside anti-Semitism, if it was in his best political interest. When chided by an American Jew in 1919 that such cold-blooded use of racial hatred for political purposes was "monstrous," Dmowski cheerfully agreed: "I think that your characterization is not out of place. In fact, I *like* the word monstrous (Heller 89). "

Dmowski enjoyed telling the story of how, during his visit to New

York in 1918, he had been summoned to see "the richest and most powerful rabbi in the world." Over time and telling, the story acquired mythic proportions. Like Christ tempted in the desert by Satan's offer of power, Dmowski claimed that the rabbi had offered him total power over Poland. He could be its ruler if he swore never to persecute Jews again. Dmowski would proudly recounted how he had refused the rabbi's offer (Meissner, H. interview). His story clearly implied that Piłsudski, now trying to treat the Jews fairly, had been successfully bribed by "world Jewry."

There was one member of the family who would not believe him. Throughout the 1920s and 1930s, even after Dmowski retired from active politics, Casanova steadfastedly opposed anti-Semitism in her articles and books. She particularly deplored the violence of the notorious *Endeks*, young and unruly members of the "Endecja," who, as a random pastime, harassed, beat and even disfigured Jews during these turbulent years.

She often chatted in Polish with Jewish tradespeople and professionals, most of which apparently came from Sephardic (from Spain) stock. She reported with astonishment that their expulsion from Spain in 1492 was still fresh in their minds (*Volga* 16; *Exóticas* 31-31). Casanova seems to have felt considerable guilt about her country's past mistreatment of Jews. Her relatives, Dmowski and *ND* friends often teased her about her philo-Semitism, Spain's history:

> ...mis amigos, los nacionalistas polacos, antisemitas furibundos, ironizan amablemente mi defensa de los israelitas, recordándome su expulsión de España "por buenos"...Ni por buenos ni por malos se los echó, sinó porque así convenía a España...*(Guerra* 99)

> My friends, the Polish nationalists, rabid anti-Semites, gently mock my defense of the Israelites, reminding me of their expulsion from Spain "because they were so good".

> They weren't ejected from Spain because they were good or bad, but because it was to Spain's advantage...

Otherwise, life in the Niklewicz home, although somewhat spartan by Casanova's Spanish standards, was lively and enjoyable. Casanova was relieved that Mañita's marriage, unlike her own, was happy and successful. Her son-in-law would never be rich, but the Niklewiczes lived in a home full of love, warmth and politics -- especially politics. "Desayunábamos política, almorzábamos política, y comíamos política" 'We had politics for breakfast, lunch and dinner,' remembers Krystina Niklewicz. Since those politics were the campaigns and ideas of the right-wing National Democratic Party, and the Party spent a great deal of the decade resisting Piłsudski's efforts to run the country, Casanova spent many hours debating with the rest of the family, albeit good-naturedly.

115

She would have enjoyed less political activity and more humane philosophies (Niklewicz, K. interview).

Another War (1919-1920)

One of Piłsudski's concerns after the signing of the Treaty of Versailles was the securing of Poland's eastern borders against the Soviets. The new Soviet Union was as opposed to the idea of an independent, Catholic Poland as the czarists had been. Piłsudski rightly feared that if the Soviet Union became stronger, Poland's independence would not last, and that the Soviets would then threaten the rest of Europe (Watt 107-108).

After Casanova's return to Warsaw in late 1919, Poland entered an uneasy state of partial war with the Soviet Union. As she wrote to *ABC*, it seemed incredible that, so soon after one war Poland would now willingly rush into another. She drew the philosophical conclusion that war must be a constant of human nature. Initial Polish victories consoled her, but she bitterly noted that "Solo los fuertes mandan y dominan, y para ser fuertes los Estados no se les exige que tengan conciencia" 'Only the strong rule and dominate, and when nations are strong, they are not required to have a conscience' (8 July 1920).

She had one important journalistic "scoop" that summer. Before Poland invaded the Ukraine, Piłsudski had signed a secret military pact with Simon Petlyura, "the tiger of the Ukraine," commander of the anti-Soviet Ukrainian guerrilla forces. This romantic but sinister figure stopped in Warsaw for a few days. Readers of *ABC* were able to read a long interview with "este hombre terrible" 'this dreadful man' (17 July 1920). She found him interesting, if not trustworthy. (*ABC* 18 July 1920) Casanova made the sign of the cross on his forehead (the traditional Polish farewell to soldiers going to the front), and sternly admonished him not to give in to the temptation to betray Poland (Despite her blessing, Petlyura was assassinated in Paris six years later).

By August 1920, Casanova's articles to *ABC* had acquired a desperate tone. The Red Army sent the Polish Army into retreat, and unexpectedly invaded Poland. She reported Soviet General Budënny's and his Cossacks' atrocities: they had murdered, burned, raped and looted their way into Poland. Her nephew, Franek Lutosławski (son of the late Marian), gave her an eyewitness account of the raided Ukrainian city of Zhitomir, where the Cossacks burned down a Polish hospital, killing six hundred patients. The Cossacks had been unimaginably violent and cruel to the native population of the Ukraine. And now they were in Poland.

¿Cómo han llegado hasta aquí?, me pregunto, incrédula de la realidad, y miro en el mapa las ciudades y los rios que rindieron tropas polacas desmandadas, perdidas... ("Los bolcheviques," ABC 15 September 1920.)

How have they gotten this far, I ask myself, not being able to grasp reality, as I note on the map the cities and rivers that Polish troops surrendered to them and that they passed without resistance from the disorderly and lost Polish troops...

Again Warsaw readied itself for a siege. Resigned, Casanova showed her solidarity by staying in the city and helping with the Polish Army's medical committees. As she somewhat self-consciously informed *ABC*, a member of the Red Cross and recipient of the *Gran Cruz* had certain obligations. But she admitted she was afraid. Another worry emerged after her daughter, Bela, travelled to Drozdowo to stay with her paternal grandmother Paulina Lutosławska. Unexpectedly, the countryside around Drozdowo fell into Soviet hands and all communications were cut for several months. Reports came of the total devastation of the country around Łomża.

Her *ABC* columns written during these months reflect Casanova's alternating feelings of despair, fear and pessimism (See *ABC* articles 283 to 319). The Western world refused to help Poland: it saw the war as unnecessarily provoked, and doomed to failure. She felt this universal "desertion" strongly. Stories of Cossack and Bolshevik atrocities haunted her columns. As months went by, the life of Warsaw's poor became unbearable; the wealthy did not come to their aid. Social relationships became strained to the breaking point (*ABC* 27 September 1920). The Polish people knew that Colonel Tukhachevsky of the Red Army had confidently announced that world revolution would begin "over the corpse of Poland." Modern historians have compared his aggressive military style to that of Genghis Khan or Attila the Hun. As Tukhachevsky advanced towards Warsaw, the city's atmosphere became tense and apocalyptic.

Seldom has one battle changed the course of one country's history as did Marshall Piłsudski's victory over Tukhachevsky in the battle of Warsaw. On August 16, 1920, the Red Army threatened Warsaw and the existence of an independent Poland. Forty-eight hours later, the Red Army had been shattered and the troops that had survived were fleeing Poland. Western powers that had considered the Soviet-Polish clash a "lost" war, were astounded by this reversal. Some anti-Communist historians claim that the battle of Warsaw, by stopping Soviet expansion in Eastern Europe, was as crucial to Europe as the Battle of Tours had been in the Middle Ages, when it prevented Muslim invasion of the West (Dupuy 991).

Poland's joy, and the world's astonishment at the defeat of the Soviets, were inexpressible:

...la palabra 'milagro,' 'milagro' tiembla en todos los labios...a victoria de Polonia es grande, y el mundo entero debe a sus hijos, vivos y muertos, gratitud...

("Los bolcheviques", *ABC*, 24 September 1920).

...the word 'miracle', 'miracle' trembles on everyone's lips...Poland's victory is enormous, and the entire world owes a debt of gratitude to Poland's children, living or dead.

To Casanova's added relief, Bela and the family in Drozdowo had survived the Bolsheviks' takeover of their property, and the temporary reorganization of the private estate into a Soviet-style "workers' collective.

For several weeks, Bela had been required to work as the collective's bookkeeper. She wrote a vivid narrative of her adventures and misadventures with the "Reds" (*Bolszewicy w polskim dworze*, 'Bolsheviks in a Polish Home'), which Casanova translated into Spanish. While her book was serialized by a Polish newspaper, *ABC* simultaneously published excerpts in Madrid (19, 20, 29, 30 October 1920; 6, 13, 14, 25, 26 November 1920).

Poland's miraculous victory over the Soviet army was on the front pages of the world press, and Casanova's up-to-the-minute stories were avidly read in Madrid and Latin America. Despite a disorganized, poorly-equipped army and against enormous odds, Poland had proved to the world that it could repel invasion. The Soviets would not attack Poland for another twenty years. The Polish people, under the leadership of Piłsudski, could now dedicate themselves to rebuilding their nation.

Economic Matters

1920 was a financially disastrous year, not only for Casanova, but for all of Poland. Dmowski, the Niklewicz and Lutosławski families had, at least temporarily, lost most of their capital during the war. Adding to the needs of Casanova's immediate family, little Ryszard Niklewicz's birth brought another mouth to feed. Casanova apparently wrote several letters home to friends and family in Spain, gently hinting at their hardships, but not asking for funds. To her amazement, word of her plight reached the Red Cross in Galicia, which had already collected over twenty-thousand pesetas towards the erection of a monument in her honor to be built in La Coruña. The Red Cross socialites tactfully noted her need:

La situación económica del país de su residencia, Polonia, es extremadamente crítica, y no resulta aventurado suponer que la vida para Sofía y su familia está resultando muy angustiosa. Por eso, el envío de aquella suma ha de resultar de gran oportunidad...(*Voz de Galicia*, 9 April 1920).

...The economic situation in Poland, the country she resides in, is extremely serious, and one can venture to say that life for Sofía and her family is turning out to be very distressing. Because of that, the remittance of that amount of money will be a great help...

Casanova never forgot the generosity of the Galician Red Cross. Thanks to a favorable exchange rate, this windfall enabled the family to survive for many months, although not in the style they were accustomed to before World War I.

Long after the money had been spent, Casanova remembered the gift with gratitude touched by amusement. As she told her grandchildren, she had the dubious honor of being "la primera persona en la historia que se comió su propio monumento" 'the first person in history who ate her own monument. ' (The municipality of La Coruña has somewhat made up for this by posthumously naming a street for Casanova; there is also news of a primary school named after her in Ferrol). She would never be immortalized by a statue, but Galicia's generosity helped her survive another war (Niklewicz, K. interview).

Between Two Worlds

Casanova travelled to Madrid in 1923, 1925, 1926, 1928 and 1929, spending an average of three to four months on each visit. These stays in Spain were a time of personal renewal. Unlike most expatriates, Casanova maintained close ties to her country and its culture. Repeated trips, along with a constant stream of her articles and books that appeared in Spain during this decade kept her name in the news. And while she was in Poland, she would follow Spain's political life through its daily press, and through her voluminous correspondence with friends and contacts, particularly the faithful Vicente Casanova.

During the early 1920s Spain had undergone a clear change of atmosphere. The defeat of the Spanish army in North Africa and the uncovering of financial scandals in high circles caused an enormous loss of confidence in the Spanish government. The rise of Mussolini and Italian Fascism, the emergence of Hitler and the Nazi party in Germany, the death of Lenin in 1924 were all events that Casanova noted in her columns, but which did not affect Spain much. Old acquaintances, such as the Countess of Pardo Bazán and Don Benito Pérez Galdós, died during this time.

New political figures were rising in Spain. As early as 1922, *ABC* was following with great interest, admiration and support the career of Casanova's fellow Galician (from Ferrol), General Francisco Franco. After the disasters in Morocco, General Primo de Rivera had taken over the government in a coup d'etat. The King had been forced to name him Prime Minister and Spain had suspended Parliament and entered "la Dictadura. "

Unlike many Monarchists, who distrusted the non-aristocratic Primo de Rivera, Casanova seems to have welcomed the change in direction. She felt that like Piłsudski, Primo de Rivera was "a strong man" who would bring order and peace to Spain. During a trip to Spain in 1924, on the spur of the moment she called on him at his official residence, sending in a servant with her card. Primo de Rivera recognized her name, received her cordially, and after a long conversation, he presented her with an autographed photograph, which she proudly displayed in her Warsaw salon, next to photographs of the Royal family (Meissner, H. interview).

For the next few years, until 1930, Primo de Rivera ruled a Spain where there was less personal freedom, but more "law and order. " Unfortunately, Primo de Rivera was not another Piłsudski. He did not have the gifts of leadership and organization that enabled the Polish leader to govern Poland and control factionalism and violence. At least "la Dictablanda" (a play on the words "dura," 'hard' and "blanda," 'soft') for his easy-going style of government) brought an interlude of peace. As far as can be ascertained, in Casanova's eyes Primo de Rivera's lenient rule (accompanied by a period of financial prosperity that swept the western world) made Spanish life even more enjoyable.

Compared to war-torn Warsaw, Madrid offered a lively and even brilliant cultural life. When in the capital, Casanova attended as many social and cultural events as could be crammed into her schedule. Her presence at events and openings was often noted in society pages, next to the names of other social figures and cultural celebrities such as María Guerrero, the actress, and novelist Concha Espina (whom Casanova apparently knew, but according to family memory, did not regard very highly).

Casanova enjoyed attending *zarzuelas*, the Spanish musical comedies; she also attended many of the plays that the Machado brothers wrote during the 1920s and which enjoyed enormous popular success. Her old friend Eduardo Marquina (who had written her then favorite play, "En Flandes se ha puesto el sol") was still writing and producing poetic dramas based on historical themes. In addition to long stays in Madrid, she visited friends in different cities and provinces of Spain, and usually began or ended her stay with a visit to Galicia, events that were usually reflected

120

by her *ABC* columns.

Literary Production

Along with an intense social life, during these years Casanova kept a strenuous writing schedule that would have taxed a younger person. First came her articles for *ABC*, which appeared almost every week. During the 1920s she wrote more than four hundred articles for *ABC* alone. Most dealt with Eastern Europe, and appeared under the heading "*ABC en Varsovia*" (See items 253 to 683).

Despite their generic title, these articles covered dissimilar subjects. Some were of passing interest, reporting on the theater season in Warsaw or other ephemera. Others were lengthy essays that analyzed complex post-war European, among them "Por la Europa de la paz" 'Through peace-time Europe,' which the paper featured prominently (*ABC*, 1 January 1920). Still others were short news articles describing political events such as the assassination of Poland's newly elected president, Gabriel Narutowicz (December 1922), or the death of Lenin in January 1924. About a third of the articles dealt with the events and repercussions of the Russian revolution.

Besides reporting on Eastern Europe regularly for *ABC* (and for other newspapers in Spain and Latin American that syndicated her columns, such as *La Nación* of Buenos Aires and Havana's *El Diario de la Marina*), Casanova pursued a broader writing career. Her poetic production had almost ceased with the beginning of World War I: now she concentrated her energies on writing journalistic accounts and more lucrative popular novels for a much broader audience.

Four volumes of her projected *Obras Completas* were published during this decade: *En la corte de los Zares* (1924); re-issues of *El doctor Wolski* (1925) and *El pecado* (1926); and finally, *De Rusia: Amores y confidencias* (1927).

Only four of the books she wrote during the 1920s explored Eastern European topics (*La Revolución bolchevista*, 1920; *Viajes y aventuras*, 1920; *En la corte de los Zares*, 1923; *De Rusia: Amoramores y Confidencias*, 1927). She also published five short novels of uneven literary interest in popular editions (*Episodio de guerra*, 1921; *Valor y miedo*, 1922; *Princesa Rusa*, 1922; *Kola el bandido*, 1923; *El dolor de reinar*, 1925). In addition, she reissued three earlier books (*Lo eterno*, 1920; *El doctor Wolski*, 1925; *El pecado*, 1926). And she still contributed short stories or poems to small reviews such as *Raza Española*, or to the mass-audience *Blanco y Negro*.

121

As is clear from their titles, most of these books written from Casanova's personal experiences during World War I and the Russian revolution. Most of them, despite being written in genres not usually associated with politics (such as *Viajes y aventuras*, a children's book, or *Princesa Rusa*, a sentimental romance), reflect her clear intention to tie the dangers implicit in the Russian revolution to Spain's political situation.

Despite their brisk journalistic format works such as *La revolución bolchevista*, or *De Rusia* remain fresh and readable. Others, such as *Viajes y aventuras*, were written with a more literary audience in mind, and possess great charm and style. There are still others (*Princesa rusa, Valor y miedo*) that are *feuilleton* material, aimed at a popular "woman's" audience and lacking literary merit.

La revolución bolchevista

Casanova tried to warn Spain of the "Bolshevik menace" through *La revolución bolchevista*, which is a compilation of articles from *ABC*, dating from 1917 to 1918. Most were written as the events they recorded were taking place, with few if any anti-Bolshevik arguments, but reinforced by her own spontaneous feelings. The articles feature enthusiastic accounts of the day-to-day excitement of life in revolutionary Petrograd, her celebrated interview with Leon Trotsky and a heart-rending series of articles on the execution of her brothers-in-law Józef and Marian.

But there are trenchant "post-scripts," dated Paris and Madrid 1919, that recount Casanova's meeting with an anonymous Bolshevik official in Paris. He warned her that the Soviet "infiltration" of Spain had begun:

Hallará muy cambiado su país... con levadura rusa en la fermentación de sus comarcas del mediodía... He pasado tres meses entre Andalucia, Valencia y Cataluña y aquello anda revueltísimo. Rusia ha dado el ejemplo de la revolución mundial... (169-170)

You will find your country very changed... with Russian yeast in the fermentation of its southern regions. I have just spent three months in Andalucia, Valencia and Catalonia and everything is stirred up... Russia has set the example of world revolution...

En la corte de los Zares

Her book, *En la corte de los Zares* (1924), enjoyed a vogue during the 1920s. It was if not more anti-Soviet in tone, more pro-Romanov in feeling. *En la Corte de los Zares* is a popular book: it does not pretend to be scholarly, theoretical or objective and it bears marks of the haste with which it was composed. Accounts of early Russian rulers are sketchy and unreliable. Casanova had gathered most of the historical facts and anecdotes that make up its narrative on the Royals from a "Princess Obolenskaia" (a member of the royal household that she had known in St. Petersburg, and who she kept in touch with even after the execution of the Czar and his family), and Bela had also collaborated with the research.

Casanova uses extensive, first-hand evidence gleaned during her visits to Russia, and some of the accounts and photographs are obviously authentic. Some aspects are sentimental (such as an imagined romance between a Royal Guard and one of the princesses) while Casanova's portrait of her acquaintance Princess Elizabeth, sister of the Czarina, is so idealized as to be hagiographic (235-240). At times, the book descends to the level of a *vie romancée*. *Corte* was one of her most popular books, for then as now, the public was interested in the lives and deaths of royalty, and in the tragic last days of the Romanov family.

Despite the above caveats, in the balance Casanova's accounts in *Corte* do not pander to the reader. Her obvious sympathy for the Czar's family makes the book's thesis one-sided, but becomes effective in serving the book's goal, which was to move readers to feel terror and pity for the fallen Royals. The Czarina's wistful refrain of "unidos todos" 'all of us together,' which she had repeated to her family for many months of imprisonment, haunts the reader at the book's tragic climax (283). Casanova's overwhelming compassion for the Royal family tempers her presentation of their failure as rulers. *Corte* went into three editions and was listed as a source for the "Rusia" entry in the Enciclopedia Espasa of that decade.

As is evident, Casanova's literary output and success remained at a high level during these years. She was still the only conduit of information between Spain and Poland. Given their dissimilar cultures, she sometimes found it impossible to explain one to the other. She maintained a steady Spanish audience for her work through her visibility in *ABC* and elsewhere, and year after year a sizeable sector of the reading public bought her books.

In her sixties, Casanova stood for a kind of nationalism that seemed momentarily in eclipse since the decline of Spain's empire in the previous two decades. Her earlier works, re-issued in the cynical 1920s, evoked more innocent times. After costly defeats in Morocco, *Lo eterno*'s story of a priest's self-sacrifice in Africa appeared even more poignant.

During these years, Casanova received two great honors. First, she was nominated by Spain for the 1925 Nobel Prize in Literature. Then, as now, nominations for the Nobel Prize in Literature are often politically inspired (In 1905 when her old acquaintance, the dramatist José

Echegaray, was granted the Nobel Prize, there was a furor, and Spanish intellectuals drew up a manifesto protesting the choice of a safe, "establishment" author over more deserving ones).

Casanova's literary oeuvre, although prolific and readable, did not merit a Nobel Prize. She probably knew that she got the nomination through the lobbying of her friends Blanca de los Ríos, Don Antonio Maura (then President of the Royal Academy of the Spanish Language) and the famous scholar, Don Emilo Cotarelo y Mori, but she was proud of the honor (Bugallal *Siglo* 10; *Martirio* Preface).

She was equally proud, later that year, when the Spanish king awarded her the Alfonso XII medal, Spain's highest recognition of intellectual accomplishment, meant to reward outstanding achievement in arts and letters. She took the Alfonso XII medal back to Warsaw with pride, and placed it among her treasured mementos.

Poland Again

Whenever Casanova travelled back to Poland by train, she had a few days' grace as she made her way over Central Europe to adjust to semi-obscurity and the much harsher Polish climate and life-style. At home in Warsaw, she was "Wittitta" or simply "Babunita" (an improbable combination of the Polish *babunia* 'granny,' and the Spanish diminutive ending *-ita*), and a spectator to the politics in which her family took such an active part.

Being a grandmother in Polish society is an honored and enjoyable position, bringing many pleasures and satisfactions -- unlike the right-wing politics that surrounded her. Casanova was loved, deferred to, and listened to with great respect by her five Niklewicz grandchildren (Konrad, the youngest, was born in 1922). Krysia and Andrej, the two eldest, first learned to speak using the unique mixture of *gallego* and Polish that their nurse Pepa used at home (Casanova used to joke that Pepa was the first person in history to have spoken only *gallego* and Polish). Krysia was fluent in Spanish, and longed to travel to Spain with her grandmother, whom she greatly resembled. Casanova used to talk to Krysia about Spain, lend her Spanish books and play *zarzuela* records brought back from her trips.

According to Krystina Niklewicz's recollections, Casanova thought that everything about Spain was superior to its Polish equivalent. During beautiful spring days in Warsaw, her grandmother would tell her: "Do you see the weather today? Well -- this would be the worst day of the year in Madrid!", a sentiment heartily echoed by Pepa. When Krysia finished secondary school in 1928, her grandmother proudly took her to Spain, where Krysia was surprised to discover that the weather could be as dull and changeable as Poland's.

Now in the Indian summer of her life, Casanova derived a great deal of satisfaction from her daughters's successful lives. Mañita was a born leader, a social force for the *ND*, and a devout Catholic.

Of the three girls, Bela most resembled her father in temperament and looks. She pursued a successful writing career (which sometimes drew on her family life and on her relations with her father) until she impetuously fell in love with and married an unusual and talented Polish Army officer, Colonel (later General) Romuald Wolikowski. Wolikowski had been a soldier during World War I and the Russian Revolution. He played a role in the recovery of Polish independence, and became Chief of Staff of the Fifth Army which so brilliantly defended Northen Poland during the Russian invasion of 1920. He was later named Military Attaché to the Polish Embassy under Lenin, and ended his active military career, although not his diplomatic efforts, fighting the Nazis in 1939. Bela and General Wolikowski had two children, both sons, Andrzej (born in 1924) and Grzegorz (1925).

Wolikowski and Casanova enjoyed excellent relations, and he greatly admired his "very modern" mother-in-law, who refrained from meddling in the young couple's affairs. Bela resumed her writing after the boys' early years. She published a total of seven books (five of which enjoyed popular success and went into several editions) and many articles. Some of her books touched on her unusual family experiences (Wolikowski, R. interview).

The youngest and last to be married, Halita, was beautiful and vivacious, with a touch of her mother's melancholy temperament. After finishing university studies in Economics, she married a wealthy physician from Posnań, Dr. Czeslaw Meissner. Halita and her husband eventually had five children, Andrzej, Adalbert, Teresa, Zofia and Czesław Meissner (Meissner, H. interview).

Both Bela and Halita had managed to see their father over the years, despite their mother's strenuous objections. No matter how carefully they tried to conceal these meetings from her, Casanova usually found out, sometimes in uncanny ways. The day that Halita's first child, Andrzej, was born, Casanova answered the phone in the Meissner's Posnań flat, and with a pounding heart heard Lutosławski's voice for the first time in decades. Many years later, Halita remembered her mother's angry account of the conversation, which began in Polish:

"This is Professor Lutosławski, Halina Meissnerowa's father".

"And this is Halina Meissnerowa's mother. "

Then the conversation shifted to Spanish:

"Ay, Sofitina ¿cómo estás?"

"Muy bien, he cumplido con todas mis obligaciones, y me siento muy feliz".

"Pues yo no puedo decir lo mismo."

"Sofitina, how are you?"

"Very well, I have carried out all my obligations, and I am very happy. "

"Well, I cannot say the same for myself." (Meissner, H. interview)

Viajes y aventuras

Sometime after she returned from the wars (probably in 1919), Casanova was asked by Burgos' *Biblioteca Rodríguez* to write a children's book for a series introducing current events to children. She decided to write about the child she knew best, Krystina, who between the ages of five and nine experienced more travel and adventures than most people in a lifetime. *Viajes y aventuras de una muñeca española*, published in 1920 and enhanced by charming black-and-white illustrations by Gutiérrez-Larraya, reflects Casanova's war adventures, her happiness at living with the Niklewiczes, and provides an accurate picture of their family life.

In writing *Viajes y aventuras de una muñeca española,* Casanova was doubtlessly inspired by the success that *Bohaterski Miś* 'The Heroic Teddy Bear' (1919) was receiving in post-war Poland. Written by Bronisława Ostrowska (1881-1928), it was a popular children's book that purported to follow a teddy bear's adventures in all the fighting fronts during World War I (Krzyżanowski 475). The idea of using a doll's perspective on adult affairs is not original -- "doll stories" have delighted children for centuries. Folk tales, eighteenth-century books written by the Comtesse de Ségur (1799-1874), and even a short story by Louisa May Alcott (1832-1888) are "doll-stories" and use doll-narrators as a convention.

Casanova chose Carmela, Krysia's Spanish doll, who had accompanied the family during all their travels, as the book's protagonist and as in some ways as her own spokesman. Carmela and the family weather five years of war and travails (although the deaths of three family members are not mentioned), and return to Warsaw to a flat that has remained untouched by time and war, to resume their life. The book seems to imply that even in the worst of times, "civilized" values will survive in the home, at the heart of Catholic family life. One suspects that Casanova identified with Carmela's self-deprecating closing words: "Pero soy, quien soy: una...española" 'But I am what I am...a Spaniard.' (110)

126

Polish Politics

As mentioned earlier, Casanova's family may have brought her much satisfaction, but their politics did not. Casanova was pained to witness the enormous polarization of Polish political life during the 1920s. The National Democrats' constant hostility to Piłsudski did not please her. And Dmowski's and her favorite brother-in-law, Father Kazimierz Lutosławski's close ties to the *Sejm*, made them part of some of the country's most turbulent affairs. When the first Polish constitution since independence was being drafted, Father Lutosławski, along with other *Sejm* deputies, was selected to hammer out the first draft. The constitution was obviously slanted against Piłsudski, and eventually had to be replaced.

Dmowski and Father Lutosławski played an important part in the campaign against Piłsudski's first elected President, his friend Professor Gabriel Narutowicz. Narutowicz had been elected, in part, thanks to a coalition that included the Jewish-led National Minorities bloc. The Right seized on this support, branded the new President "Narutowicz, King of the Jews," and unleashed a virulent anti-Semitic, anti-Naturowicz campaign of enormous impact. National Democratic newspapers tried to equate Judaism, Socialism and Narutowicz in the mind of the Polish masses through articles and slogans. In a Right-wing newspaper, Father Lutosławski asked Polish public opinion: "How could the Jews dare to impose their president on us (Watt 191; Machray 243)?" The campaign continued until Eligiusz Niewiadomski, an unemployed artist, murdered Narutowicz at an art exhibit a few days after he had been inaugurated as President (Niewiadomski was a nationalist fanatic but not a member of the *ND*).

Incidents such as Narutowicz's assassination clearly mark Casanova's differences from her family's politics and anti-Semitism. Intellectually, she could understand how the long-oppressed Poles, seething at the enforced 'sharing' of their land with other nationalities, resented the presence of the Yiddish-speaking, unassimilated Jews. She knew Narutowicz's murder was inexcusable before international opinion (indeed, before any moral standard), and that such anti-Semitism would be considered a stain on Poland's character. As a Christian, she could never understand how her Polish Rightist friends, so ultra-Catholic in theory, could carry in practice such unrelenting, un-Christian hatred towards the Jews. Like Piłsudski (and the majority of Poland), Casanova felt anti-Semitism was unworthy of Poland's greatness as a nation. She resisted it both in personal argument and in her articles for *ABC*.

According to Casanova's descriptions, life in Warsaw became more pleasant as the 1920s drew to a close. The city became more like the great capitals of Europe as it recovered from decades of war and poverty. There were a few years in the 1920s when the city flourished, with new large buildings, museums and theatres. The great avenues were repaved, and a series of new cafes and restaurants lined the busy streets. Then, with the depression of 1929, that pleasant period ended and Poland moved into an era of austerity.

Spain, too, suffered from the effects of the world-wide depression. Primo de Rivera's plans had fallen apart by 1929. When he presented his resignation as a gesture to King Alfonso, it was unexpectedly accepted. After Primo de Rivera went into exile, the king realized that he did not have the support of any of the influential sectors of Spanish society.

Casanova felt the change when she returned to Spain in 1929. The death that year of her beloved patron, Queen Mother María Cristina, had marked the end of the old times. Now not even the Church would support the king. The intellectuals were drawing together to promote a second Republic. And the Monarchists themselves did nothing to delay the inevitable. Casanova feared that the Russian Revolution would usher radical changes into a Spain eager for anything new or different from the status quo. Still, despite her worries, she was confident that Spain would in time overcome the forces that were beginning to tear her apart.

Chapter 11

The Spanish Republic

The 1930s brought Spain (and Casanova's work) to the brink of political explosion. There were polemics in the press, a proliferation of new political parties, arguments between old friends, antagonisms within families, hostility between social classes. The Monarchists were unable to resist the wave of militantly pro-Republican feeling that swept the nation, and the country turned to the Left.[8]

Sofía Casanova was in Spain during the months that brought about the decisive change in government. She arrived late in 1930, and spent a few weeks in the North of Spain, where she immediately felt the change in political mood and the polarization of feelings:

Va a estallar la revolución...Vamos a la república...

Observo, indago, escucho... me oriento en este dia caótico de mi patria, y espero...(*ABC*, 11 September 1930)

The revolution is about to break out... We are heading for the Republic...I watch, I question, I listen...I orient myself during these chaotic political times of my country's, and I wait...

Her optimism was shaken by the events of December, 1930, when a small Aragonese garrison was seized by pro-Republican soldiers early in December. By the middle of the same month, the rebellion had been quelled, and the two main leaders executed. Public opinion rose against these summary executions. There were ugly rumors that the king had personally intervened in the trial, preventing the officers' stay of execution. The two became folk heroes and martyrs of the Left. Public opinion went against the king. Except for *ABC* and a handful of minor Monarchist newspapers, the press violently condemned him. The government had to call for elections which were set for March 12, 1931.

Casanova was deeply grieved by the violence of the event, and by the anarchy and unrest that was overtaking every aspect of Spanish life: "Nunca los años de guerra y revoluciones en Rusia y en Polonia han conturbado mi ser como los sucesos de estos dias" 'Never during years of revolution and wars in Russia and Poland was I as troubled as I have been by the events of these past days' (*ABC*, 15 January 1931).

Casanova was stung by the king's lack of foresight. He and his advisors had let power slip through their fingers while they engaged in intrigues or frivolous pursuits. For Casanova, the ineptitude and short-sightedness of the Monarchists (who did nothing to stem the tide of events) was as painful as the increasing power of the Left. The Monarchists had no issues, no platforms, no strategies or plans to improve Spain's troubled situation. On the other hand, the intense and increasingly violent Left had too many conflicting theories. A large number of the electorate, through apathy, made the situation worse. "España es un pais... que se empeñan en destrozar todos, todos los españoles" (*ABC*, 21 February 1931) 'Spain is a country that every single Spaniard is bent on destroying. '

The evening after the elections, it became clear that the Republicans had won. On April 13, as the king's advisors negotiated his departure with representatives of the new Republican government, huge crowds began to celebrate the coming of the Republic in the streets of Madrid. By three o'clock, the new Republican flag had been raised, and countless red flags and banners waved everywhere. As the day wore on, and the work day ended, a holiday atmosphere took over: *Madrileños* embraced, crying "¡Viva la República!" Streets were noisy with celebration, but aristocratic neighborhoods and the area around the Palace were eerily quiet. Yet, as Casanova was to point out many times to her adversaries abroad, the king did not abdicate, but merely surrendered his power temporarily to the Republic. He wrote in a manifesto published the next day by *ABC*:

Las elecciones celebradas el domingo me revelan claramente que no tengo hoy el amor de mi pueblo. Mi conciencia me dice que ese desvío no será definitivo, porque procuré siempre servir a España... Un rey puede equivocarse, y sin duda erré alguna vez, pero se bien que nuestra patria se mostró en todo momento generosa ante las culpas sin malicia... quiero apartarme de cuanto sea lanzar a un compatriota contra otro en fratricida guerra civil... suspendo deliberadamente el ejercicio del Poder Real... y me aparto de España. (*ABC*, 14 April 1931)

Sunday's elections clearly show me that today I do not have my people's love. My conscience tells me that this aberration will not be permanent, because I have always tried to serve Spain... A king can make a mistake, and I certainly erred at times... but I know well that our country has always been generous towards mistakes made without malice... I want to withdraw from whatever could send a fellow countryman against another in a fratricidal civil war... I purposefully suspend the exercise of Royal Power... and I withdraw from Spain...

With these enigmatic phrases, and without any warning, King Alfonso slipped out of Madrid, alone. In retrospect, many of the king's actions seemed incredible to the Monarchists. His passive surrender of power and immediate departure, compounded by his virtual desertion of the queen and their children (who spent an uneasy night in the almost-unguarded Palace, surrounded by unpredictable crowds), were an embarrassment to the Monarchists and a cause for jubilation for the Left. When on the next day the queen with her children undertook the long and difficult train journey out of Spain (with one child gravely ill with hemophilia and required a medical escort), their hapless circumstances were covered extensively by the national and international press and were damaging to the king's already disgraced reputation.

Casanova was so moved by the events that in her first article published after the king's departure she could not bear to mention the royal family directly. She was preparing to leave for Poland again, this time with deep foreboding. She could envision it all: the take-over by the Left, the coming of anti-clericalism, factionalism, destructive dissent, "international-ism" -- in short, the Republic would leave Spain open to Bolshevik takeover. Setting aside her lifetime attachment to the queen mother, and her devotion to the royal family, she was intellectually sure that the Monarchy had been the only stabilizing force in the country. The only positive characteristic of the Republic that she could find was that it had been born "sin sangre" 'without blood,'(*ABC*, 5 May 1931).

During those jubilant spring days she mingled with the crowds. Their red flags and public enthusiasm uneasily reminded her of the first days of the March Revolution. She listened to what the *madrileños* and *madrileñas* were saying, and reported two women "of the people" rejoicing about the departure of the royal family, "who had everything," while they had nothing. In her column she responded to their claim:

Los Reyes tenían de todo: alegrías y penas inconsolables, dolores íntimos y responsabilidades que no conocéis vosotras... los Reyes dejan España llorando, y vosotras, bravas madrileñas, teneis la felicidad de seguir viviendo y trabajando en vuestra Patria, comiendo el pan de vuestros campos y viendo crecer al sol los hijos de vuestras entrañas. (*ABC*, 5 May 1931)

The Royal family had everything: joys and inconsolable sorrows, private griefs and responsibilities unknown to you... the king and queen leave Spain in tears, and you, my good *madrileñas* have the happiness of being able to stay, living and working in your homeland, eating your country's bread and seeing your children grow under its sun.

Casanova identified the deposed king and queen with the end of order. At the age of seventy, she witnessed the end of the one Spanish institution besides the Church that had remained a constant in her life. It was a terrible blow to her spirit, and it hardened many of her attitudes.

131

As she recovered, she mobilized her attack against the forces now ruling Spain. From then on her interest in Spanish politics became intense: her *ABC* articles shifted noticeably in subject. Through her *ABC* column and books, and in every way open to a woman of her social class and professional status, she participated in the growing reaction against the Republic.

The Not-so-loyal Opposition

Casanova's regular column in *ABC* made her a member of the opposition press. Sadly, the Republic, which was (at least in theory) committed to freedom of the press, spent a great deal of its five and a half years of rule suppressing it and violating the "freedom of the press" clause of the 1931 Constitution.

Casanova had been back in Poland only a few weeks when news reached the Polish press that churches and convents were burning in Spain. Opposition papers such as *ABC* and *El Debate* were suspended or had their offices ransacked. Photographs from this time show the *ABC* premises plundered and looted.

She read the foreign newspapers available to her, and was disturbed to read about the desecration of churches and tombs. She fell ill and refused to receive visitors, who were seeking to hear her explanation of these bizarre events. There was no mail from Spain. She discovered that *ABC* had suspended publication for a few weeks, beginning a pattern that would be repeated several times until the coming of the Civil War. *ABC* would have publication suspended by the Republican government, and for several anxious weeks Casanova would have to depend on foreign news services and weeks-old personal letters for information. *ABC* was suspended for twenty-five days in 1931, for one-hundred-and-eleven days in 1932, closed down for two weeks by the Republican workers in its staff in 1934, constantly checked by Republican censors, and finally taken over by the Republicans in July, 1936. Casanova's column would not appear during these periods of suspension; therefore, from 1931 to 1936 she published a smaller number of articles than usual. This constant tug-of-war with censorship made the writers and editors of *ABC* take an even more militant stand against the Left, and indeed against any kind of social change, than they had before the imposition of Republican censorship.

These drastic measures taken by the Republicans had been provoked in part by *ABC*'s strong anti-government stand. (In fact, the nation-wide wave of church-burnings and the looting of *ABC*'s editorial offices had

132

been touched off by the first meeting of the Monarchist Club, attended by *ABC*'s editor and several of its columnists.) The day after king Alfonso's departure, the paper editorialized:

Seguiremos y permaneceremos donde estábamos: con la Monarquía constitucional y parlamentaria, con la libertad, con el orden, con el derecho, respetuosos de la voluntad nacional, pero sin sacrificarle nuestras convicciones. La Monarquía es el signo de todo lo que defendemos: es la historia de España. Los hombres y los azares pueden interrumpir, pero no borrar, la Tradición y la Historia, ni extirpar las raices espirituales de un pueblo, ni cambiar su destino. (*ABC*, 14 March 1931).

We will be, and we remain, where we stood before: with constitutional and parliamentary Monarchy, with law, with order, respecting national choice but without sacrificing our convictions to it. The Monarchy stands for all we defend: it is the history of Spain. Men and chance can interrupt tradition and history, but they cannot erase them, or pull out the spiritual roots of a nation, or change its destiny.

Somewhere between the words "without sacrificing our convictions" and the mindless violence of the mob that burned down the *ABC* building, lay the heart of the problem that beset Spain. There was no Spanish tradition of political compromise, of respect for the opinions or rights of others. Was Spain, as some have claimed, so deeply influenced by Catholic thought and its absolute interpretations, that there was little room for deviation from the ideal? The Republican throngs in the streets and the aristocratic Monarchists both thought it wrong to compromise what they viewed was the "correct" way. As Ramiro de Maeztú (also an *ABC* columnist) put it, the situation in Spain was black and white: "O la Cruz, o la hoz y el martillo... O con la Revolución, o con la Contrarrevolución" (de Maeztú 90) 'Or with the Cross, or with the hammer and sickle... or with the Revolution, or against it' (de Maeztú, who wrote these words for his regular column for *ABC*, was murdered in 1936, at the outbreak of the Civil War).

Looking back on the issues that Casanova and other *ABC* writers debated during the turbulent 1930s, it is obvious that the intransigence of the Left was matched by the stubbornness of the Right. The Left chose to strike uncompromisingly at issues which the Right refused to give up. To deny Spanish Catholics the right to celebrate Holy Week or Christmas processions was to cast down a gauntlet, which the Right was quick to take up. The secularization of education, the harassment of Jesuits, the banning of public religious displays, the impending appearance of divorce laws, agrarian reform -- all were responses to major problems, but were so radical and uncompromising that they inevitably produced a backlash.

Casanova's columns during the 1930s, like those of Maeztú and other writers of the Right for *ABC*, ring with an intensity that, were it not tempered in her case by her usual humanity, realism and sincerity, would be called fanatical. Her social and political ideas of earlier periods remain in vestigial form. Her drift from Monarchist liberalism towards authoritarianism, her growing admiration for Hitler and Fascist leader José Antonio Primo de Rivera do not surprise us, given the context of Spanish history and her own personal history. What is surprising is that her commitment to progress and anti-authoritarianism lasted as long as it did. Coming from a family long connected to the army, deeply attached to the royal family, fervently Catholic and nationalistic, her shift from a liberal stance to an alignment with the Nationalists, Franco, and Spanish reactionaries, is predictable.

Yet within the same columns that praise Hitler's "example" of leadership, sneer at parliamentarism, and minimize the poverty of Spanish peasants, there are conflicting, more liberal aspects of her political thought. Despite her call for a reaction against the Left, she wanted to avoid at all costs the violence of civil war, and the chaos of revolution. Out of Christian belief she pleaded for direct social action on the part of the Right to alleviate the maladies that afflicted the nation.

As Casanova pointed out to her readers, the conservative and moderate elements in Spanish life did nothing to alleviate national or local problems. On the other hand, the various parties of the Left were socially involved and filled this vacuum to their advantage:

¿Quiénes van a nuestras regiones contaminadas de la lepra roja para instruir a las masas engañadas y rechazar, frente a frente de los agitadores, las falaces promesas de su repertorio? (*ABC*, 13 January 1933).

Who are the ones going to our regions (that have been) contaminated by Red leprosy, to instruct the misled masses, and to reject, face to face with the agitators, their deceitful promises?

Despite her fundamental political naivete, some of Casanova's ideas would have been effective. For example, she suggested a systematic program of Catholic information and social action (based on similar programs she had seen in Poland), paralleling the system of the Left. But since she envisioned it as armed "con alas de ideal, pies desnudos de humildad franciscana" (*ABC*, 4 January 1934) 'with the wings of an ideal, the bare feet of Franciscan simplicity,' her idealistic conception had no chance of ever being implemented in the real world of politics.

One of the problems she faced was Spain's lack of experience in social change and its reliance on outmoded political models. When she advised the Right to organize itself and to promote education, understanding and religion in the provinces where the Left had already made inroads, she had before her the successful example of Polish society, with its literacy campaigns, well-organized Catholic and civic organizations, and post-war reconstruction. At that time the readers of *ABC* as well as its editors and writers did not have such models (and still didn't after the Civil War ended), so her moment never came to pass.

Notwithstanding her opposition to the Republic on almost every issue, of all *ABC*'s regular columnists, Casanova was almost the only one to grant some grudging approval to Republican reforms. Most writers of the Right decried the agrarian reform laws, which had enraged the rich landowners, particularly in Andalucia. Casanova still had some hope that the laws would improve the abysmal conditions of Spanish agricultural workers: "lo que se es que urge dar al campesino paz, seguridad en su hacienda, y respeto a la ajena," (*ABC*, 24 February 1933).'All I know is that we must give the farmer peace, security in his own land, and respect for that of others'. She knew that without some reforms, or concessions, the Right would never prevail.

Themes and Variations (1930-1936)

As the 1930s progressed, and as Spanish public opinion became increasingly polarized, Casanova wrote from Poland about topics that had interested her for decades, and introduced several new ones.

The Russian Revolution and its repercussions remained a persistent concern. Being ideally located in Eastern Europe to follow its events, she read widely on the subject, reviewed books on Russian history that were not available in Spain, kept up with Russian and Polish newspapers, and constantly met and spoke to travellers from the East. She maintained a steady, disparaging stream of comment on the Russian *Piatiletka,* the five-year development plan. She also reported on Russia's efforts to export revolution, and on the "failure" of Russian educational policies.

During the 1920s, Stalin, the epitome of all that Casanova feared in the Russian Bolshevik temperament, had seized power. Since he was a Georgian, and not a White Russian, she also saw in him the "barbaric" Asian Russian strain that she feared would destroy Western civilization.

Above all, she was obsessed with possible Russian influence in Spanish affairs. Until 1931, there had been little Russian influence in Spain. With the emergence of the Republic, a torrent of pro-Soviet information and propaganda flooded the country. In 1934, Casanova would write that "Ya me dan la razón quienes, desde hace catorce años, oyeron mis advertencias y las leyeron en estas columnas" (*ABC*, 4 January 1934) 'Now I am acknowledged to have been correct by those who, for the last fourteen years, heard my warnings, and read them in these columns.'

Another lifetime concern -- her avowed pacifism -- came to the fore during these troubled years. A month seldom went by without a plea for world peace somewhere in her articles. An article on the new theories of Einstein and Freud would debate the roots of war in the human psyche. Her Easter and Christmas articles often dealt with peace, expressing wishes that the following year would bring that elusive condition. She cited the invasion of Abyssinia (now Ethiopia) by Mussolini in 1935 as an appalling example of the senseless need for war: "¡Qué angustia y que vergüenza -- repito -- sentimos ante tamaño mal!" (*ABC*, 10 September 1935) 'What anguish, and what shame -- I repeat -- we feel before such a great evil!'

Casanova's concern for peace remained tied to her belief that if women were more involved in politics, life would be far more humane. She felt that they were the more civilized sex, and that their humane qualities had kept them in submission to the more "primitive" males for centuries. After each war, it was the women who survived, and paradoxically suffered more:

Las mujeres no quieren la guerra, y nos opondremos a ese crimen legalizado for códigos bárbaros. Recorran los estadistas sanguinarios esos centenares de cementerios... y preguntad a las madres... que piensan de la guerra. Que piensan de la guerra las madres de los trece millones de muertos, las de once millones de inválidos que sufren hambre y limosna. (ABC, 13 September 1933).

Women don't want war, and we will oppose that crime, legalized by barbaric codes of law... Let those blood-thirsty legislators tour those hundreds of cemeteries... and ask the mothers... what they think of war. What do they think of war, the mothers of those thirteen million dead, the mothers of the eleven million cripples who go hungry and beg for a living...

Although she claimed "No soy feminista..." (ABC, 4 November 1931) 'I am not a feminist,' and often praised self-sacrificing mothers who stayed at home, Casanova clearly identified with active, achievement-oriented women: indeed, she was one herself. Of course, she had the example of Polish women before her, and during the war, she reported how energetically women had participated in Polish relief, education and nursing. Now, following World War I, Polish women received the same education as men, occupied more responsible jobs, and had more influence on the legislative process. Dr. Ela Balicka helped draft laws against the death penalty in the *Sejm*. Casanova followed this breakthrough with an article deploring legislation being considered by the Spanish *Cortes Constituyentes* which was to make women *eligibles*, "eligible for election," but not *electoras*, "able to vote" (*ABC*, 1 August 1931; *ABC*, 4 November 1931). In a reversal of the Circe legend, she felt that women made men nobler -- and better citizens.

Another major concern, the "Black Legend" of Spain, was a holdover from earlier years of discomfort abroad. Using the classical idiom, Casanova considered herself a *desfacedora de entuertos*, "righter of wrongs," against slurs of Spain's reputation abroad. During the 1930s, when the international press focused on Spain's politics and problems, her pro-Spanish activities doubled.

Spain had not been taken seriously -- or understood -- abroad since the seventeenth century. Unlike France, which always had its cultural ambassadors, or pre-independence Poland, who had a Chopin or a Paderewski publicizing its cause, Spain never promoted its image and interests abroad. This, tied to the real inferiority of achievement and wealth that Casanova felt first-hand, led her to react violently to the wave of articles that greeted Republican Spain. However, since the readers of the Spanish press were part of an insular society having little contact with the rest of Europe, they did not feel the onus of this old legend, or of its modern variations. Casanova, however, wanted to keep them abreast of what was being said against Spain abroad (*ABC*, 12 December 1931).

Linked to this sensitivity to Spain's reputation abroad, was her concern about Spain's insouciance and lack of awareness of the country's "blessings." Casanova had spent the greater part of her life living in Eastern Europe, experiencing the harshness of nature, famines, epidemics and war, problems that had not touched Spain for generations. She often referred to Spain as *España privilegiada*, "privileged Spain." She castigated the irresponsible Spain whose citizens attended bullfights on the day that Cuba was snatched away from Spanish hands, and whose merchant class had callously reaped benefits from World War I's carnage while the rest of Europe suffered.

Of course, one can say that the level of poverty and suffering in rural Andalucia during the 1930s could have matched that of rural Poland. Casanova saw Spain as an oasis and haven, a vision not shared by the peasants and workers of Spain, who could hardly survive on its arid soil nor prosper within its obsolete economic and social system. The wretchedly poor Andalucian, Aragonese and even Galician farmers she wrote about would have been enraged at her version of their conditions:

Nosotros los que conocemos los pueblos realmente hambrientos -- hambrientos de pan, de abrigo, de libertad y de justicia -- no nos asustamos ante el hambre de esas masas campesinas, que no carecen de lo indispensable a su existencia. En las cortijadas no tiene el jornalero aceite, vino, legumbres, fruta, conejos, a falta de pollo y solomillo. Si hay viñas, agua y sal -- ¿por qué se quejan de hambre los campesinos andaluces? (*ABC*, 24 February 1933)

Those of us who know the really hungry countries -- hungry for bread, for shelter, for freedom and justice -- are not afraid before the hunger of these agrarian masses, who do not lack the essential means for their existence. In the humble houses of Sevillan day-laborers, isn't there olive oil, wine, vegetables, fruit, rabbits, even if there is no chicken or steak? If there are grapevines, water and salt -- why do the Andalucian farmers complain of hunger?

Although reminiscent of the *ancien régime*'s "let them eat cake," her perspective contains some valid observations. In retrospect, the Spanish public and press during the 1930s tended to focus on the frivolous and irresponsible. As conflicting political forces gathered strength and the threat of civil war grew, most popular newspapers were obsessed with sports, bullfighting, films and other amusements. Casanova was correct in pointing out this fatal lack of concern.

Outside of Spain, the 1930s brought a new series of international issues to her attention. The German propaganda machine worked day and night to influence public opinion. In Warsaw Casanova listened on the radio to German propaganda broadcasts and to Adolf Hitler's speeches. As part of her lifetime stance of detachment from the opinion of Poles around her, she appears to have totally ignored the obsessive concern of all Polish political parties (*ND* included) over German rearmament, despite its obvious threat to Poland's security. Rearmament did not surprise her. Unlike them, *she* had always known that the unfair penalties imposed on Germany after World War I would eventually come back to haunt the victors.

On the other hand, she liked what she heard about Hitler's avowed intentions to stamp out Communism. Hitler's rhetorical threats against Russia thrilled her: using an almost-Wagnerian image, she asked "¿La lanza de Hitler podrá traspasar el corazón del monstruo?" (*ABC*, 26 March 1933) 'Will Hitler's spear penetrate the heart of the monster?'

She wished that Spain would have a leader of Hitler's power and she envied the unity that Germany presented to the world through its

138

propaganda. In an article titled "Ejemplo," (*ABC*, 3 December 1933) 'Example,' she listed positive aspects of Nazism that could bring Spain order and direction. She argued that Spain needed another Primo de Rivera, a strong man in the mold of Hitler, a *Führer* for Spaniards. Of course, she wasn't alone: there were many others in Spain who admired Hitler. Spain was so lacking in leadership and national purpose that Casanova and others lost perspective. They believed the oratory of a mass movement politician who would later strike out at the heart of their personal beliefs and privileges.

There was one policy of Hitler's, one troubling mania, that Casanova did not condone. Germany had begun to persecute the Jews as early as the 1920s, and by the 1930s Hitler's anti-Semitism was becoming violent. In the abstract, Casanova could understand why Germany (like Poland) would want to oust all "foreigners" from its soil. However, Hitler's abuses were inexcusable. In "Ejemplo" she idealistically called on him to curb his anti-Semitism, and not to stain his international reputation.

What Casanova wrote during the five and a half troubled years of the Spanish Republic and the rise of Hitler, labels her at best a Monarchist and a credulous Germanophile, at worst an apologist for the Right and a proto-Fascist. On the other hand, one can also say that many of her views, such as philo-Semitism and pacifism, remained the same. Her compassion towards the Jews is particularly striking. And along with Casanova, Hitler's powers as a "fakir" also mesmerized English Prime Minister Neville Chamberlain and millions of other Europeans. Hitler and history proved Casanova, Chamberlain and the credulous masses that they had been wrong. After 1939, Casanova was among those who most regretted the consequences of this lapse in judgement.

Finally, she was not the only Spanish writer who admired Germany, whose writings became apocalyptic in tone during the 1930s, and who lost their long-held objectivity. Spain was enmeshed in a passionate family conflict and any attempt at moderation was eventually abandoned. Casanova, like other writers of the Right and Left, did not see her writings as a means of convincing those who held different opinions: she wanted to sound a call of alarm and action to her readers and her government.

Como en la vida

During the 1930s, Casanova's literary output declined somewhat as political writing consumed most of her time. In 1930 *Más que amor* was reissued as *Idilio epistolar*. The novel's passionate tone, and its delicate psychological study of stages in a love affair, had aged well.

In 1931, with the publication of *Como en la vida*, Casanova proved that at the age of seventy, her powers as a novelist had reached a new peak. She may have at one point intended *Como en la vida*, a short novel, to be her last work of fiction. To compose what was nominally a love story, she drew on earlier themes and on different aspects of her long life. *Vida* is the only one of her fictional works that is set both in Galicia's provincial society that she knew so well, and also in Madrid and the great European capitals. Although the main character, Fernando Monforte de Andrade is a man, the unique combination of Galician and Eastern European themes, the tension between Europe and Spain, and between modernity and tradition, clearly reflect Casanova's concerns. In addition, certain characters are based on real people, and parts of the work are clearly autobiographical.

Las catacumbas de Rusia roja

Just as self-contradictory, if perhaps less successful as a novel is its sequel, *Las catacumbas de Rusia roja* (1933), which clearly had more polemic intentions. *Catacumbas* was prefaced by Quevedo's famous lines, long a favorite of Casanova's: ¿No ha de haber un espíritu valiente? / 'Shouldn't there be one brave spirit?'

Clearly, Casanova's book was going to say what she felt about the Russian threat during a time when Russian propaganda was becoming widely disseminated in Spain. Her book presents a ferociously anti-Communist picture of Russia. And as a self-standing sequel to *Como en la vida*, *Catacumbas* is an idiosyncratic combination of anti-Communist *roman a thèse* and romance. It takes up where we left off with Colonel Zarief and Princess Alix Aborin, characters from *Como en la vida*, but takes place entirely in Eastern Europe.

In the heated atmosphere of the 1930s, this anti-Communist novel was a peculiar mirror image of the Socialist Realist novel which was just then evolving into its standard form. The Social Realist novel's goal was to present a perfect image of life in Russia, the workers' paradise. Zarief, the main charactoer in *Catacumbas*, is the White Russian equivalent of the heroic Bolshevik worker-heroes, who quote Lenin as they demolish czarist institutions, and who cheerfully work industrial miracles in farmers' collectives, defense plants and steel factories. In the novel's anti-Bolshevik atmosphere, it is not surprising to find that when one of Stalin's colleagues, Sergei Pawlowicz, commits suicide, he leaves a terse note for his Bolshevik friends, "Me voy asqueado de vosotros." (190) 'I leave sickened by you.' Communist Russia, according to Casanova, was venomous and unredeemable.

Prelude to Disaster

Casanova, with some trepidation, decided in 1933 to spend a few months in Spain after a two-year absence. She noticed many changes, some great and some trifling, and shared them with her readers (*ABC*, 26 October 1933). She worried about the Communist influence in Spain: the Spanish Communist Party, although numerically weak, was organizing. The Comintern sent several "advisers" to Spain for the first time (*ABC*, 1 January 1934).

She had again arrived in time for elections that year. Despite her claims of not being a feminist, she was pleased that for the first time women had the vote and could make a difference in the elections: "En ellas va a oírse la voz de las mujeres, y el porvenir de España. Confianza." (*ABC* 26 October 1933) 'In them one will hear the voice of women, and the future of Spain. Have confidence.'

When the November elections for the *Cortes* (legislative bodies) took place, it became obvious that the newly-enfranchised Spanish women were voting conservatively. This sharp turn to the Right, a natural swing to the opposition party common in the history of established democracies, made the Spanish Left less willing to participate in parliamentary politics.

Part of Spanish public opinion was now polarized between those who admired Hitler, and those who admired Lenin and Stalin. The anniversary of the dissolution of the Inquisition was celebrated by the Left and mourned by the Right. The extreme Left was adopting the clenched fist and the red flag of revolution, while the extreme Right wore blue shirts and extended their arm in the Fascist salute.

In 1933 Hitler had not yet invaded neighboring countries or begun the devastating "Final Solution". Stalin's purges and *gulags* were yet to come. If Casanova and other backers of the Right accepted the "example" of Germany at face value, the Left was happy to spread the good news of "Comrade Stalin" and the "workers' paradise" in its press. Among some groups in Spain, foreign ideology (whether German or Russian) was accepted as ammunition without question or discrimination.

Casanova's writing style changed during this time. The nationalistic rhetoric that swept over the Spanish Right, both in its subtle and its blatant manifestations, had an impact on her style. Casanova had always loved the high-flown and ornate language of the Golden Age, and now imitated the rhetoric of the *Falange*, the party led by the charismatic son of Primo de Rivera, José Antonio. For example, the Falange's anthem's closing lines, and its motto, were "España - una, grande y libre" ("Spain - united, great and free"). Casanova's dream for a Spain that was "indivisible, fuerte, cristiana" (*ABC*, 29 June 1933) 'indivisible, strong, Christian' closely followed this slogan.

When she returned to Poland in 1934 for Christmas, Casanova had much to ponder. She compared the sober but more or less democratic political life of Poland, sternly led by strong-man Piłsudski, to the chaotic political life in Spain. Her country was being overwhelmed by assassinations, church-burnings, strikes, censorship and anarchy from all sides (*ABC*, 10 January 1935).

Even more alarming events occurred in 1935. Hitler was beginning open persecution of Jews. Thousands of German Jews streamed into Poland, throwing Polish anti-Semites into a frenzy, touching off a series of anti-Semitic laws. Casanova knew what the Right could not accept. that millions of Polish Jews could not be expected to leave, if they had no place to go. She noted that in the fourteenth century the Polish king Casimir the Great was granted his name partly because of his generosity to the Jews. She conceded that a tiny minority of troublesome, Communist Jews existed in Poland, but there should be respect and peace for the rest (*ABC*, 31 July 1935).

When Piłsudski died in June 1935, his death was an enormous loss for Poland and for Sofía Casanova. She described the event and the funeral in great detail for *ABC* ("El mariscal de Pilsudski ha muerto, *ABC*, 6 June 1935; "El hombre," 13 June 1935; "Sombra y luz", 6 July 1935, etc.). Column after column mourned him elegiacally. As she feared, the repercussions from his death were felt immediately. There was no other public figure who commanded the respect and power that the Marshal had exacted from the Polish nation. Paderewski had died, Dmowski was not in good health and had retired from public life. The country was swept by a wave of violent anti-Semitism, a series of financial crises and political quandaries.

Every week she reported a new, unpleasant form of discrimination against Jews: Christian medical students, a minority in the University of Warsaw's medical school, demanded Jewish corpses for autopsies (*ABC*, 24 January 1932). At other times side issues such as Jewish ritual slaughter of cattle became the subject of virulent attacks on the Jewish population. She begged the young *Endek* hot-heads to pursue Polish goals without persecuting the Jewish minorities (*ABC* 4 December 1933).

Sometimes Casanova reflected certain stereotypes or prejudices current in Polish society. She thought Jews were "more musical" than other races (*ABC* 21 May 1932), that they controlled world finance (ABC 21 May 1931) and that they owned "ninety-five percent" of all Polish financial institutions (*ABC* 9 April 1932). And by 1936 she thought that Christian morality and the Talmud were "incompatible." But in general her warm, spontaneous and long-standing sympathy for the Jews of Poland remains of Casanova's most admirable and consistent social concerns.

In her seventy-fifth year, Casanova was as active and as energetic as a person twenty years younger. She argued with a new generation of grandchildren that anti-Semitism was unfair and un-Christian, although in 1936 she once weakened her stand and allowed that although violence against Jews was unacceptable, if Poles wanted to boycott Jewish businesses, they could. Nonetheless, her basic sense of fairness and Christian generosity towards the Jews had not failed. She still identified with those "foreigners" in a hostile land. As a realist, she asked their detractors how they expected to replace the indispensable Jews. (*ABC*, 9 April 1936).

News coming out Spain was not good. In the first few months of 1936 there had been more than two hundred political assassinations, almost two hundred church-burnings, over ninety lootings of newspapers and political clubs, and one hundred and thirty-six strikes affecting every sector of Spanish life. There was a marked turn to the Left in the February elections. In a gesture that shocked Casanova, the new government freed all political prisoners and many common criminals. Death and arson spread over Spain. The parties of the Left bitterly fought among themselves over every issue. Commenting on a news agency article that claimed thirty thousand political prisoners had been freed (a greatly exaggerated figure) she hoped that the Right had only lost a battle, and not the war (*ABC*, 19 September 1936). The military, led by Francisco Franco, secretly began to plan a conspiracy to overthrow the Republic.

The articles that Casanova wrote that last year for *ABC* contained all her major themes: philo-Semitism (*ABC*, 9 April 1936), a defense of Spanish culture (*ABC*, 2 April 1936), praise for Poland's Catholic traditions (*ABC*, 21 June 1936), outrage at the Abssinian war (*ABC*, 10 June 1936). Her last regular article for *ABC* (dated 11 July 1936) was ostensibly about the inauguration of a monument to the Polish patriot Kiliński. But since it was written with an eye on the Spanish censors that

143

had again muzzled *ABC* after the elections, its real message was to be read between the lines. It called for a strong leader that a country -- any country -- could rally around. Unknown to her, of course, at that very moment a Spanish "strong man" like the kind she yearned to see in power, was putting the last touches on a plan that would affect Spain for decades to come.

The Spanish Civil War began during the summer of 1936. On July 17, José Calvo Sotelo, the Monarchist leader and head of the parliamentary opposition against the Republic, was assassinated, apparently by forces favorable to the Republican Government. By July 19 the familiar notice imposing censorship appeared in *ABC*, which had fewer pages than usual and no advertisements. There were also some confused notices concerning a military uprising that the government claimed to have defeated. Then *ABC* did not appear again until July 25, when in huge head lines it proclaimed itself *ABC REPUBLICANO*.

Ni rastro queda en este periódico de los que tenaz y astutamente combatieron al regimen que guia a la España nueva...*ABC* (fué) el paladín del privilegio, de la plutocracia y del absolutismo clerical. Este número de la nueva etapa se forja con acuciosa premura, porque nos domina el ansia de ser voceros de la epopeya que escribe el pueblo con gloria inmarcesible...*(ABC,* 25 July 1936).

No trace is left in this newspaper of those who tenaciously and craftily fought the regime that leads the new Spain...*ABC* used to be the champion of privilege, of plutocracy, and of clerical absolutism...This issue of the new stage (of *ABC)* is being put together with eager haste, because we are overcome with the ardent desire to be spokesmen for the epic that the people are writing with unfading glory...

The rhetoric of the Left had supplanted the rhetoric of the Right. The Civil War had begun, and *ABC*, along with Madrid, was in the hands of the Republicans. Casanova's long career as an *ABC* columnist was now over.

Chapter 12

World War II and its Aftermath

Sofía Casanova was so confident of the Nationalists' strength and of the justice of their cause, that she thought the Spanish Civil War would not last long. She and many of her Polish friends and relatives kept up with the news by radio, cheering each Nationalist victory. General Franco became their hero, and *La Cruzada* 'The Crusade' to rescue Spain from the Republicans their personal crusade. Catholic Poland was passionately interested in the Civil War. To the Polish Right, it was a "just" war, without the national self-interest that tainted other European conflicts. Because of the Spanish Left's widely publicized anti-clerical excesses, Catholic Poland as a whole was anti-Republican.

Krysia translated a book by the controversial Cardinal Segura, *El Caso de España*, into Polish. Andrzej Niklewicz translated "Cara al sol" ('Facing the Sun,' the Falange's anthem) into Polish, and taught it to Catholic youth groups. When a Nationalist friend travelled to Spain and wrote an anti-Republican book, *Heroic Spain*, the "Reds" (or "rojillos", as Sofia called them) in the Spanish Embassy protested to the Polish government, and the book was confiscated by the authorities. Nonetheless, Casanova and her circle of friends rejoiced at the free publicity it received (Niklewicz, K. interview). According to her grandson Adalbert Meissner, during these years Casanova worked on a novel, *Juanito - República*. He remembers that she considered the novel (never published, and apparently lost in 1944 during the Warsaw uprising) among her better works.

Bela and her husband, General Wolikowski visited the battlefields of Nationalist Spain for three months in 1936. (Wolikowski apparently went as a representative of the Polish Army). Here they met with General Franco. Franco inquired after Casanova and commended her as "Spain's intellectual ambassador to Eastern Europe" (Niklewicz, K., interview; Wolikowski, R. interview). After their return, Bela travelled all over Poland, speaking about the importance of the *Cruzada*. Mañita and Sofía in Warsaw, and Halita in Posnań, were involved in shipments of clothes, money and bandages to the Nationalists' field hospitals.

Casanova was largely ignorant of the viciousness of the Civil War. She seems to have heard only about some of the incidents and battles against the Nationalists. As the months dragged on and the "Crusade" became a dreary war of attrition, she puzzled over the length of the conflict, which she had thought would be almost instantly won by the Loyalists (Niklewicz, K. interview).

Fulfilling a deeply-held wish, she visited Nationalist Spain and its battle zones in November 1938. Both her brothers had temporarily moved to La Coruña and she stayed with them for a few weeks. She found La Coruña unchanged, and enjoyed being entertained by old friends such as José Luis Bugallal. Early in December she visited the *pazo* where she was born, and had her photograph taken standing on the threshold of its chapel. At seventy-seven she looked somewhat frail but determined (Bugallal *Siglo* 13-14; Niklewicz).

From La Coruña Sofía Casanova went to Burgos where she was received with many honors by General Franco. The *Caudillo* autographed his photograph for his fellow Galician, who took it home to Warsaw and proudly displayed it next to those of the Royal Family and General Primo de Rivera's. Reportedly, Casanova also lectured on the Bolsheviks in San Sebastián and Bilbao during this, her last trip to Spain. She then returned to Poland, to spend the Christmas holidays with her family. She retained this last memory of Spain and of General Franco's warm welcome, for the rest of her long life *(Bugallal Siglo 13-14; Niklewicz).*

August, 1939

It took Hitler's *blitzkrieg* only a month to destroy what it had taken an independent Poland twenty years to build. After years of strained relations with Stalin, Hitler signed a pact of alliance with the Soviet Union, which in its secret clauses divided Poland between the two countries. Casanova left evidence of her early admiration for Hitler, but there is no written record of her reaction to his improbable *volte face* towards her nemesis, Stalin.

Casanova had not written for publication since the takeover of *ABC*. But with the beginning of the German invasion of Poland, on September 1, 1939, she began a series of desperate letters to her brothers in Spain. Since there was no mail service she was not sure they would ever receive them, but she wanted a record of the tense days before another war. She was impressed by the courage of the Polish people, but pessimistic about their ability to fight Germans, their ancestral conquerors. Memories of Warsaw's evacuation in 1915 were still vivid in her mind. Now there would be no escape to the East: Poland was trapped between two enemies.

The mood was intense and apocalyptic. Young Alex Jordan (Tadeusz

146

Alexander Lutosławski, son of Professor Lutosławski and his second wife, Wanda Peszyńska) was in Warsaw during the last few days before the war. In an article written decades later, he described the mood as not one of despair or even of sullen defiance, rather of genuine euphoria fed by the rediscovery of tremendous national unity. Morale was high, as when any group of people share a common danger:

..I recall a party I attended in Warsaw in June 1939. All of us there were approaching twenty, and were members of a class thought effete in many countries, and enjoying more options than most, among them that of leaving the country in time. Juliette de Mesa, the dazzling daughter of a Polish mother and Cuban father, was telling us about the civil war in Spain, where she had volunteered to serve as a nurse with the forces of Francisco Franco. As she described the horrors of the Spanish Civil War, we all knew that our turn was next. We knew that we would soon have to fight for our lives, and we were perhaps better informed about the odds than the general public. It was a challenge we accepted and perhaps even welcomed. I have never seen a more carefree, joyful band of boys and girls; we had plenty of Heidsieck, and there was dancing and singing in Polish and in French, the vernacular of Warsaw society at that time...No one was posturing or pretending, the *joie de vivre* was truly not dimmed by looming danger. (Jordan "Under the Cannon" 1141)

On August 31, 1939, war broke out between Germany and Poland. The Army was mobilized, reservists were called up, and the streets of Warsaw were crowded with hundreds of thousands of people. Sofía Casanova was moved and saddened by the sight of Polish soldiers marching to an almost certain defeat. She once again saw her hopes for peace and harmony evaporate.

By September 8 the Germans were near Warsaw, and began air raids on the city. The sound of sirens and bombs shook the city every night. At the age of seventy-eight, Casanova spent sleepless nights running down the five flights of stairs to the basement of her building during terrifying raids that dwarfed her memories of the first aerial bombings in 1914. She wrote dozens of letters to her brothers from that basement, from the home of the Portuguese Ambassador (a friend who offered to take her in for a few days), and from the homes of other Polish society friends she visited as the buildings shook from explosions and German planes roared over the city:

...agitadas las ideas y la sensibilidad...trozos del pasado, volvían a la mente con negro presentimiento del mañana. ¿Por qué estoy aquí? ¿Por qué? (*Martirio* 33)

...my ideas and sensibilities were shaken...fragments of a past come to mind with dark foreboding about the future. Why am I here? Why?

When she returned home, she spent one last uneasy evening in her private drawing room, her *Hiszpania*, with its works of art, books and furniture from Spain. Her sleep was interrupted by mad flights down to the basement, where dozens of families and neighbors crowded. A mass panic, reminiscent of 1915, had seized Warsaw. The Polish radio broadcast horrifying stories about the cruelty and power of the Germans (*Martirio* 28-29). On the fifth day of the attack, she realized that staying in Warsaw was impossible. Someone had delivered a letter from Halita, begging her to come and stay with her and her children in a villa about forty miles outside of Warsaw: "Ven, te necesito; ven en seguida; ayúdame y trae el retrato del Generalísimo Franco" 'Come, I need you; Come right away; Help me and bring General Franco's portrait.' She again chose a few items, some the same ones she mentioned taking during her flight in 1915: a photograph of her mother, and some books. The only new item was Franco's photograph. She arrived in the village of Grelewo on September 8, 1939 (*Martirio* 36-37).

Halita was staying there with her five children, ranging from five to fifteen (Halita's husband, a doctor, had been mobilized by the Army). For a few days they hid in a rented villa, along with a few other refugees from the capital, whose varied lives and personalities she described in detail. Every night the German *Luftwaffe* bombed the area, forcing them to flee the upper stories and find shelter in the basement. The motley group of displaced persons clustered around the radio, trying to find some hope in the optimistic government broadcasts and barely tolerating one another's foibles.

During the day, those stranded there believed that despite the current desperate situation in Poland, the nation would survive, helped by England and France, and that Poland would be saved. When Casanova disagreed, she was roundly denounced as not having enough faith in Poland's military power. She regretted never being able to share her Polish hosts' incurable optimism, after so many years of sharing their tragic history:

Yo les quito las ilusiones, les soy antipática. Mi destino en Polonia ha sido y es cruel, singularmente al desmentir errores concernientes a España y al intentar curar de ilusiones a los fantaseadores fanáticos del absurdo. Mi 'pesimismo' --dicen proprios y ajenos-- se considera como desconocimiento de todas las magnitudes históricas y políticas de Polonia. Sin embargo, yo...

I take away their illusions, they find me disagreeable. My fate in

148

Poland has been and continues to be cruel, particularly when I contradict errors about Spain, and when I try to cure fanatical dreamers of the absurdity of their ilusions. My 'pessimism' - say family and others - is considered ignorance of Poland's historical and political greatness. Still, I... (*Martirio 55*)

During the day soldiers and civilians would stop by their villa and give them the latest news. Some claimed that Germans had given parts of Poland to the Soviets. This was dismissed out of hand as an impossible rumor.

For Casanova, these days spent stranded in an obscure country villa among boarders she did not know, without real news or contact with the world, were almost worse the siege of Warsaw. At one point they ran out of food. She was haunted by memories of her war experiences, of the evacuation to Minsk and Moscow, of the Russian Revolution, even by stories she had read about the Spanish Civil War. Then the radio broadcasts ceased: Warsaw had fallen to the Nazis.

Late one night, without bloodshed or drama, a German artillery division arrived and took over their villa. Their group was allowed to stay for the moment. A few hours later they heard that Poland had surrendered (*Martirio* 66-67).

Casanova, Halita and the rest of the family stayed through the beginning of October. There were rumors that Warsaw had been razed. Sofía Casanova was desperate to see Krysia, her favorite grand-child. Against Halita's passionate protests, she rented a peasant's wagon and returned to the city by herself, to find Krysia and her brother Andrzej, who had also stayed behind. Returning to Warsaw on a cold and rainy fall day, she found that the Germans had devastated district after district. Nonetheless, most of the city was still standing. Their apartment house had been hit directly by a bomb and one hundred and twenty of their neighbors had been killed. Miraculously, Krysia and her brothers Andrzej and Konrad were unharmed. But their apartment, including all of Casanova's books, works of art and mementos collected over a lifetime of achievement and travel, had been destroyed (*Martirio* 73-74).

As the situation stabilized, Mañita also returned to Warsaw with her children. Drozdowo had fallen into Soviet hands once again, and they had been given two hours to leave their ancestral home in the hands of the Bolsheviks. Casanova and the Niklewiczes rented a large apartment, and tried to carry on with their lives. From her window, Casanova wrote to her family in Spain, she could see that Warsaw was suddenly overrun with Nazi flags (*Martirio* 87). Having been politically active all his life, Mieczyslaw Niklewicz immediately became involved with the underground against the Germans. Bela and Halita's husbands, both in the Polish Army, had fled the country, and the sisters faced the hardships of occupation alone, with the responsibility of their families. Sensitive and talented Bela narrowly missed being sent to a Siberian prison by the Soviets and managed to escape into the German section of Poland. Pobre Bela mía. Vuelve desconocida, con dolor de cada fibra de su

> cuerpo y de su alma. Quiere reponerse pronto y trabajar como una obrera en una fábrica. Los niños, aturdidos, pero fuertes, dan ánimo a la madre. (*Martirio* 84)

My poor Bela. She has returned a stranger, with sorrow in every fiber of her body and soul. She wants to recover soon and go to work in a factory. The children, bewildered, but strong, give their mother courage.

Bela's exiled husband, General Romuald Wolikowski, as the head of the Polish Mission to Russia, was to be instrumental in rescuing more than one hundred thousand war prisoners from Russian prisons and labor camps. But Bela was not to to see him again until she left Poland in 1950. (Cormack; Niklewicz)

Since Hitler's Germany and Franco's Spain had diplomatic relations, Sofía Casanova was able to write home. An unexpected blow came almost immediately. After sending *ABC* an article describing the brutal German occupation and its effects on daily life, Casanova received polite but firm directions from Madrid. *ABC* would not print any article that had anti-Nazi topics or comments. Thunderstruck, Casanova chose to remain silent for the rest of the war (Niklewicz; Meissner).

She also received word that Francisco Franco was taking a personal interest in her case, and offered to repatriate her (*Martirio* 17). She declined reluctantly but gratefully, writing to the Spanish Ambassador in Berlin that her health prevented her from travelling, but that she would appreciate his protection. In return, the Ambassador sent her an official notice to fasten on her door, stating that her home was under special diplomatic custody. Also thanks to the Embassy's intervention, they were allowed to shop in stores reserved for German officers. This was a way to fend off starvation, yet in occupied Warsaw it carried with it a heavy moral price for a family of committed Nationalists. To Mañita's great shame, in order to feed her large family, she had to be seen entering the hated enemy stores.

Despite these few benefits, daily life was grim and unpleasant. The Nazis plundered Poland, taking from it foodstuffs, industrial equipment, cattle, and manpower. And in a short time, they established six concentration camps in Poland, to exterminate Polish and European Jews,

150

Christian Poles and any number of other groups of people. Could Roman Dmowski, who had died in 1939, have ever dreamt that when his proposed "solution" of the Jewish problem in Poland was finally implemented as part of Hitler's "final solution," it would involve the death of millions of his own people?

One million Polish citizens were sent to work camps in the Soviet Union. Others, including as Mañita's son Ryszard Niklewicz, were sent to concentration camps in Germany. During those dark days, Casanova lived with Mañita and her family in Warsaw: Pepa stayed in Posnań with Halita and her children.

In June 1941, Hitler turned against his erstwhile ally Stalin, and invaded the Soviet Union. To Casanova's disgust, Spain sent forty-seven thousand soldiers, many of them Falange aristocrats, to support Germany and fight Stalin in the *División Azul* 'Blue Division,' so called because of their uniforms' color. They left Spain in July of 1941, came through Warsaw, and by the hundreds flocked in to visit Sofía Casanova, to pay tribute to the famous *ABC* correspondent whose pre-Civil War columns they had admired. She was appalled to see Spaniards wearing the hated Nazi uniform, and tried to dissuade them from fighting for Hitler's forces, but they were adamant and enthusiastic.

When only a few hundred survivors straggled back several months later, as the war turned against Germany, the *División* gallantly offered Casanova an opportunity to return to Spain with them. Again she declined, but asked them to take her grandson Andrzej Wolikowski, then sixteen, to join his father abroad (Niklewicz, K. interview).

At the age of eighty, Sofía Casanova was still spry and resourceful. The entire Niklewicz family was involved in the Underground against the Nazis, and she helped as much as she could. They held clandestine meetings regularly in their home, helped by the clearly-stated diplomatic immunity the Spanish Embassy had unwittingly given her. Whenever a 'Blue Division' friend stopped to say good-bye on the way to Spain, the elderly and aristocratic Casanova would improbably ask them for their gun "as a keepsake." A surprising number agreed to this, never knowing that Sofía and Mañita would turn their handguns over to the underground Polish Home Army.

When the Warsaw Insurrection began on August 1, 1944, the population of the city fought the Germans for sixty-three days. Casanova fled to Drozdowo with Halita, Pepa, and the children (although in a state of genteel disrepair, the main building of the estate had come back into the hands of the family). During the insurrection, Bela lost her other son, Grzegorz Wolikowski, shot by the Germans in the streets of Warsaw.

Another generation of Polish men was dying as part of the "human sacrifice" that history claimed from Poland. The city (or what was left of it after the air raids of 1939, the destruction of the Ghetto in 1943, and five years of occupation) was systematically razed, block by block, even after the cease-fire and deportation of most of its inhabitants.

At the age of eighty-five, almost blind, and under harsh conditions, Sofía Casanova continued to write. She had to devise a special system to focus her dimming eyes. She clipped her paper to a piece of cardboard ("el cartoncito") and held it at a distance in mid-air with her left hand as she wrote with her right (A. Meissner, letter, n. d., ca. December 1988). Early in June, 1944, a single article by Sofía Casanova appeared, with no comment, on the lead page of *ABC*. It was dated from Warsaw, in the spring of the same year. Without mentioning the Nazi occupation, Casanova described the tension that gripped the city. But spring was near, she wrote, and men couldn't change that. "El tiempo manda...y los hombres no pueden detener al sol en su ruta...la primavera llegará...(*ABC* 6 June 1944) 'Time is the ruler...and men can't stop the sun on its journey...Spring will arrive...' The article indicted war and predicted the end of Nazi rule, without any overt political statement. Despite its positive message, its tone was one of deep sadness if not resignation.

When it seemed that Poland could take no more punishment, the Conference of Yalta in 1945 allowed Russia to settle accounts with its old possession, Poland. By 1947 the country was a Soviet satellite. The "Cold War" had begun and the Iron Curtain fell around Poland, stranding Casanova behind it.

Sofía Casanova was completely cut off from the West and out of touch with Spain, which did not have diplomatic relations with Communist Poland. She was silenced by the Polish Communist government, which warned her that she could not be published either in Poland or abroad. Casanova's advanced age and nationality may have saved her from greater problems, but her daily life (and her family's) was subject to the same indignities as other Polish citizens -- prying neighbors, inflexible bureaucrats, constant fear of interrogation or prision, substandard and degrading living conditions, continual worries about food and government interference. One can only guess at her and her family's reaction to the deeply unsympathetic Russian occupation, which now appeared permanent. Twenty years of Polish independence had been an aberration, and they had were back to ignoble pre-1915 conditions.

Now it was Catholic Poland's turn to dismay Francoist Spain with its plight as a Communist satellite. In post-war Spain, Sofía Casanova, depicted with sympathy in newspaper and magazine articles, acquired the air of a mythical figure. Much was made of her being marooned behind the Iron Curtain. *ABC* reportedly received hundreds of letters inquiring after her fate.

To Casanova's surprise, shortly after the end of the war someone in Spain, who was apparently not authorized by her or her family (and who added to her political troubles with the Communist authorities), published the letters that she had written to her Spanish family in Madrid. Adalbert Meissner had typed the letters into manuscript form and sent the manuscript to the Casanovas in Madrid by a circuitous route. The letters, titled "Polvo de escombros" 'Dust from Ruins,' make up the first half of the book *El martirio de Polonia*, published in Madrid in 1945.

Casanova's anguished personal narrative contrasts with the book's more objective second half, written by a "Miguel Branicki", apparently a pseudonym for a member of one of the great Polish families. The book sold well enough to go into a second edition in 1946.

In 1947 her brother Vicente died in Madrid. She could write only with great difficulty, since she was almost totally blind by now, but sent occasional letters to friends and relatives in Spain. Although they had last seen each other in 1938, José Luis Bugallal in La Coruña proved to be a faithful correspondent. She would write him long letters inquiring about La Coruña, Madrid, Galicia. She longed to read the work of the new, post-war novelists, poets, and playwrights. Very occasionally she received reading matter from Spanish visitors to Warsaw, which her daughters would read to her. She wrote him of her heartbreak when Bela left Poland forever in 1950, to join her husband and son in France, and then settled with them in remote Alberta, Canada (Bugallal 17). That April both Pepa and Dr. Meissner, Halita's husband, died in Posnań.

Life passed by very slowly. She lived with Halita, Halita's daughter and two children. As she wrote to Bugallal in 1955:

> Si te contara la atmósfera asfixiante en que vivo, mis privaciones del intelecto y del cuerpo, os conmovería, y no puedo hacerlo, no lo haría si tuviera libertad, para no entristeceros...(Bugallal *Siglo* 18)
> If I told you about the suffocating atmosphere in which I live, of my intellectual and physical deprivation, it would move you, and I can't do it, nor would I do it if I had freedom, as not to sadden you...

Her great-grandson Piotr Niklewicz, born to Riczard Niklewicz and his wife in 1944, remembers these last years. During the early fifties, Sofía Casanova would spend the summers in Drozdowo with Mañita and the rest of the family:

> Altogether she seemed to have her own life, distant from us children, but also from the other residents of (Drozdowo). It was an old, large

153

manor house, always full of guests. My grandmother (Mañita) often said she fully appreciated her luck to be able to keep this house in spite of all the political changes in Poland...these were the times of Joseph Stalin! She felt it her obligation to share it with her less lucky family and friends. And so she did.

Sofía Casanova took part only superficially in the social life of Drozdowo. I remember her sitting in a remote part of the garden, in the shade of an old tree, reading, or just deep in her thoughts. She was highly esteemed by the others. She always had the best place at the table...the best peaches from the tree growing in front of the house were given...to Sofía Casanova and her friend Elżbieta Balicka (both in their eighties). Although we all knew she was a poet, this rarely was the topic of conversation at the table. My family and their friends...were more down to earth, not much literary or artistically oriented.

During the late 1940s and early 1950s, Casanova had a last burst of poetic inspiration. From her youth she remembered favorite poems by Rosalía: "A solas repito: airiños, aires...A tientas copio alguno pedazos de *Vida*, de mis recuerdos y cantares, versos de ayer y de hoy... (Bugallal *Siglo* 20) 'All alone I repeat: airiños, aires...Blindly I copy extracts from *Vida*, from my memories and songs, verses from yesterday and today.'

Her *Poesías Inéditas* contain poignant evidence that she meditated on the end of a romantic relationship. Was it Wincenty Lutosławski, Alfredo Vicenti or some other old love that she wrote about in "La bondad del tiempo" 'The kindness of Time?' "Te perdí en el vacío / me has perdido en el tiempo / y el pasado no existe / cuando muere el recuerdo / come estrella caída de los cielos" "I lost you in the void / you lost me in Time / and the past doesn't exist / when remembrance dies / as a star fallen from the heavens.' (*Inédita*)[9]

She wrote to Bugallal in 1955 that "una crisis íntima me acaba en la soledad y el hondo descontento de cuanto me rodea" ("A personal crisis weakens me in my loneliness and my deep discontent with all that surrounds me"). This "personal crisis" was perhaps Wincenty Lutosławski's last illness: he died in Cracow on 28 December, 1955 (Bugallal *Siglo* 18; *New York Times Obituary*, 5 January 1955). After his second wife's death some months earlier (which in Casanova's mind lessened the immediacy of his state of mortal sin), they had corresponded and agreed to forgive and forget. But their reconciliation (if one can call it that) came too late. They were each too old and too sick to travel, and he died without seeing Casanova again (Niklewicz, K. interview).

In 1952, through a letter from Bela in Canada, Sofía Casanova learned that the Royal Academy of Galicia had named her, on April 16, an "Académico de Honor". She wept when she heard that she was still remembered and honored in her native province, and wrote to Bugallal:

...te estoy escribiendo...para que expreses a esos nobles...amigos, mi emoción y my gratitud. Yo, una personalidad escondida, no puedo ni escribir ni hablar, sostenida por quienes no me olvidan. ¿Mi obra? Incompleta, desgarrada -- como mi vida -- por íntimos dolores y guerras. ¿Mis versos? Dispersos, perdidos...Gracias de corazón y con vosotros siempre mi alma. (Bugallal *Siglo* 21)

'I am writing to you...so that you can express to those noble...friends, my emotions and gratitude. I, a hidden personality, cannot write or speak, (but) am sustained by those who don't forget me. My work? Incomplete, torn -- like my life -- by intimate sorrows and wars. My poetry? Scattered, lost...Thanks from the heart and I am with you always...'

As Casanova grew older her inner life became more serene. Bugallal was touched to read in one of her letters that, while blind and suffering so many indignities and deprivations, she constantly thanked God for all the graces He conceded her (Bugallal *Siglo* 20). As she readied herself for the next life she so fervently believed in, she decided she wanted to die and be buried in Spain. In 1957 Halita wrote to Bugallal that she was still trying to get Sofía, now ninety-five, to Galicia. But the complex diplomatic maneuvers took too long.

The winter of 1957 was an unusually cold one in Europe. For the first time in decades, Sofía Casanova was ill and not able to dress up and celebrate the New Year with friends and family. "Mal empezamos el año" ("We are beginning the year on the wrong foot"), she told Halita. She developed bronchitis, and then pneumonia. She entered a Catholic hospital, and there wrote a last, jovial letter to Bela in Canada, telling her about the excellent care she was receiving, telling her that she had died and gone to heaven, and found angels wearing nurses' uniforms. But she must have also been afraid, for she wrote herself a little note: "Vamos, Sofía, hay que ir adelante, aunque por caminos tempestuosos." 'Come, Sofía, we must go on, even through stormy roads.'

She knew it would be her last illness and that she would never go back home.[10] She serenely tried to console a grieving Halita: "Sé que voy a morir: no llores, Halita, no llores." 'I know that I am going to die: don't cry, Halita, don't cry.'

Lucid to the end, she died on January 16, 1958, thanking Halita and the other family members that surrounded her bed for their care. She was buried far away from Galicia, on a bitterly cold but sunny Posnań morning, as she had foreseen over seventy years before:

Porque presiento que nunca
Veré el cielo de mi tierra,
Ni han de sollozar sus brisas
En mi tumba solitaria! (*Poesías 15*)
For I have a premonition that
I will never see the skies of my native land,
and that its breezes will not weep
on my solitary tomb!

Conclusion

Casanova's accomplishments earn her a unique place in Spanish history and letters. She was "the only Spanish female" (or male) reporter to cover not only World War I but the Russian revolution, as well as World War II and its aftermath. Throughout her long life she garnered a long series of achievements and 'firsts' that brought her into contact with significant political and literary figures, who often enthusiastically supported her efforts.

One measure of a writer's greatness is his or her ability to transcend personal, cultural and historical limitations. Sofía Casanova was born into perhaps the most regressive and patriarchal society in Europe. It is startling to realize how much support Casanova enjoyed, unlike other Spanish women writers (such as Pardo Bazán and Concha Espina). Her talents as a poet, writer and journalist were recognized from her earliest years. Perhaps her beauty, modesty and social connections enhanced her value with traditionalists. In any case, after her marriage in 1887, geographical distance and financial independence helped her to transcend some of the limitations imposed on women by Spanish society.

There are at least two areas in which Casanova's contributions to Spanish culture are unmistakable, and in which she succeeded. First, for more than seven decades she was one of the few conduits of information between Spain and Poland, and a passionate advocate for each country. In addition, as a Spanish foreign correspondent she was an outspoken opponent of war and one of the first women in Spain to express the belief that it was up to women to avert war.

There are other areas where Casanova was not able to overcome the limitations that her cultural and historical background imposed on her. She was torn between her resentment of the way Spanish women were treated and her ambivalence towards feminism, a lack of ease which is reflected in her novels and which affected their quality and their success. Finally, Casanova's slow progression from liberal and progressive humanitarian ideas, to her final embrace of Fascism and Franco after 1936 ended her lifetime role as a more or less non-conformist woman's voice within the ranks of the Monarchist press.

Sofía Casanova: A Link between Spain and Poland

Since the Renaissance, Polish intellectuals and artists have been interested in Spain -- but the same cannot be said of their Spanish counterparts. Traditionally, there has been little knowledge of Poland and its affairs in the Spanish peninsula. Information about Poland, and attitudes about its culture and art, have often been filtered through France, a country that sheltered the great Polish emigrations of the nineteenth and twentieth centuries.

Before Casanova's time, only one individual, Dr. Józef Leonard, a Polish émigré living in Madrid, had actively bridged the gap between Spain and Poland. Dr. Leonard, a teacher of the young Rubén Darío in Nicaragua, was actively involved in Spanish intellectual life between 1868 and 1881. He became foreign editor of *La Gaceta de Madrid*, the government's official paper, he wrote for the progressive *Revista de España* and was associated with the Institución Libre de Enseñanza in its earliest stages.

Apparently unwittingly, Casanova succeeded Leonard in his position as a literary and journalistic link between the two cultures. She also upheld some of the progressive, anti-authoritarian political stands he had advocated. Before World War I, Casanova seems to have been the only Spaniard keeping the "Polish Question" before the Spanish public. As ardent a nationalist as any Polish citizen, she insisted that her articles for *ABC* be titled "Desde Polonia," even though the partitioned country did not exist as one entity at that time.

Casanova spent a great deal of time before 1919 reminding Spain that Poland still existed, as she liked to put it "in the hearts of her people," despite the country's subjugation by three invaders. Her articles brought the harsh realities of life in Eastern Europe to the attention of Spanish public opinion. Casanova sent reports about the daily executions of Polish patriots, descriptions of the censorship imposed on Poland by the brutal Russian military, and a sense of the unhealthy social atmosphere bred by oppression (*Exóticas* 35).

Casanova saw only one side of the Polish-Russian dilemma, and presented only one side (that of Polish nationalism) to her Spanish readers. Catholic Poland's peculiar situation among its Slavic, non-Catholic oppressors, made her confuse Polish feelings of superiority vis à vis other nations with the highest tenets of Western civilization. She shrugged off evidence that over the centuries Poland had threatened Russian hegemony, and taken away parts of Russia, siding with Russia's enemies.

Hand-in-hand with her one-sided Russo-Polish view of the conflict, her writing reflects the fact that Poland, open to the west, considered the Russians "Asiatic barbarians," and bitterly resented these less-educated invaders. The Russians were indeed less cultured than the Poles when they conquered their land. Poles saw themselves as the champions of Europe

158

against Eastern (what Casanova called "Asian") barbaric hordes. Most Poles, educated or not, viewed Russia with a mixture of contempt and aversion, and so did Sofía Casanova.

Over the centuries, Roman Catholicism had brought to Poland the Latin language, literature, art and philosophy, leaving a legacy that Casanova identified with and defended against Slavonic "foreign" influence. Casanova was thrilled whenever she found any connection between the Catholic cultures of Spain and Poland. She wrote to polymath Don Marcelino Menéndez y Pelayo in 1903 to let him know about the publication by the Cracow Academy of Sciences of an edition of the Latin works of the Spanish Renaissance humanist, Pedro Ruiz de Moros (Ruiz de Moros had lived and taught in Poland during the sixteenth century when Poland and Spain had intellectual relations). She was just as proud to report the finding of a seventeenth-century statue of a Spanish Virgin of Guadalupe, worshiped by Polish Catholics in her own times ("La virgen de Guadalupe y la de Koden," *ABC* 19 June, 1924).

On the other hand, Casanova's understanding of Russian Orthodox religious practices, of Russian society and of Slavic culture in general, can at best be described as deficient and condescending, at worst biased and heavy-handed. In *El doctor Wolski*, *Sobre el Volga helado*, *Exóticas* and *Las catacumbas de Rusia roja*, Casanova's contempt for Russian culture and manners emerges as proof of her prejudice. For her, as for many Poles, Russia was embodied in its worst ambassadors, the *niekulturny* ("uncultured") military invaders. Everything Russian, beginning with its "coarse peasant food," was objectionable: Russian manners were described as servile (*Wolski* 10), and Anna Karenina as a "typically adulterous" Russian woman (*Guerra* 265). Russian Orthodoxy is frequently dismissed as primitive, hollow and full of pagan excesses (*Viajes* 58-59). It should not surprise us that she found Soviet orthodoxy to be equally violent, anti-religious and debased (*Catacumbas* 193-194), since she found its source within the depths of Russian culture. It was this one-sided image of Russia and Communism that she disseminated in Spain between 1919 and 1936.

A Radical Pacifist

Casanova is unique among her Spanish peers because of her outspoken pacifism. Her beliefs stemmed from a combination of radical Catholic ideals and her proto-feminist convictions. Casanova's thinking went beyond condemning war simply because it was evil. In addition to her Christian belief that war and killing were proscribed by her religion, she clearly linked violence and aggression to masculinity, and urged women as a group actively to oppose war.

Casanova was a Catholic radical and idealist, a deeply religious thinker who read the Gospels and believed she understood their moral imperatives. "Thou shalt not kill," or "All men are brothers" were not simply maxims, but powerful imperatives of conduct among people. Christian ethics were one of the few forces in daily life that kept society from degenerating into chaos. "En estos horrores de la guerra, el Cristianismo se ahoga en sangre" (*Guerra* 20) 'Amid these horrors of war, Christianity drowns in blood,' she wrote.

On the other hand, as Casanova knew from her experiences abroad, during the early part of the century the issue of peace had been added to traditional feminist concerns. By 1914 peace had become an important topic in international women's circles, awakening women to their responsibility to promote peace. International women's organizations established committees and held international conferences on the subject, and peace became a major feminist issue (there is no evidence that Casanova was involved in any of these activities, but she was aware of them through the press and through personal contacts).

When war broke out in 1914, earlier feminist gains enabled French, English and American women to nurse the wounded, drive ambulances and jeeps, organize other women,, and in general support the war effort. It is well known that a smaller number of American and British women took a public stance opposing the war, and wrote about their beliefs.

Spain, however, remained neutral during the war, and Spanish women remained at home -- with the exception of Sofía Casanova. Casanova was an articulate and compassionate pacifist whose credibility was enhanced by her service as a Sister of Charity and by her position as a widely-read war correspondent. She had a significant impact on public opinion, drawing enormous attention to her ideas and herself. Almost single-handedly, and without aligning herself to any party, she confronted the evils of war and tried to inspire Spanish women to take up their responsibilities to achieve peace.

As a woman, she refused to accept what she called the "science" of gaining land or commercial power, through the death of other human beings (*Guerra* 127). It was clear to her that women were closer to the teachings of compassion, and that they held the key to the future through their influence. She bitterly noted that "masculine heroics" were much more popular than what she called her feminine objectivity, and that her true descriptions of the horrors of war were less palatable than patriotic rhetoric. She called male dominance of society "ley natural" 'natural law'

160

but chafed under its rule. However, her most daring suggestion for women to advance anti-war views was a call to "women everywhere" to show a white banner or scarf in public -- certainly not a call to militancy (*Rev. Rus.* 29).

Two decades after World War I, she still exhorted women to combat warfare and militarism. She believed that if women were more active in the political process, public life would be far more humane ("Condicionalmente," 1 Aug., 1931) After wars, she noted, it was women who survived, and who paradoxically suffered more. Women didn't want war, and would always oppose it: she spoke for the mothers of the thirteen million men who had died in World War I ("Los sabios y la guerra". 13 Sept., 1933).

Sofía Casanova: A Paradigm for Feminine Consciousness

Like Cecilia Böhl de Faber, Rosalía de Castro and countless other Spanish women before her, Sofía Casanova was deeply torn between her allegiance to the traditional society around her, and her feelings of creative autonomy and self-expression. Spain had moved towards the emancipation of women much more slowly than other European countries. From the 1860s to the 1890s, and later on after World War I, while women elsewhere were fighting for equal educational opportunities and the right to vote, Spanish women were largely uneducated and politically inert. Although feminism was mentioned (usually derisively) in the Spanish press, there was an almost total lack of interest in the subject among Spanish women until the 1920s.

In this cautious context, and given Casanova's anomalous position within Spanish society, it is not surprising that she eschewed feminism and that she publicly deplored what she called the excesses of suffragettes, whose "antics" alienated both men and women from what she considered the true message of feminism -- that women should have equal opportunities to contribute to society. But as even as she criticized suffragettes, she would praise the efforts of emancipated Polish women who worked outside of the home and helped build the Polish nation, but remained excellent wives and mothers and did not lose sight of their feminine responsibilities (*Volga* 36).

Less obvious are the mechanisms through which Casanova unconsciously expressed her deep estrangement from the way Spanish society impeded the development of women. Through what a psychologist could call displacement, she created pallid, submissive, almost masochistic heroines (Mara in *El doctor Wolski*, Princess Alix Aborin in *Catacumbas*, Consuelo in *Lo eterno*, Blanca in *Como en la vida*) whose unhealthy passivity reflected her visceral but repressed understanding of the real situation of women in Spain. These characters' submission to the dominant male, their unhappiness and sometimes even their death, reflect her resentment of the patriarchal ways that she had escaped, that she could not bring herself to criticize directly to her audience, and even to herself.

"España heroica"

Although by temperament she was a progressive thinker, a champion of the underdog, a defender of women and a pacifist, Sofia Casanova was also by birth a member of the Catholic, nationalist and monarchist class that ruled Spain until 1936. After 1898 her patriotism became even more noticeable, and informed all her writings.

But Casanova was torn between the demands of this patriotism, and her desire for social justice. There is in Casanova's works a tension between her impulse to venerate Spain and her desire to right its social and political wrongs. Passionate as she was about her country, her comparisons of "España privilegiada" 'privileged Spain' with the industrious and politically aware Polish citizenry are obvious and pointed.

Despite her tendencies towards political independence, at the end of her life Casanova remained solidly within the ranks of the Right. Although she regretted the effects that the Civil War had on the Spanish people and could not understand Franco's support of the Nazis, she admired him personally and backed the Loyalists against the Republic. During her sad last years, an official non-person in the oppressive atmosphere of Communist Poland, Franco's Spain appeared to her as a beacon in the "darkness" that had fallen over the rest of Europe. As she wrote in a sonnet that *ABC* published in 1957:

> Del hoy la vida es duda y es lamento,
> sangra la noche, es negro el firmamento,
> la ley es odio, la verdad terror,
> la paz es guerra, la victoria triste
> mas en España existe
> de Europa la conciencia y el honor.
> Today life is doubt and lament,
> the night bleeds, the skies are black
> hatred is law, truth terror,
> peace is war, and victory sorrowful;

but the conscience and honor of Europe
endure in Spain (*ABC*, 2 April 1957).

Final Subjects

What ultimately makes Casanova a subject worthy of study lies beyond
these political issues. The evidence of her long and successful professional
career reminds us that our perceptions of the role of women in Spain's
past have been distorted by the repression of the Franco years, and also
by our own contemporary reactions against anything the Francoist
establishment claimed to value. We must take another look at the
stereotypes of the past and examine literary topics and personalities that
would have been considered nonexistent or unsympathetic as recently as
fifteen years ago, in order to find their real content and values.

Casanova's unique life and personality, full of adventure and drama,
are reflected in her literary works. Perhaps this is why the works that
most reflect her personality (*Más que amor, Viajes, Como en la vida*), are
the ones that stand up best to the test of time. During her long and
productive life, Sofía Casanova created a literary corpus that merits
renewed scrutiny. She was a fluent, able and perceptive writer in almost
every genre that she attempted. We have yet to collect all her poetic
works, and place them in the greater context of Spanish poetry.

"Life is stranger than fiction," Sofia Casanova's granddaughter
Krystina Niklewicż would say about her grandmother's unique life. Sofía
Casanova's career in Spain was strongly influenced by one accidental but
all-important encounter with her future husband, Wincenty Lutosławski
when she was in her early twenties.

That one crucial event and subsequent marriage took her out of her
native land and helped launch a life driven by innate energy and enter-
prise. Stimulated by the events around her, she made studied choices that
led her to self-definition and allowed her to follow her passionate desire
to make a contribution to her adopted country, to her homeland, and to the
world. Casanova chose to retain her links to Poland. She chose to be there
when World War broke out, she volunteered to work as a nurse in a
hospital. She willingly took on unpopular causes in her articles for the
Spanish press, and later on she again chose to remain in Poland after
World War II. Her life and her works bear the examples of many of her
bold decisions and her unflagging commitment to her ideas.

In Casanova's vast journalistic output, still mostly uncollected and largely unexamined, we can see the activity of a curious, energetic and insightful thinker. Her sense of fairness led her to take public stands that were unpopular, but which she felt she had to take. Scrutinizing a wide range of societies, concepts and ideologies, she gave her Spanish audience her honest and sincere analysis, which encompassed both the negative and the positive: Russian barbarism, Polish anti-Semitism, women's responsibility to avert war, Spain's relative backwardness and its potential for greatness: all these were grist for her mill.

Spain was such a central part of Casanova's identity and experience that she could have said, like Unamuno, "Me duele España" 'Spain hurts me'. By a whim of fate, she lived almost her entire life away from her country, cut off from her cultural roots. She tried to live out her long isolation with dignity and courage. Like many expatriate authors, she succeeded in creating an experience, a continuity and a literary oeuvre out of the disparate elements available to her. In her literary work, in her allegiance to Spain and in her devotion to her family, she found the stability and commitment necessary for a meaningful life.

Yet toward the end of her life, Sofia Casanova felt that she had failed. In her old age, she despaired at having been cut off from her audience, without the sense of fulfillment achieved by many writers at the end of their careers. Used to constant communication with Spain during a lifetime abroad, her enforced silence made obscurity even more excruciating (Bugallal *Siglo* 21).

From a larger perspective, Casanova felt that she had failed at her idealistic goals of warning Spain about Bolshevism, of stimulating her country out of its apathy, of improving social conditions, and of defending Spain against its detractors abroad. Despite her Herculean efforts, she was not able to spare her countrymen from the horrors she had witnessed in other countries. She felt she had failed to contribute significantly towards resolving Spain's social problems, and that she had been unable to promote the social and human values that she held dear. One could argue that the fault lay in Spanish public opinion, since Casanova had done her part in alerting it. But that did not assuage her sense of failure.

All of Casanova's work is informed by an underlying passion: she wanted to educate Spain, to enlighten her country, to improve it so that it could fulfill what she viewed as its rightful destiny of greatness. Casanova tried for decades to carry out this self-imposed mandate. Her heroic efforts may not have yielded the return she sought, but we think more of her rather than less, because of the sheer audacity of her desire and ambitions.

Finally, we must recognize that beyond the many features that made

Casanova a remarkable woman for her times, there are other traits that contributed to the high quality of her work. The humanitarian feelings that tempered her vision, and the honesty with which she wrote, give her writing a universality that transcends politics. Casanova had two unflagging passions: to defend the oppressed and to tell the truth as she saw it.

Her identification with the underdog (the poor, women, the Polish nation, the Jewish people) gave her work its universality and its enduring interest. In addition, her commitment to seeking out the truth in the face of propaganda or unyielding tradition informs her entire career as a writer. We hope that in spite of the obscurity imposed upon her works until very recently, new generations of scholars will certainly recognize her uniqueness and through future analysis enrich our understanding of her work and ideas.

It is fitting to close with a quote from her poem, "Visión," that reflects the essence of her sorrowful witness to the failings of humankind. Casanova expected much from humanity, and was often distressed by human imperfection. Hers was a dark vision of humanity:

Si demasiadas sombras tiene este cuento,
perdonad: viste luto mi pensamiento.
(Fugaces 125-129)

If this story has too many shadows,
Forgive: my thoughts are dressed in mourning.

Notes

1. For Spanish encyclopedia articles, see "Casanova de Lutosławski (Sofía)," *Enciclopedia Universal Ilustrada Europeo-Americana*, 1912 ed.; See also "Pérez de Eguía Casanova, Sofía," *Enciclopedia Gallega. Vol. II. Diccionario Bio-Bibliográfico de Escritores*, 1953. Two literary histories that do include information on Sofía Casanova are: José María de Cossío, *Cincuenta años de poesía española (1859-1950)* (Madrid: Espasa-Calpe, S. A., 1962); Federico Carlos Saínz de Robles, *Ensayo de un diccionario de literatura. Tomo II. Escritores españoles y latinoamericanos* (Madrid: Aguilar, 1964).

For recent bio-bibliographical accounts of Sofía Casanova and her works see: Janet Pérez, *Contemporary Women Writers of Spain* (Boston: Twayne Publishers, 1988) 19-21; Carolyn L. Galerstein, ed. *Women Writers of Spain. An Annotated Bio-bibliographical Guide* (Greenwood Press: New York, Connecticut, London, 1986) 69-72.

María del Carmen Simón Palmer has recently done bibliographical research on Casanova. See "Tres escritoras españolas en el extranjero," *Cuadernos Bibliográficos*, XLVII (1987): 157-180; See also "Sofía Casanova, autora de La Madeja," *Actas del Tercer Congreso Internacional de Estudios Galdosianos, II* (Las Palmas: Exmo. Cabildo Insular de Gran Canaria, 1990) 569.

For a recent reissue of Casanova's articles written during the Russian Revolution see: M. Victoria López-Cordón, ed. *Sofía Casanova. La revolución bolchevista (Diario de un testigo).* (Madrid: Editorial Castalia, Biblioteca de escritoras, 1989).

2. I will follow common Spanish usage throughout this book and call Rosalía de Castro "Rosalía," while referring to Sofía Casanova by her last name.

3. "El intruso," a short story about one of the thousands of derelicts that crowded into Russian cities during the winter, seems to have been first published during this period. It was later collected in *De Rusia* (1927)

4. For further information on Lady Caroline Fitzgerald, see: David J. O'Donoghue. *The Poets of Ireland. A Biographical Dictionary with Bibliographical Particulars.* Published by the Author (London, 1892-3). O'Donoghue describes Fitzgerald as being "an Irish-American poetess, now Lady Edmund Fitzmaurice," and lists her as author of *Venetia Victrix, and other Poems* (London & Edinburgh, 1889) 74.

5. We have not been able to locate these items.

6. Sofia Casanova's articles for *ABC* during this period (as collected in *De la revolución rusa en 1917* and *La revolución bolchevista*, unless otherwise noted) are the factual and anecdotal basis for this chapter, along with *Viajes de una muñeca española*, and *En la corte de los Zares*. I have also consulted standard histories and studies of the Russian Revolution, particularly: Seton-Watson, *History of the Russian Empire, 1801-1917*; Wandycz's *Polish-Soviet Relations, 1917-1921*; Nicholas V. Riasanovsky, *A History of Russia* (London and Toronto: Oxford University Press, 1967); Adam B. Ulam, *The Bolsheviks: The Intellectual and Political History of the Triumph of*

God's Playground: A History of Poland in Two Volumes (New York: Columbia University Press, 1982). Needless to say, all opinions (unless so noted) and errors are my own.

7. In a letter dated 20 September 1989, K. Niklewicz reiterated to the author her belief that although Dmowski publicly claimed to want only "unity," not independence for all three sections of partitioned Poland, he harbored a deep personal desire for Polish independence: it was "asunto de táctica" ('a question of strategy'). His followers knew his feelings and believed that with his "conciliation" policies he was laying a foundation for Polish independence. But like many others, Casanova wanted an independent Poland above all.

8. For the historical background for this chapter, I have relied principally on *ABC*'s annals for this period (including Casanova's articles). I have also consulted several standard Spanish general histories, including Tuñón de Lara, *España*; Carr, *Spain*; Joaquín Arrarás, *Historia de la Segunda República Española Tomos 1 y 2*; Gerald Brennan, *The Spanish Labyrinth: An Account of the Social and Political Background of the Civil War*; Gabriel Jackson, *The Spanish Republic and the Civil War. 1931-1939*; Hugh Thomas, *The Spanish Civil War*.

9. As of 1987, the collection of unpublished poems and other Casanova manuscripts, given to the Real Academia Gallega in 1971 by Krystina Niklewicz, is apparently lost or misplaced (Simón Palmer, *Escritoras* 170). These and other excerpts were transcribed from K. Niklewicz's own notes and private papers by the author.

10. Although Krystina Niklewicz was not in Posnań at the time of her grandmother's death, she believes that Casanova died "en casa de Halita atendida por ella y sus hijas" 'in Halita's home, nursed by (Halita) and her daughters" (K. Niklewicz, letter, 20 April 1920).

Sofía Casanova: An Annotated Bibliography of her Works

Poesías. Madrid: Imprenta de A.J. Alaria, 1885.
> Casanova's first book. Dedicated to Alfonso XIII and Queen María Cristina. Divided into "Intimas" and "Varias." Themes include alienation, pessimism, unsuccessful search for a soulmate, sympathy for the downtrodden, evocations of Spanish history and tradition.

El doctor Wolski: páginas de Polonia y Rusia. Madrid: Sucesores de J. Cruzado a cargo de F. Marques, 1894.
> A novel that portrays the professional and romantic problems of "Dr. Wolski" (Wincenty Lutosławski), an idealistic Polish physician foiled by Nature in his attempts to improve the human race through eugenics, hygiene, etc.. Two attempts at bearing the optimal child fail. Wolski's relationship with Ivan Ivanovich, his Russian friend, is used to explore their philosophical differences, relations between Poles and Russians, common antagonism towards the Czar.

Fugaces. La Coruña: Biblioteca Gallega. Andres Martínez, Editor, 1898.
> Casanova's second book of poetry. Selections from *Poesías* ("Juventud") as well as twenty-three new poems written abroad ("Ausencia," 1887-1897). Poems of nostalgia, spiritual aridity, human suffering, an absent God.

Bartek el Vencedor. Traducción Directa del Polaco por Sofía Casanova. Madrid: R. Velasco, Impresor, 1902.
> Translation of a short novel by Henryk Sienkiewicz. Casanova's introduction explains patriotic intention behind translations from the Polish.

Bartek el Vencedor. Madrid: Librería Fernando Fé, 1903.

Sobre el Volga helado. Narración de viajes. Madrid: R. Velasco Imp., 1903.
> Narrative of Sofía Casanova's and Wincenty Lutosławski's 1892 trip from Poland to St. Petersburg, Nizny Novgorod, Moscow, Kazan by sleigh over the frozen Volga. Observations on Polish and Russian manners and society.

Más que amor. Cartas. Madrid: R. Velasco, Impresor, 1908.
> Epistolary novel. Chronicles development of long-distance idyll between "María," a Spanish widow living in Poland (Sofía Casanova) and "Carlos de Vargas" (Spanish editor and poet Alfredo Vicenti), a Madrid politician. Although they have seen each other only twice in twelve years, they correspond, fall in love at great distance, and

finally reunite in Aranjuez and Madrid. María tries to overcome her distrust, but basic incompatibility between men and women prevails. They agree to separate, but maintain their correspondence. Skillfully written with bittersweet psychological insights into cultural isolation, loneliness, a woman's desire for autonomy and a man's need to dominate. Reissued in 1931 under the title of *Idilio epistolar*.

Więcej niż miłość: powieść wspolczesna. Kraków: G. Gebethner i Sp., 1908. Polish translation of *Más que amor*, excerpted by *Gazeta Codziena*, a Warsaw newspaper. Censored by the Russian authorities for anti-czarist ideas.

Lo eterno. Narración española. Madrid: 1908.

Short novel: describes the struggles of a young priest unsure of his vocation, who falls in love with a young woman, helps her to overcome her problems and marry the man she loves. He goes on to find his true vocation as a missionary in Africa and holy death.

Enrique Sienkiewicz. ¿Quo Vadis? Primera versión española directa del polaco por Sofía Casanova. Madrid: La novela de ahora, Casa Editorial de Saturnino Calleja Fernández, 1908.

Princesa del amor hermoso. El cuento semanal (24), año XII, 1909.

Kowalewska, Zofja. Una nihilista. Novela Rusa. Traducida por Sofía Casanova. Madrid: M. Perez Villavicencio, 1909.

"La mujer española en el extranjero." Madrid: R. Velasco, impresor, 1910.

Casanova's lecture on negative stereotypes of Spanish women in European literature (the jealous mistress, Carmen, etc.), delivered at the Ateneo de Madrid on April 9, 1910. Deplores lack of education, attitudes of Spanish women: states that women should not be subservient to men, but rather men's friends and colleagues.

El Pecado. Biblioteca de Autores Gallegos, Vol. X. Madrid: Imprenta de Alrededor del Mundo, 1911. Collection of 11 short stories, mostly dealing with *gallego* themes.

El Cancionero de la dicha. Madrid: R. Velasco Impresor, 1911.

Casanova's third book of poetry. Prefaced by *an ofrenda de poetas*, eight poems (including one by Manuel Machado), celebrating her art. "Versos de lejanos días" and "Ausencia" repeat poems from *Fugaces*. Middle section, "Cancionero de la dicha." shows *Modernista* influence. "Los días de hoy" has topical and political poems.

El cancionero de la dicha. Segunda edición. Madrid: Biblioteca de Manuel Polo y Perez, 1912.

Exóticas. Madrid: Sucesores de Hernando, 1913.

Collection of articles on Eastern Europe (politics, literature, censorship, social issues) along with some more personal writings published in Madrid during the first decade of the century.

"La madeja. Comedia frívola en tres actos y en prosa." Madrid: R. Velasco, 1913. Dissimilar lives (an American heiress, an innocent Spanish bride, an experienced bachelor) cross into eternal "web" of love, jealousy, romance. Casanova's only play. Premiered at the Teatro Español on March 11, 1913, at the request of Don Benito Pérez Galdós.

"La madeja. Comedia frívola en tres actos y en prosa." *Los Contemporáneos*, 241, 1913.

De la guerra: Crónicas de Polonia y Rusia. Madrid: R. Velasco, imp., 1916. Collected newspaper articles: World War I in Poland, the German invasion.

De la revolución rusa en 1917. Madrid: Renacimiento, 1918.
An eyewitness account of the Russian revolution, published in *ABC*.

"Impresiones de una mujer en el frente oriental." Madrid: Imprenta Gráfica Excelsior, 1919. An impassioned anti-war account, delivered to a Spanish military audience.

Sobre el Volga helado. La Novela Corta (165), año 4, 1919. Reissue.

Triunfo de amor: novela inédita de Sofía Casanova. La Novela Corta (186), año 4, 1919.

Lo eterno. La Novela Corta (218), año 5, 1920. Reissue.

Viajes y aventuras de una muñeca española en Rusia. Ilust. Gutiérrez Larraya. Burgos: Hijos de Santiago Rodríguez, 1920.
A children's book: probably inspired by a Polish book, *The Heroic Teddy-bear*. A Spanish doll's and her owners' travels take them from Spain to France, Germany, Poland, Russia and back to their Polish home. Child's eye view of the senselessness of war. Illustrations.

La revolución bolchevista. Madrid: Biblioteca Nueva, preface 1920.
A day by day acount of the Bolshevik takeover.

Episodio de guerra. Prensa Popular. *La Novela Corta* (299), 1921.

Princesa rusa. Madrid: Publicaciones Prensa Gráfica, II, No. 56, 1922.

Kola el bandido. La Novela semanal (7 July), 1922

En la corte de los zares: del principio y del fin de un imperio. Madrid: Librería y Editorial Madrid [cop. 1924]. Popular narratives and articles describing the history and last days of the Romanov Dynasty.

Obras completas. Volumen I. En la corte de los zares. Madrid: Biblioteca Rubén Darío, 1924. Reissue.

Obras completas. Volumen II. El doctor Wolski. Madrid: Librería y

Editorial Madrid, S. A., 1925. Reissue.

Obras completas. Volumen III. El pecado. Madrid: Librería y Editorial
Madrid S.A., 1926. Reissue.

Obras completas. Volumen IV. De Rusia: amores y confidencias. Madrid:
Librería y Editorial Madrid (S.A.), 1927. Reissue.

El dolor de reinar. La novela semanal (213), 1925.

Idilio epistolar. Novela. Madrid: M. Aguilar, editor, 1931.
Reissue of *Más que amor.*

Como en la vida. Madrid: M. Aguilar, editor, 1931.
Contrasts simple, traditional life in a Galician *pazo* with rootless lives
of Eastern European émigrés. Fernando, a Spanish diplomat,
abandons his fiancee, Blanca, for Princess Alix, a Russian émigré.
When Alix betrays him, he returns to Spain and enlists, hoping to
redeem himself and his country. Casanova probably intended this
novel to be her last, and wove into it lifelong themes.

Las catacumbas de Rusia roja, por Sofía Casanova. Novela. Madrid:
Espasa-Calpe, S.A., 1933.
Princess Alix (from *Como en la vida*), in love with White Russian
leader Zarief, dies in her effort to help him rescue Russia from the
Bolsheviks.

El doctor Wolski: páginas de Polonia y Rusia. Madrid: Editorial Madrid,
1935.

El martirio de Polonia. Madrid: Ediciones Atlas, 1945.
Casanova's journal, kept during the German *blitzkrieg* in
1939. Smuggled out of Poland, then published in Madrid without her
permission.

El martirio de Polonia. Segunda edición. Madrid: Ediciones Atlas, 1945.
Second edition.

Como en la vida. Revista semanaria. Novelas y cuentos. (851), 1947.
Reissue.

Poesías Inéditas. Real Academia Gallega, La Coruña.
57 unpublished new poems, revisions, fragments of old and new
poems.

M. Victoria López-Cordón, ed. *La revolución bolchevista (diario de un
testigo).* Madrid: Editorial Castalia, Biblioteca de escritoras, 1989.

Articles by Sofía Casanova for ABC

1. "La guerra en Rusia" 8 April, 1915.
2. "Las batallas. Los hospitales. Los mártires" 13 April, 1915.
3. "De la guerra en Rusia" 16 April, 1915.
4. "Prisioneros y heridos. Las operaciones" 23 April, 1915.
5. "¡Domingo de resurrección!" 29 April, 1915.
6. "El espionaje" 5 May, 1915.
7. "La batalla de los Cárpatos" 14 May, 1915.
8. "Las desdichas de Polonia" 24 May, 1915.
9. "Lo que piensan los rusos de los alemanes" 29 May, 1915.
10. "Incertidumbre dolorosa" 7 June, 1915.
11. "Tren militar" 19 June, 1915
12. "Desde las posiciones del Naref" 24 June, 1915
13. "A orillas del Naref" 1 July, 1915
14. "Los gases asfixiantes. El espanto de las víctimas"
    7 July 1915
15. "La ciudad aterrada" 14 July, 1915
16. "La evacuación" 2 August, 1915
17. "Momento supremo" 17 Sept., 1915
18. "El avance alemán" 18 Sept., 1915
19. "En los caminos de la retirada" (I) 13 Oct., 1915
20. "En los caminos de la retirada" (II) 15 Oct., 1915
21. "La vida en Moscú. La situación política" 12 Nov., 1915
22. "La destitución del Gran Duque. El cierre de la Duma"
    13 Nov., 1915
23. "Polonia, problema internacional" 2 Dec., 1915
24. "Problema internacional" 5 Dec., 1915
25. "La corte de los Zares" 12 Dec., 1915
26. "La opinión en San Petersburgo" 13 Dec., 1915
27. "La paz en la guerra. La Princesa Urusof" 22 Dec., 1915
28. "La noche de Navidad" 20 Feb., 1916
29. "Primavera de odios" 24 May, 1916
30. "Diario de viaje" 13 June, 1916
31. "Del pasado glorioso" 15 June, 1916
32. "Una nota subjetiva" 16 June, 1916
33. "Heroicidades inhumanas" 20 June, 1916
34. "En las posiciones" 22 June, 1916
35. "Pascua Florida" 29 June, 1916
36. "La vida en las posiciones" 4 July, 1916

175

29 May, 1919

272. "El fracaso de Europa" (V) 2 April, 1920
273. "El fracaso de Europa" (VI) 6 April, 1920
274. "Habla Merezewsky" 30 April, 1920
275. "Los imperialistas vencidos" (I) (Koltchak) 5 May, 1920
276. "Los imperialistas vencidos" (II) 7 May, 1920
277. "El triunfo de Rusia" 9 May, 1920
278. "España en Polonia" (I) 12 May, 1920
279. "España en Polonia" (II) 13 May, 1920
280. "La espera trágica" (I) 30 May, 1920
281. "Nada cambia" 8 June, 1920
282. "¡Guerra!" (La gran ofensiva polaca) 10 June, 1920
283. "Los nuevos hombres" (I) (El jefe del estado polaco) 14 June, 1920
284. "Los nuevos hombres" (II) (El jefe del estado polaco)
      18 June, 1920
285. "Los nuevos hombres" (III) (El jefe del estado polaco)
      20 June, 1920
286. "Los nuevos hombres" (IV) (El jefe del estado polaco)
      23 June, 1920
287. "El desastre de la ofensiva" (I) 15 July, 1920
288. "El desastre de la ofensiva" (II) 16 July, 1920
289. "Los nuevos hombres" (I) (El atamán ukraniano, Peltura)
      17 July, 1920
290. "Los nuevos hombres" (II) (El atamán ukraniano, Peltura)
      18 July, 1920
291. "Los nuevos hombres" (III) (El atamán ukraniano, Peltura)
      20 July, 1920
292. "Perfiles del caos" (I) 24 July, 1920
293. "Perfiles del caos" (II) 26 July, 1920
294. "Perfiles del caos" (III) 28 July, 1920
295. "Páginas de la guerra" (El exterminio de Polonia) 12 Aug., 1920
296. "Fe en la defensa" (I) 14 Aug., 1920
297. "Otra vez el peligro" 17 Aug., 1920
298. "Los bolcheviques" (I) 18 Aug., 1920
299. "Los bolcheviques" (II) 19 Aug., 1920
300. "Ante el avance de los bolcheviques" (I) 24 Aug., 1920
301. "Ante el avance de los bolcheviques" (II) 25 Aug., 1920
302. "Ante el avance de los bolcheviques" (III) 27 Aug., 1920
303. "Los bolcheviques" (IV) 14 Sept., 1920
304. "Los bolcheviques" (V) 15 Sept., 1920
305. "Los bolcheviques" (VI) 16 Sept., 1920
306. "La batalla de Varsovia" 17 Sept., 1920

307. "Los bolcheviques" (VII) 22 Sept., 1920
308. "Los bolcheviques" (VIII) 24 Sept., 1920
309. "Los bolcheviques" (IX) 28 Sept., 1920
310. "Los bolcheviques" (X) 29 Sept., 1920
311. "Los bolcheviques en Lomza" (I) 19 Oct., 1920
312. "Los bolcheviques en Lomza" (II) 20 Oct., 1920
313. "Los bolcheviques en Lomza" (III) 29 Oct., 1920
314. "Los bolcheviques en Lomza" (IV) 30 Oct., 1920
315. "Los bolcheviques en Lomza" (V) 6 Nov., 1920
316. "Los bolcheviques en Lomza" (VI) 13 Nov., 1920
317. "Los bolcheviques en Lomza" (VII) 14 Nov., 1920
318. "Los bolcheviques en Lomza" (VIII) 25 Nov., 1920
319. "Los bolcheviques en Lomza" (IX) 26 Nov., 1920
320. "Intervalo de paz sin paz" (I) 10 Dec., 1920
321. "Intervalo de paz sin paz" (II) 12 Dec., 1920
322. "Intervalo de paz sin paz" (III) 23 Dec., 1920
323. "Intervalo de paz sin paz" (IV) 24 Dec., 1920
324. "El poeta de Lituania" (I) 30 Dec., 1920
325. "El plebiscito en Lituania y Silesia" 7 Jan., 1921
326. "El poeta de Lituania" (II) 11 Jan., 1921
327. "El plebiscito en Alta Silesia" 25 Jan., 1921
328. "Latidos de fiebre" 3 Feb., 1921
329. "Rusia ayer y hoy" (I) 17 Feb., 1921
330. "Rusia ayer y hoy" (II) 23 Feb., 1921
331. "Rusia ayer y hoy" (III) 24 Feb., 1921
332. "Rusia ayer y hoy" (IV) 1 March, 1921
333. "Rusia ayer y hoy" (V) 6 March, 1921
334. "Triunfo y dudas" 16 March, 1921
335. "Estancamiento" 18 March, 1921
336. "Mirando a Rusia" (I) 26 March, 1921
337. "Mirando a Rusia" (II) 31 March, 1921
338. "La gran alianza" 3 April, 1921
339. "Luz y tinieblas" 9 April, 1921
340. "El feminismo triunfante" (I) 13 April, 1921
341. "El feminismo triunfante" (II) 16 April, 1921
342. "El feminismo triunfante" (III) 5 May, 1921
343. "El feminismo triunfante" (IV) 8 May, 1921
344. "El feminismo triunfante" (V) 15 May, 1921
345. "Las flores de la reina" 22 May, 1921
346. "Norteamérica y los niños hambrientos" (I) 24 May, 1921
347. "Norteamérica y los niños hambrientos" (II) 31 May, 1921

389. "Entre Rusia y Alemania" 16 March, 1922
390. "Complicaciones de la felicidad" 24 March, 1922
391. "El teatro ruso" 28 March, 1922
392. "Dominio espiritual en América" 8 April, 1922
393. "Detalles de la catástrofe" 21 April, 1922
394. "España y Rusia" 29 April, 1922
395. "Comentarios al tratado de Rapallo" 14 May, 1922
396. "De lo que no se habla" 20 May, 1922
397. "Los monárquicos rusos" 28 May, 1922
398. "Moscú y Roma" (I) 7 June, 1922
399. "Moscú y Roma" (II) 11 June, 1922
400. "El metropolitano de Lwow" 14 June, 1922
401. "Las viudas" 5 July, 1922
402. "Crisis de autoridad" 18 July, 1922
403. "Historia y aclaraciones" (I) 23 July, 1922
404. "Historia y aclaraciones" (II) 25 July, 1922
405. "La pésima política" 16 Aug., 1922
406. "El desenlace" 24 Aug., 1922
407. "Los hijos de Don Juan" 8 Sept., 1922
408. "Dos culturas" 28 Sept., 1922
409. "Errores del poder prusiano" 30 Sept., 1922
410. "Huellas de Alemania" 29 Oct., 1922
411. "Niños polacos y alemanes" 2 Nov., 1922
412. "Los ladrones" 10 Nov., 1922
413. "Las cárceles" 19 Nov., 1922
414. "América y Mickiewicz" 21 Nov., 1922
415. "Primeras lecciones" 24 Nov., 1922
416. "Amor del romancero" 17 Dec., 1922
417. "La renuncia de Pilsudski" 19 Dec., 1922
418. "Silueta de luz" 20 Dec., 1922
419. "El 'comandante'" 24 Dec., 1922
420. "El nuevo presidente" 29 Dec., 1922
421. "A rey muerto..." 3 Jan., 1923
422. "Lo dulce y lo práctico" 26 Jan., 1923
423. "El asesinato del Presidente" 2 Feb., 1923
424. "Poesía y amores" 7 Feb., 1923
425. "Camino de España" (I) 16 Feb., 1923
426. "Camino de España" (II) 17 Feb., 1923
427. "Camino de España" (III) 2 March, 1923
428. "La fiera y el hombre" (I) 14 March, 1923
429. "El prendimiento o el beso de Judas" 25 March, 1923

430. "Madrid" (I) 20 April, 1923
431. "Madrid" (II) 26 April, 1923
432. "Rusia" (I) 10 May, 1923
433. "Rusia" (II) 12 May, 1923
434. "El mariscal Foch en Polonia" 26 May, 1923
435. "A través de Europa" (I) 14 June, 1923
436. "A través de Europa" (II) 29 June, 1923
437. "A través de Europa" (III) 1 July, 1923
438. "Otros hombres" 13 July, 1923
439. "Cortejo de reyes" (I) 18 July, 1923
440. "Cortejo de reyes" (II) 24 July, 1923
441. "¿El patriarca renegado?" 8 Aug., 1923
442. "Conventos y juderías" (I) 16 Aug., 1923
443. "Conventos y juderías" (II) 21 Aug., 1923
444. "Se ve el incendio" 7 Sept., 1923
445. "Vida en las juderías" (I) 15 Sept., 1923
446. "Vida en las juderías" (II) 23 Sept., 1923
447. "Esperando" 19 Oct., 1923
448. "Pensando en alta voz" 24 Oct., 1923
449. "El príncipe y el aldeano" (I) 2 Nov., 1923
450. "El príncipe y el aldeano" (II) 3 Nov., 1923
451. "La gran batalla" 29 Nov., 1923
452. "Se vive" 1 Dec., 1923
453. "Ecos del triunfo" 13 Dec., 1923
454. "Las víctimas sin culpa" 2 Jan., 1924
455. "La renovación de lo idéntico" 16 Jan., 1924
456. "Antes de la filípica" 6 Feb., 1924
457. "Vladimiro Uljianow Lenin" 7 Feb., 1924
458. "Misterios de la realidad" 12 Feb., 1924
459. "Libros de mujeres" 19 Feb., 1924
460. "Una mañana..." 16 March, 1924
461. "La contribución de lo bello" 28 March, 1924
462. "La hora de la mujer" 16 April, 1924
463. "Fin de un suplicio" 8 May, 1924
464. "El enigma de Oriente" 15 May, 1924
465. "Ráfaga de luz" 7 June, 1924
466. "La virgen de Guadalupe y la de Koden" 19 June, 1924
467. "¿El fin justifica los medios?" 1 July, 1924
468. "Los diplomáticos" (I) 23 July, 1924
469. "Los diplomáticos" (II) 26 July, 1924
470. "Los diplomáticos" (III) 27 July, 1924

471. "Zarpazos de la fiera" 19 Aug., 1924
472. "Amante y asesina" 22 Aug., 1924
473. "Ha ocurrido algo..." 12 Sept., 1924
474. "Los alarmistas...alegres" 1 Oct., 1924
475. "Los enemigos de España" 30 Oct., 1924
476. "Teatro nacional" 2 Nov., 1924
477. "Lo efímero y lo eterno" 6 Dec., 1924
478. "Lo que cambia" 31 Jan., 1925
479. "Impresiones de Rusia" (I) 19 Feb., 1925
480. "Impresiones de Rusia" (II) 20 Feb., 1925
481. "Impresiones de Rusia" (III) 27 Feb., 1925
482. "El altar de la patria" 27 Feb., 1925
483. "Impresiones de Rusia" (IV) 14 March, 1925
484. "Impresiones de Rusia" (V) 27 March, 1925
485. "Los niños rusos" 16 April, 1925
486. "Rusia pintoresca" 9 May, 1925
487. "Europa y Galicia" (I) 12 June, 1925
488. "Europa y Galicia" (II) 13 June, 1925
489. "Europa y Galicia" (III) 16 June, 1925
490. "Las fronteras" (I) 18 July, 1925
491. "Las fronteras" (II) 21 July, 1925
492. "Las fronteras" (III) 30 July, 1925
493. "Desde Polonia" (Guerra!) 20 Aug., 1925
494. "El gran balneario de Panticosa" 21 Aug., 1925
495. "La ley agraria" 25 Aug., 1925
496. "Desde Polonia" (Los adoptantes) 28 Aug., 1925
497. "No cambian mis vecinos" 23 Sept., 1925
498. "Desde Polonia" (Hija de española) 25 Sept., 1925
499. "Entran mis vecinos..." 16 Oct., 1925
500. "El comisario Chicherin" 24 Oct., 1925
501. "La victoria para las españolas" 27 Oct., 1925
502. "De Rusia" (I) 13 Dec., 1925
503. "De Rusia" (II) 24 Dec., 1925
504. "De Rusia" (III) 27 Dec., 1925
505. "Empieza el año" (I) 20 Jan., 1926
506. "Expectación" (II) 27 Jan., 1926
507. "Con ellos y España" 20 Feb., 1926
508. "La amiga Rusia..." 27 Feb., 1926
509. "La joven aliada..." 3 March, 1926
510. "Triunfo del teatro español" 28 March, 1926
511. "Triunfo del teatro español" 2 April, 1926

512. "El feminismo de una diplomática" 9 April, 1926
513. "Tenemos que insistir" 24 April, 1926
514. "De Rusia misteriosa" 29 April, 1926
515. "Pensando en un rey" (I) 5 May, 1926
516. "Pensando en un rey" (II) 16 May, 1926
517. "Las mujeres" 19 May, 1926
518. "La política y la Dictadura" 26 May, 1926
519. "La batalla" 2 June, 1926
520. "Los motivos y la situación" 10 June, 1926
521. "Que Dios perdone" 16 June, 1926
522. "Algo de las causas" 13 July, 1926
523. "El dictador entre bastidores" 28 July, 1926
524. "La nueva etapa" 7 Aug., 1926
525. "Lo que dice Zinowiew" 17 Aug., 1926
526. "Diplomáticos y 'ministras' hispanófilos" 20 Aug., 1926
527. "La obra de Dzierzynski" 3 Sept., 1926
528. "Visita de españoles" 10 Sept., 1926
529. "Alto en la subida" 22 Sept., 1926
530. "Secreto de los Zares" 13 Oct., 1926
531. "Algo de Galicia aquí" 14 Oct., 1926
532. "Pedazos de epopeya" 21 Oct., 1926
533. "Camino de España" 9 Nov., 1926
534. "Del noviazgo" 17 Nov., 1926
535. "Chopin y la bandera" 14 Dec., 1926
536. "Coronas y desterrados" 15 Dec., 1926
537. "Huella en la sombra" 18 Dec., 1926
538. "Realidad y misterio" 21 Dec., 1926
539. "España en el extranjero" 1 Jan., 1927
540. "Educación y poesía" (I) 13 Jan., 1927
541. "La educación y la poesía" (II) 19 Jan., 1927
542. "Como nos ven en el extranjero" 22 Jan., 1927
543. "Polonia lucha" 25 Jan., 1927
544. "Del país de los Soviets" (I) (Cosas de Rusia) 16 Feb., 1927
545. "Del país de los Soviets" (II) (Cosas de Rusia) 18 Feb., 1927
546. "Del país de los Soviets" (III) (Cosas de Rusia) 19 Feb., 1927
547. "Del país de los Soviets" (IV) (Cosas de Rusia) 23 Feb., 1927
548. "La fiesta de la Planta" (I) 16 March, 1927
549. "La fiesta de la Planta" (II) 18 March, 1927
550. "Rusos y chinos" (El jefe de los nordistas) 19 March, 1927
551. "Los niños en España y Rusia" 22 March, 1927
552. "Demanda de perdón" 2 April, 1927

553. "Lo viejo de lo nuevo" (I) 6 April, 1927
554. "Lo viejo de lo nuevo" (II) 7 April, 1927
555. "Un asesino arrepentido" (La expiación) 12 April, 1927
556. "Detalles del conjunto babilónico" 5 May, 1927
557. "Las impresiones del camino" 6 May, 1927
558. "Camino adelante" 11 May, 1927
559. "Mujeres" (I) 20 May, 1927
560. "Viendo la vida" 24 May, 1927
561. "Mujeres" (II) 9 June, 1927
562. "La perversa política" 11 June, 1927
563. "Mujeres" (III) 20 June, 1927
564. "Intimamente" 21 June, 1927
565. "Un asesinato político" 23 June, 1927
566. "Las negras rutas" 8 July, 1927
567. "Un congreso católico" 19 July, 1927
568. "Un poeta" 20 July, 1927
569. "Fantasmas imperiales" 10 Aug., 1927
570. "Novelas de la realidad" (I) 11 Aug., 1927
571. "Novelas de la realidad" (II) 13 Aug., 1927
572. "Males que exijen remedio" 19 Aug., 1927
573. "Otros mares" (I) 8 Sept., 1927
574. "Otros mares" (II) 13 Sept., 1927
575. "La pesca" (Del Báltico al Cantábrico) 16 Sept., 1927
576. "La ruta de Dantzig" 23 Sept., 1927
577. "Pilsudski, el misterioso" 29 Sept., 1927
578. "La última sesión del 'Seim'" 4 Oct., 1927
579. "Viejas ciudades" 11 Oct., 1927
580. "La danza de los siglos" 13 Oct., 1927
581. "Las sombras de los días" 19 Oct., 1927
582. "Mar adentro" 21 Oct., 1927
583. "El aniversario bolchevique" 5 Nov., 1927
584. "El eterno desconocimiento de España" 11 Nov., 1927
585. "La muerte del diablo" (I) 23 Nov., 1927
586. "La muerte del diablo" (II) 30 Nov., 1927
587. "La muerte del diablo" (III) 3 Dec., 1927
588. "La guerra bolchevique" (I) 17 Dec., 1927
589. "La guerra bolchevique" (II) 21 Dec., 1927
590. "La guerra bolchevique" (III) 23 Dec., 1927
591. "La guerra bolchevique" (IV) 6 Jan., 1928
592. "De cara a Rusia" (I) (Los hombres) 10 Jan., 1928
593. "De cara a Rusia" (II) (Los hombres) 21 Jan., 1928

188

634. "De norte a sur" (Inverosímil) 23 Nov., 1928
635. "De norte a sur" (La dulzura de elogiar) 30 Nov., 1928
636. "De norte a sur" (I) (Otra vez Rasputín) 11 Dec., 1928
637. "De norte a sur" (II) (Otra vez Rasputín) 14 Dec., 1928
638. "De norte a sur" (III) (Otra vez Rasputín) 20 Dec., 1928
639. "De norte a sur" (IV) (Otra vez Rasputín) 25 Dec., 1928
640. "El teatro judío" (Representación de una leyenda hebraica)
     10 Jan., 1928
641. "De norte a sur" (El gran duque Nicolás) 17 Jan., 1929
642. "De norte a sur" (España y Polonia) 24 Jan., 1929
643. "De norte a sur" (Francisco) 29 Jan., 1929
644. "De norte a sur" (I) (La caza) 16 Feb., 1929
645. "De norte a sur" (II) (La caza) 20 Feb., 1929
646. "De norte a sur" (III) (La caza) 22 Feb., 1929
647. "De norte a sur" (Jubiloso después) 1 March, 1929
648. "Ciudades europeas" (La polaca Wilno de admirable historia y
     territorio pintoresco) 3 March, 1929
649. "De norte a sur" (La paz) 8 March, 1929
650. "De norte a sur" (I) (Episodios de guerra) 14 March, 1929
651. "De norte a sur" (II) (Episodios de guerra) 16 March, 1929
652. "De norte a sur" (III) (Episodios de guerra) 20 March, 1929
653. "De norte a sur" (I) (Horas de Andalucía) 6 April, 1929
654. "De norte a sur" (II) (Horas de Andalucía) 10 April, 1929
655. "De norte a sur" (III) (Horas de Andalucía) 17 April, 1929
656. "De norte a sur" (IV) (Horas de Andalucía) 20 April, 1929
657. "Del teatro" 23 April, 1929
658. "Lejos de España" (Las grandes rutas europeas) 25 April, 1929
659. "De los claros días" 30 May, 1929
660. "¡Qué hacen las agencias?" 15 June, 1929
661. "Mirando lejos" 26 June, 1929
662. "Eva belicosa" 27 June, 1929
663. "Un viaje" 13 July, 1929
664. "Las espinas del triufo" 20 July, 1929
665. "El teatro en Varsovia" (La nueva comedia de Bernard Shaw)
     25 July, 1929
666. "Del teatro ruso" ("El poder de las tinieblas") 1 Aug., 1929
667. "Se miran las esfinges" (I) 16 Aug., 1929
668. "Se miran las esfinges" (II) 22 Aug., 1929
669. "Noticias" 30 Aug., 1929
670. "Pinceladas" 18 Sept., 1929
671. "De uno a otro extremo" 26 Sept., 1929

753. "ABC en Dantzig" 16 March, 1933
754. "Al lado de la revolución" 26 March, 1933
755. "Arrecia el fuego" 12 April, 1933
756. "El más triste proletariado" 20 April, 1933
757. "Poema contra el amor" 21 May, 1933
758. "ABC en Polonia" 28 May, 1933
759. "De Rusia" 10 June, 1933
760. "ABC en Polonia" 5 July, 1933
761. "ABC en Dantzig" 20 July, 1933
762. "ABC en Polonia" 15 Aug., 1933
763. "ABC en los Cárpatos" 10 Sept., 1933
764. "Los sabios y la guerra" 13 Sept., 1933
765. "ABC en Varsovia" 15 Oct., 1933
766. "Camino de España" 26 Oct., 1933
767. "España" 15 Nov., 1933
768. "Ejemplo" 3 Dec., 1933
769. "En la hora definitiva" 4 Jan., 1934
770. "Reinvindicación espiritual" 13 Jan., 1934
771. "El mejor sistema" 20 Jan., 1934
772. "Unas palabras" 17 Feb., 1934
773. "Sin ellas" 4 March, 1934
774. "El ideal y los aranceles" 29 March, 1934
775. "Amigo de España" 6 April, 1934
776. "Camino de ruinas" 6 May, 1934
777. "La visita de Barthou" 10 May, 1934
778. "Siempre igual" 20 May, 1934
779. "Por la justicia" 10 June, 1934
780. "ABC en Varsovia" 13 June, 1934
781. "El triunfo de España" 27 June, 1934
782. "Judíos y cristianos" 5 July, 1934
783. "El vértigo" 19 July, 1934
784. "Junto al volcán" 21 July, 1934
785. "El agua enemiga" 10 Aug., 1934
786. "ABC en Varsovia" (Oyendo las campanas) 18 Aug., 1934
787. "Página rural" 9 Sept., 1934
788. "En los aires" 14 Sept., 1934
789. "El modernismo amoral" 27 Sept., 1934
790. "Triste comparación" 24 Oct., 1934
791. "¡Viva España!" 31 Oct., 1934
792. "De lejos y cerca" 3 Nov., 1934
793. "La horrible perspectiva" 29 Nov., 1934

794. "ABC en Varsovia" 18 Dec., 1934
795. "Los crímenes de Petersburgo y Moscú" 5 Jan., 1935
796. "El oso, herido" 31 Jan., 1935
797. "Naranjas españolas" 17 Feb., 1935
798. "Mirando a Rusia" 23 Feb., 1935
799. "ABC en Varsovia" 16 March, 1935
800. "ABC en Varsovia" 20 March, 1935
801. "La sonrisa del Lord" 13 April, 1935
802. "Los días sin calma" 11 May, 1935
803. "Los amigos de ocasión" 1 June, 1935
804. "El mariscal de Pilsudski ha muerto" 6 June, 1935
805. "El hombre" 13 June, 1935
806. "Sombra y luz" 6 July, 1935
807. "Mirando en torno" 31 July, 1935
808. "Camino abierto" 3 Aug., 1935
809. "De cara al Báltico" 30 Aug., 1935
810. "No sólo en Abisinia..." 31 Aug., 1935
811. "¡Guerra, guerra!" 10 Sept., 1935
812. "Esperando" 9 Oct., 1935
813. "Realidades" 19 Oct., 1935
814. "El gran escándalo" 15 Nov., 1935
815. "La sensibilidad" 20 Dec., 1935
816. "ABC en Varsovia" 10 Jan., 1936
817. "Comentarios" 17 Jan., 1936
818. "Hay que mirar el fondo" (E.T.) 17 Feb., 1936
819. "La lógica de lo ilógico" 18 March, 1936
820. "Después de la batalla" 19 March, 1936
821. "ABC en Varsovia" 2 April, 1936
822. "Un tema nuevo" 9 April, 1936
823. "La política" 10 April, 1936
824. "Al día" 10 June, 1936
825. "Lo nuevo en lo eterno" 21 June, 1936
826. "Un recuerdo" 8 July, 1936
827. "Los vencedores" 11 July, 1936
828. "Mirando a Rusia" 13 July, 1936
829. "En guerra" 14 Feb., 1940
830. "Lejos y cerca" 6 June, 1944

Sofía Casanova: A Selected Bibliography

Alayeto, Ofelia L. "Sofía Casanova: A Link between Polish and Spanish
Literatures (1861-1958)." Diss., City University of New York, 1983.

---. "The Poetry of Sofía Casanova." *Monographic Review/Revista
Monográfica*, Vol. 6 (1990).

---. "Sofía Casanova: An Annotated Bibliography." *Bulletin of Bibliography* 44 (1987)

Bugallal y Marchesi, Jose Luis. ---. "Sofía Casanova. Un siglo de gloria
y de dolores." La Coruña: Litografía e Imprenta Roel, S.A., 1964.

---. "Sofía Casanova. Un siglo de gloria y de dolores." *Boletín de la Real
Academia Gallega* 327-332, 1958 (141-172).

---. "Ha muerto Sofía Casanova," *ABC*, 25 January 1958.

---. "La santa que murió de saudade," *ABC*, 25 January 1958.

---. "Sofía Casanova, gloria de España en la *saudade*." Vida Gallega, III
(1958).

Casanova, Vicente. "El pino del Norte. Zarzuela en un acto, dividido en
tres cuadros, en prosa y en verso. Estrenada en el Teatro de Apolo
la noche del 27 de febrero de 1907." Madrid: R. Velasco, Impresor,
1907.

"Casanova de Lutosławski (Sofía)." *Enciclopedia Universal Illustrada
Europeo-Americana*, 1912 ed.

Cossío, Jose María de. Cincuenta años de poesía española (1850-1950).
Madrid: Espasa-Calpe, S. A., 1962.

---. "La labor poética de Sofía Casanova," *ABC*, 2 February 1958.

Criado y Domínguez, Juan Pedro. *Literatas españolas del siglo XIX*.
Madrid: Imprenta de Antonio Pérez Dubrull, 1889.

D'Ors, Eugenio. *Obra Catalana Completa*. Barcelona, Ed. Selecta,
[1950], 874.

Galerstein, Carolyn L., ed. *Women Writers of Spain. An Annotated Bio-
bibliographical Guide*. Greenwood Press: New York, Connecticut,
London, 1986.

G., M.. *Z. C. L. (Wywiad). Tyg. Pol.* 6 (1927).

Gicgier, Tadeusz. "Desde Polonia." *Stolica*, 43 (1970).

Jabłonowski, W. "Zofia Casanowa." *Tyg. Ilustr.* 39 (1909).

Jedrzejewski, Clément. Personal interview. April 1980.

Jordan, Alex (Tadeusz Lutosławski). Personal interview,
December 1980.

González Faro, Luz Marina. *Panorama Antológico de Poetisas Españolas
(Siglos XV al XX)*. Madrid: Ediciones Torremozas, 1987.

Łączyńska, A., "Babunita." *Kierunki*, Rok 3, Nr. 7 (1958).

Lazo, Alfonso. *La revolución rusa en el diario ABC de la epoca*. Sevilla: Publicaciones de la Universidad de Sevilla, 34 (1975).

"Lutosławska Zofia." *Polski Słownik Biograficzny*. Wrocław, Warszawa, Kraków, Gdańsk. Zakład Narodowy Imienia Ossolińskich.

Lutosławski, Wincenty. *Jeden Łatwy Żiwot*. Warszawa: F. Hoesick, 1933.

M. "Z teatru hiszpańskiego." *Świat* 31 May 1913.

Marriage certificate, Sofía Casanova and Wincenty Lutosławski.

Meissner, Halina (Halina Lutosławska). Personal interview, December 1980.

Mendoza, Carlos. "Bibliografía." *La Ilustración Ibérica*, 649 (1895).

Miciński, Tadeusz. *W. Mroku Gwiazd. Kolosseu. Orland Szalony. Lucifer. Kain. Krol w Osyaku. Noce Polarne. Minotaur*. Zatona Tec. Poezni Gebethnera: Kraków, 1902.

Niklewicz, Krystina. Personal interview. December 1980.

Niklewicz, Peter. Personal interviews, December 1980-January 1981.

Novo y García, Jose. *Por Galicia. Cuartillas y apuntes*. La Coruña: Andrés Martínez, editor, 1896.

Ossorio y Bernard, D. Manuel. *Ensayo de un catálogo de periodistas españoles del siglo XIX*. Madrid: Imprenta y Litografía de J. Palacios, 1903-1904.

Pérez, Janet. *Contemporary Women Writers of Spain*. Boston: Twayne Publishers, 1988.

Pérez de Ayala, Ramón. *Obras Completas, Tomo I*. Madrid: Aguilar S.A. de Ediciones, 1964, 1299.

"Pérez de Eguía Casanova, Sofía," *Enciclopedia Gallega. Diccionario Bio-bibliográfico de Escritores. Vol. II*. Santiago de Compostela: Editorial de los Bibliófilos Gallegos, 1953. Listed as *EG*.

Pieczara, S. "Polonica, hiszpańskie," *Spraw. Pozn. Tow. Przj. Nauk.* Nr. 4 (1961).

Pitollet, Camille. "Unas notas sobre Sofía Casanova." *Boletín de la Biblioteca de Menéndez Pelayo*, 34 (1958), 134.

Porębowicz, E. "Powieść hiszpańska na temat polski," *Świat*, Nr. 21 (1894).

Saínz de Robles, Federico Carlos. *Ensayo de un diccionario de la literatura. Tomo II. Escritores españoles e hispanoamericanos*. Madrid: Aguilar, 1964, 220.

Sánchez Reyes, Enrique. "Cartas de mujeres a Menéndez Pelayo." Boletín de la Biblioteca de Menéndez Pelayo. Año XXX, enero-junio (1955), Nums. 1 & 2.

---. "Mementos de Actualidad." Boletín de la Biblioteca de Menéndez
    Pelayo. Año XXXIII, (1958), Nums. 1 & 2: 182-185.
Simón Palmer, María del Carmen. "Sofía Casanova, autora de La
    Madeja." *Actas del Tercer Congreso Internacional de Estudios
    Galdosianos, II.* Las Palmas: Exmo. Cabildo Insular de Gran Canaria
    (1990): 569.
---. "Tres escritoras españolas en el extranjero." *Cuadernos
    Bibliográficos*, XLVII (1987): 157-180.
Wittlin, Dr. Halina. Telephone interview, May 1980.
Wolikowski, General Romuald. Telephone interview. December 1981.

Works Cited

Allan, Gay Wilson. *William James. A Biography*. New York: The Viking Press, 1969.

Álbum de la Caridad. La Coruña: Imprenta del Hospicio provincial, 1962.

Carr, Raymond. *Spain 1808-1939*. Oxford: At the Clarendon Press, 1966.

Castro, Rosalía de. *Obras Completas. Recopilación y estudio bibliográfico*. Madrid: Aguilar, 1966.

Cormack, Dr. George. Speech given at the Presentation of an Honorary Doctorate from the University of Alberta to General Romuald Wolikowski, June 4, 1981.

Coronado, Carolina. *Poesías*. Méjico: Imprenta de Juan R. Navarro, 1851.

Cywiński, S. "Trzydzietolecie Eleusis," *Myśl Narod.*, 20 (1933).

"Dr. Lutosławski, philosopher, dies." *New York Times Obituary*, 5 January 1955.

Dupuy, R. Ernest and Dupuy Trevor N., Eds. *The Encyclopedia of Military History*. New York: Harper and Row, Publishers, 197O).

"Eguía (Francisco Ramón de)". *Enciclopedia Universal Ilustrada Europeo Americana*, 1958 ed.

"Eguía (Nazario)." *Enciclopedia Universal Ilustrada Europeo Americana*, 1958 ed.

Fines, Sue Ashton. "Lucifer, Man and Christ in the Works of Tadeusz Micinski." Ph.D. Diss. Stanford University, 1974.

Halecki, O.. *A History of Modern Poland. From the Foundation of the State in the First World War to the Present Day*. New York: Alfred A. Knopf, 1966.

Heller, Celia S. *On the Eve of Destruction: Jews in Poland Between the Two Wars*. New York: Columbia University Press, 1977.

James, Williams. *Essays on Faith and Morals*. Cleveland: Meridian Books, 1962.

---. Letters to Wincenty Lutosławski. Beinecke Library, Yale University.

---. "One Year Later. Poland under the Cannon". National Review. 2 October, 1981 (1138-1141).

Krzyżanowski, J. A.. *History of Polish Literature*. Warsaw: PWN: Polish Scientific Publishers, 1978.

Kulakowski, Mariusz. *Roman Dmowski w swietle listo i wspomnien*. London: Staraniem Instytutu Romana Dmowskiego w Ameryce. Nakladem Gryf Publications Ltd., 1972.

Literatura Cubana. Madrid, Barcelona: Editorial Las Américas, N.D.

Lutosławska, Izabel. *Bolszewicy w polskim dworze*. Warszawa, Niklewicz i S-ka, 1921.

Lutosławski, Wincenty. *Jeden Łatwy Żywot*. Warszawa: F. Hoesick, 1933.

---. *The Origin and Growth of Plato's Logic, with an Account of Plato's Style and the Chronology of his Writings*. London: Longman's Green, 1897.

---. *The World of Souls*. London: Unwin & Allan, 1924.

Mickiewicz, Adam. *Dziady*. Kolomyja: na skladzie w ksiegarni--, 1906.

Miłosz, Czesław. *The History of Polish Literature*. London: The Macmillan Company, Collier-Macmillan Ltd., 1969.

Mollenhauer, Bernhard. "Lutosławski and the Knight among Nations," American Slavic and Easter European Review, 18, (1954), 145-151.

Nettl, J. P. *The Soviet Achievement*. New York: Harcourt, Brace & World, Inc., 1968.

Niklewicz, M. "Pani Mañita," *Wiadomosci*, April 1980.

O'Donoghue, David J. *The Poets of Ireland. A Biographical Dictionary with Bibliographical Particulars*. London. Published by the Author, 1892-3.

Pérez de Ayala, Ramón. *Obras Completas. Tomo I.* Madrid: Aguilar S. A. de Ediciones, 1964.

Pigoń, Stanisław. "Niesamowie Spotkanie Literackie, Tadeusz Miciński--Wincenty Lutosławski", Mile Zycia Drobiazgi. Poklosie. Warszawa: PIW, 1964

Przybyszewski, Stanislaw. *Moi Współcześni. Wśród Obcych.* Warszawa: Wydawniczy, Bibljoteka Polska, 1926.

Nettl, J. P. *The Soviet Achievement*. New York: Harcourt,Brace and World, Inc., 1975.

Reddaway W. F., ed. *The Cambridge History of Poland. From Augustus II to Piłsudski (1697-1935)*. Cambridge: at the University Press, 1951), pp. 403-407

Reed, John. *Ten Days that Shook the World*. New York: Vintage Books, 1960.

Risco, Vicente. *Manual de Historia de Galicia*. Vigo: Editorial Galaxia, 1971.

Suárez de Tangil y de Angulo, Fernando. "Don Francisco Ramón de Eguía y Letona 1750-1827, Conde del Real Aprecio," *Revista de Historia y de Genealogía Española* (1916), p. 201.

Tuchman, Barbara W. *The Guns of August*. New York: The Macmillan Company, 1962,

Urbański, Edmund Stephen. "Dr. Józef Leonard and his Cultural-Political Activities in Spain between 1868 and 1881." Paper read at the Polish Institute, Columbia University, New York, November 25, 1966.

Velasco Zazo, Antonio. *Salones madrileños del siglo XIX: Estudio* Madrid: Librería General Victoriano Suárez, 1947.

Wandycz, Piotr S. *Soviet Polish Relations, 1917-1921*. Cambridge: Harvard University Press, 1969.

Watt, Richard M. *Bitter Glory: Poland and Its Fate, 1918-1939*. New York: Simon and Schuster, 1979.

Index

Falange 142, 145, 151
Faro de Vigo 3
Gómez de Avellaneda, Gertrudis 6, 13, 15
Hitler 34
Ibsen 17, 47
Ilustración Ibérica 32, 195
Jordan, Alex 34, 194
Lenin 29, 88, 90, 92-95, 106, 119, 121, 125, 140, 141, 177, 184
Lutosławska (Wolikowski), Bela 13, 15, 35, 48, 63, 76, 78, 83, 92, 100,
    117, 118, 123, 125, 145, 150, 151, 153-155
Lutosławska (Meissner), Halita 2, 37, 38, 54-56, 63, 76, 78, 83, 92,
    100, 125, 145, 148, 149-151, 153, 155
Lutosławska (Niklewicz) Mañita 29, 35, 43, 45, 51, 55, 62, 63, 67, 77,
    78, 100, 113, 114, 115, 125, 145, 149-151, 153, 154, 198
Lutosławski, Wincenty 2, 3, 12, 16-43, 45, 48, 50-55, 67, 78, 79,
    98, 102, 113, 116, 118, 125, 127, 147, 154, 163, 169,
    194, 195, 197, 198
Machado, Antonio 2, 9, 61, 108, 120
Machado, Miguel 2. 9. 6. 108, 113, 120
María Cristina of Spain vi, 15, 63, 64, 128
Miciński, Tadeusz 195
Młoda Polska movement 44
Niklewicz, Krystina 195
Niklewicz, Peter 195
Núñez de Arce 13, 15, 16, 48
Ors,' Eugenio d' 9
Pardo Bazán, Emilia 1, 6, 17, 24, 38, 57, 62, 105, 119, 157
Pérez Galdós, Benito 9, 62
Pigoń, Stanisław 198
Poland 2, 3, i, ii, iv, vi, vii, 2, 3, 5, 7, 8, 13, 15, 16, 18-29, 32,
    34, 38, 39, 42-46, 48-51, 53-56, 62-68, 73-75, 77-79, 86,
    88, 98, 100-102, 108, 109, 111-121, 123-129, 131, 132,
    134, 135, 137-139, 142, 143, 145-154, 157-159, 162, 163,
    169, 171, 172, 197-199
Primo de Rivera, General vi, 120, 128, 134, 139, 142, 146
Primo de Rivera, José Antonio 142
Przybyszewski, Stanisław 198
Rasputin 80, 84, 85, 99, 175, 189
Reed, John 96, 198
Reymont, Stanisław 45, 47, 96, 198
Romanov family 123

Scripta Humanistica®

Directed by
BRUNO M. DAMIANI
The Catholic University of America
COMPREHENSIVE LIST OF PUBLICATIONS *

1. Everett W. Hesse, *The "Comedia" and Points of View.* $24.50
2. Marta Ana Diz, *Patronio y Lucanor: la lectura inteligente "en el tiempo que es turbio."* Prólogo de John Esten Keller. $26.00
3. James F. Jones, Jr., *The Story of a Fair Greek of Yesteryear.* A Translation from the French of Antoine-François Prévost's *L'Histoire d'une Grecque moderne.* With Introduction and Selected Bibliography. $30.00
4. Colette H. Winn, *Jean de Sponde: Les sonnets de la mort ou La Poétique de l'accoutumance.* Préface par Frédéric Deloffre. $22.50
5. Jack Weiner, *"En busca de la justicia social: estudio sobre el teatro español del Siglo de Oro."* $24.50
6. Paul A. Gaeng, *Collapse and Reorganization of the Latin Nominal Flection as Reflected in Epigraphic Sources.* Written with the assistance of Jeffrey T. Chamberlin. $24.00
7. Edna Aizenberg, *The Aleph Weaver: Biblical, Kabbalistic, and Judaic Elements in Borges.* $25.00
8. Michael G. Paulson and Tamara Alvarez-Detrell, *Cervantes, Hardy, and "La fuerza de la sangre."* $25.50
9. Rouben Charles Cholakian, *Deflection/Reflection in the Lyric Poetry of Charles d'Orléans: A Psychosemiotic Reading.* $25.00
10. Kent P. Ljungquist, *The Grand and the Fair: Poe's Landscape Aesthetics and Pictorial Techniques.* $27.50
11. D.W. McPheeters, *Estudios humanísticos sobre la "Celestina."* $20.00
12. Vittorio Felaco, *The Poetry and Selected Prose of Camillo Sbarbaro.* Edited and Translated by Vittorio Felaco. With a Preface by Franco Fido. $25.00
13. María del C. Candau de Cevallos, *Historia de la lengua española.* $33.00
14. *Renaissance and Golden Age Studies in Honor of D.W. McPheeters.* Ed. Bruno M. Damiani. $30.00
15. Bernardo Antonio González, *Parábolas de identidad: Realidad interior y estrategia narrativa en tres novelistas de posguerra.* $28.00
16. Carmelo Gariano, *La Edad Media (Aproximación Alfonsina).* $30.00
17. Gabriella Ibieta, *Tradition and Renewal in "La gloria de don Ramiro".* $27.50
18. *Estudios literarios en honor de Gustavo Correa.* Eds. Charles Faulhaber, Richard Kinkade, T.A. Perry. Preface by Manuel Durán. $25.00
19. George Yost, *Pieracci and Shelly: An Italian Ur-Cenci.* $27.50

70. Henry Thurston-Griswold, *El idealismo sintético de Juan Valera*. Prólogo por Lee Fontanella. $44.50
71. Mechthild Cranston, *Laying Ways*. Preface by Germaine Brée. $26.50
72. Roy A. Kerr, *Mario Vargas Llosa: Critical Essays on Characterization*. $43.50
73. Eduardo Urbina, *Principios y fines del "Quijote"*. $45.00
74. Pilar Moyano, *Fernando Villalón: El poeta y su obra*. Prólogo por Luis Monguió. $46.50
75. Diane Hartunian, *La Celestina: A Feminist Reading of the "carpe diem" Theme*. $45.50
76. Victoria Urbano, *Sor Juana Inés de la Cruz: amor, poesía, soledumbre*. Edición y prólogo de Adelaida López de Martínez. $43.50
77. Magda Graniela-Rodríguez, *El papel del lector en la novela mexicana contemporánea: José Emilio Pacheco y Salvador Elizondo*. $46.50
78. Robert L. Sims, *El primer García Márquez: un estudio de su periodismo de 1948-1955*. $48.00
79. Zelda Irene, Brooks, *Poet, Mystic, Modern Hero: Fernando Rielo Pardal*. $49.50
80. *La Celestina*. Edición, introducción y notas de Bruno M. Damiani. $45.00
81. Jean P. Keller, *The Poet's Myth of Fernán González*. $47.50
82. Zelda Irene Brooks, *Carlos Alberto Trujillo: una voz poética de América del sur*. $39.50
83. Maksoud Feghali, *Le phénomène de construction et de destruction dans "Le Songe" de Du Bellay*. Preface by Michael J. Giordano. $49.50
84. Louis Imperiale, *El contexto dramático de La Lozana andaluza"*. Preliminary Note by Bruno M. Damiani. Preface by Marco De Marinis. $49.50
85. Alberto Traldi, *Fascismo y ficción en Italia: cómo los novelistas italianos representaron el régimen de Mussolini*. $49.50
86. Philip Cranston, *Naissances / Births*. $35.00
87. Marjorie Ratcliffe, *Jimena: A Woman in Spanish Literature*. $63.50
88. Víctor Infantes, *En el Siglo de Oro. Estudios y textos de literatura áurea*. $59.50
89. Ofelia L. Alayeto, *Sofía Casanova (1861-1958): Spanish Woman Poet, Journalist and Author*. Preface by Janet Pérez. $54.50
90. María Pilar Celma Valero, *Literatura y periodismo en el fin de siglo 1880-1907*. $85.50
91. María Rubio Martín, *Estructuras imaginarias en la poesía*. $47.50
92. Mercedes Rodríguez Pequeño, *Los formalistas rusos y la teoría de los géneros literarios*. $43.50
93. Gonzalo Corona Marzol, *Aspectos del taller poético de Jaime Gil de Biedma*. $44.70
94. Isabel Paraíso Almansa, *Cómo leer a Juan Ramón Jiménez*. $45.50

BOOK ORDERS

* Clothbound. *All book orders*, except library orders, must be prepaid and addressed to **Scripta Humanistica**, 1383 Kersey Lane, Potomac, Maryland 20854. *Manuscripts* to be considered for publication should be sent to the same address.

www.ingramcontent.com/pod-product-compliance
Lightning Source LLC
Chambersburg PA
CBHW020810100426
42814CB00001B/7